Transforming
Theological Education

Langham

GLOBAL LIBRARY

Transforming Theological Education

A Practical Handbook for Integrative Learning

Perry Shaw

Langham
GLOBAL LIBRARY

© 2014 by Perry Shaw

Published 2014 by Langham Global Library
an imprint of Langham Creative Projects

Langham Partnership
PO Box 296, Carlisle, Cumbria CA3 9WZ, UK
www.langham.org

ISBNs:
978-1-78368-957-6 Print
978-1-78368-956-9 Mobi
978-1-78368-955-2 ePub

British Library Cataloguing in Publication Data

Shaw, Perry, author.
  Transforming theological education : a practical handbook
  for integrative learning.
  1. Theology--Study and teaching.
  I. Title
  207.5-dc23

  ISBN-13: 9781783689576

Cover & Book Design: projectluz.com

Contents

Preface

Crisis, Opportunity and Thanks

In 2006 my world fell apart and I had a complete emotional breakdown. While a number of factors contributed to this personal crisis and the anxiety depression that ensued, a substantial element was my disillusionment with the world of theological education to which I had devoted much of my life's energies.

By God's grace and with help from friends and the medical profession, my health recovered in less than a year. But many questions remained. My reading pointed to the fragmentation and contextual irrelevance of most ministerial training programmes. My own experience had seen student after student entering college passionate for ministry and leaving passionate for academia, with little idea how to empower the church and often with no genuine desire to do so. I seriously considered giving up completely on institutional theological education, seeing theological schools as counterproductive for preparing effective leadership for the church. However, it soon became evident that, for better or for worse, the churches still looked to theological colleges for their leaders, and consequently the solution lay not with rejection but with seeking change from within.

The years since this crisis have offered me the opportunity to be involved in just such creative work. The start came when I joined the faculty at the Arab Baptist Theological Seminary (ABTS) in late 2007, shortly after the arrival of Elie Haddad as the new provost (subsequently president). Elie comes from the business world but is also a highly astute theological thinker, and his vision for change provided a context for me to work with the young and highly qualified faculty in curricular experimentation. The result has been a dynamic curricular process that continues to this day. Most of the ideas that are presented in this book are not mere theory but have been field-tested on the ground at ABTS. We have learned much from both our successes and our struggles. I cannot adequately express my thanks to Elie and to other key ABTS leaders, such as Paul Sanders, Martin Accad, Hikmat Kashouh and Bassem Melki, as well as to the highly committed ABTS faculty, who have supported and promoted these changes. I must also acknowledge the crucial role of Rana Wazir and Patricia Hazem, registrar and academic administrator at ABTS, who have carried much of the burden of making the changes happen on a day-to-day basis.

The second series of opportunities also began in 2007 when I was first invited to lead faculty-training events, initially in South Asia but increasingly over the ensuing years in other global contexts. Virtually all the material discussed in this book began in faculty-training workshops, and it is through the questions and challenges posed by participants that I have been able to develop and enhance the approaches that have been taken. I express my special gratitude to the leadership and faculty of the Indian Pentecostal Church Theological Seminary Kottayam and the Lanka Bible College and Seminary, who in 2007 first worked with me and who helped shape my own thinking, as well as to the numerous other colleges who since then have welcomed me and contributed to mutual learning.

Beyond the leadership and faculty at ABTS and at the numerous schools I have visited, there are several people whose support and interest have helped in the completion of this book. I would never have begun writing without the encouragement of Tim Stafford, and his experience in the publishing industry has been an invaluable resource. Manfred Kohl first opened the doors for me to international consultancy and has been a consistent encouragement over the years. Debbie Kramlich and Bob Heaton read the draft manuscript and provided numerous substantive suggestions. Many of the ideas in the book were first developed as a part of an online graduate programme for the London School of Theology, and I am grateful to Marvin Oxenham, who helped me to shape the material into some sort of systematic structure and gave me a reason to write. Luke Lewis and Vivian Doub of Langham Partnership have walked with me through the editing and publication process. My children, Christopher and Phoebe, have endured years of mealtime conversations about the issues addressed in this book. And the support and insights of Karen, my partner in life and ministry, colour every page of what is written; without her indomitable patience this project would never have come to completion.

The Overall Shape of the Book

Genuine intentionality in leadership training entails multiple levels of institutional and educational planning and implementation. The first section of this text addresses general philosophical and educational principles and how these work out in broader institutional concerns. It is crucial that the whole faculty develop a broad appreciation of these issues in order for a school to move towards fulfilling its mandate: that of preparing and equipping men and women to guide the church to have a more effective impact on the surrounding society.

Robert Ferris (2006) has claimed that "the faculty are the curriculum": the most formative learning that occurs in any programme of study is that shaped and facilitated by the instructors in the classroom. Sadly, it is here that many schools fail to reach their potential, as faculty members are bound to traditional and generally ineffective instructional approaches. The second section of this book seeks to expand the "toolbox" of teachers, such that class instruction takes seriously the missional mandate of the church and is focused more on learning than on teaching.

Introduction

The Arab Baptist Theological Seminary Pilgrimage

While throughout this book I will be referring to several models and programmes, the dominant point of reference will be the laboratory I have been provided as faculty member, educational engineer and acting academic dean: the Arab Baptist Theological Seminary. It is therefore important at the outset to describe something of the pilgrimage we have gone through together at ABTS.

ABTS was founded in Lebanon in 1960. During most of the extended period of the Lebanese Civil War (1975–1990), the school continued largely through the singular efforts of the then president Ghassan Khalaf. However, the damage done to Lebanon in general and the school in particular was such that the long-term financial and structural viability of ABTS remained questionable through much of the 1990s. With the arrival of Paul Sanders, first as academic dean and then as provost, ABTS went through a period of recovery and consolidation from 2000 to 2005. The school attained a level of financial stability and a number of key faculty members were recruited.

In March 2004 I was invited to lead a series of workshops in which I introduced the faculty to the notion of cognitive, affective and behavioural learning, and to the process of establishing learning outcomes as the driving force of a course syllabus. Over the following months, these curricular elements were incorporated into the language of ABTS faculty. In 2006 the annual Overseas Council Institute for Excellence in Christian Leadership Development focused on curriculum, and I was invited to present plenary sessions on multidimensional learning and the hidden curriculum. Following this conference, and knowing of my ready availability, a group of three Lebanese schools (including ABTS) invited me to facilitate a series of joint workshops. The focus of these workshops was an in-depth investigation of how ministerial training for Christian leadership might take seriously contextual challenges. The workshops included faculty, senior students, alumni, local pastors and significant lay leaders from the churches. For ABTS it resulted in a major revision of the school's vision and mission statement and the formulation of a profile of an ideal graduate. The following year, the school also adopted a series of educational values as lenses for evaluating curricular decision-making. These have all been formative in the shaping of the integrative curriculum that was subsequently developed and implemented.

ABTS Vision, Mission and Values

- Our vision is to see God glorified, people reconciled and communities restored through the church in the Arab world.

- Our mission is to serve the church in our region as it realizes its biblical mission of having Christ acknowledged as Lord, by offering specialized learning resources and equipping faithful men and women for effective service.

- Our seven core educational values are authentic worship, the missional church, Christlike leadership, empowerment, reflective practice, community cohesion, and personal and spiritual development.

By the beginning of 2008, ABTS had a strong faculty with a good level of shared pedagogical understandings. It also had in place statements of vision, mission and values, and a solid profile of the ideal graduate, shaped in dialogue with significant stakeholders and endorsed by the ABTS board. A faculty retreat was planned for February 2008 and aimed at a complete revamping of the curriculum. In preparation for the retreat, the school's then academic dean, Martin Accad, prepared an extensive questionnaire which he distributed to approximately one-third of the student body, gaining valuable information on where the students had come from and where they were planning to serve upon graduation. We also prepared a statistical survey of alumni. This information played a significant role in the retreat's discussions, and also led to a shift from what had previously been a traditional single-track pastoral-training programme to the incorporation of three specialist tracks in the new curriculum.

It was towards the conclusion of the first day of the retreat that a four-lens integrative approach emerged (fig. I.1), and the rest of the retreat became focused on how this could be implemented. It rapidly became evident that a foundational year was necessary, and a two-tiered structure – Year 1 of foundations, Years 2/3 of integrative theological education – was in place by the end of the retreat. Through the remainder of 2008, the curricular shape was set out in detail, affirmation in principle was received from the board, and key stakeholders were consulted to assess community response. The decision was also taken to shift from a semester delivery to five-week modules. This has proved

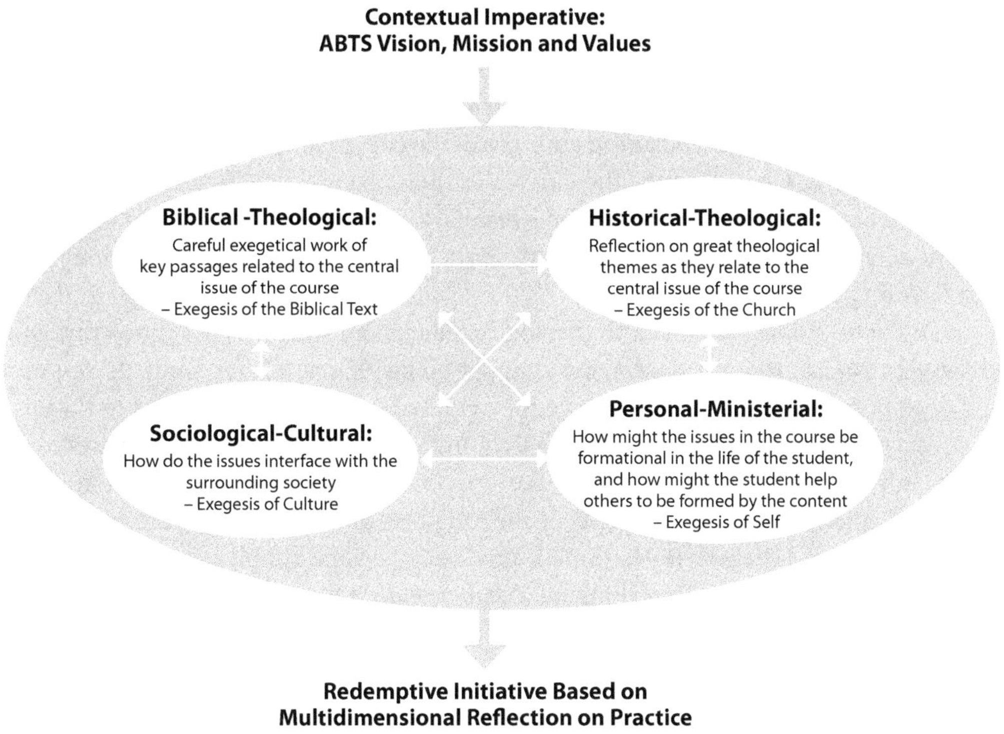

Contextual Imperative:
ABTS Vision, Mission and Values

Biblical -Theological:
Careful exegetical work of
key passages related to the central
issue of the course
– Exegesis of the Biblical Text

Historical-Theological:
Reflection on great theological
themes as they relate to the
central issue of the course
– Exegesis of the Church

Sociological-Cultural:
How do the issues interface with the
surrounding society
– Exegesis of Culture

Personal-Ministerial:
How might the issues in the course be
formational in the life of the student,
and how might the student help
others to be formed by the content
– Exegesis of Self

Redemptive Initiative Based on
Multidimensional Reflection on Practice

Figure I.1 Arab Baptist Theological Seminary curricular lenses

significant educationally, in promoting integrative thinking (as students focus on only one theme each module), and logistically, in that it greatly facilitates the scheduling process.

The February 2009 faculty retreat was dedicated to syllabus formation for each of the first-year modules. Faculty worked in teams, and syllabi were sketched for each of the modules and the courses within these modules (what we called "units"). These were further developed in teams during spring 2009. Final versions of the syllabi emerged in the first round of implementation of the first-year curriculum during the 2009–2010 academic year. A similar process was adopted at the 2010 faculty retreat for the Year A integrative modules and the three specialist tracks, and at the 2011 faculty retreat for the Year B integrative modules. The first group of BTh and MDiv graduates completed their studies in June 2012. The general consensus is that the process of shifting from a traditional "silo" approach to an integrative context-sensitive approach has been more straightforward than expected, and among both students and faculty there is a high level of satisfaction with the academic, formational and ministerial skill development that has resulted.

The General Shape of the Curriculum

The curriculum began with the basic premise that genuine formation of faithful men and women takes place only when multidimensional learning is intentionally designed and incorporated through a balanced embrace of the cognitive, affective and behavioural learning domains. Consequently, the curriculum has taken seriously the need to bring integration between academic excellence, personal formation and growth, and the development of leadership skills and qualities. We have sought to make such integration more than "ink on paper".

In the traditional approach to theological education, students are trained through a relatively fragmented curriculum, the assumption being that it is the students' responsibility to bring the pieces together once they graduate. While some manage to do this, most do not. When confronted with conflicts and challenges, many graduates respond in the only way they know – through the uncritical application of standard cultural patterns. Rather than acting as agents of the kingdom of God through careful "critical contextualization" (Hiebert 1994, 75–92), graduates become simply a reflection of the societies in which they live. In seeking to address the need for genuine integrative reflective practice which appreciates the church's great theological heritage, the ABTS faculty conceptualized core modules which would bring together a variety of lenses in dialogue with context (fig. I.1).

We believe that the ABTS vision, mission and values are both theologically sound and contextually relevant, and so we sought in these statements the foundational theme for each of the second-/third-year integrative modules. The theme is then studied through each of the four foundational lenses: biblical-theological, historical-theological, sociological-cultural, and personal-ministerial. This is not a strict 25%/25%/25%/25% division. Emphases vary according to the specific issues at stake. However, as the goal is the formation of leaders who can reflect on ministry through multiple lenses, each lens is brought to bear as much as possible. The culmination of each integrative module is a major integrative paper which is somewhat in the shape of problem-based learning: students begin by describing realities within their ministry contexts, and are then asked to reflect on these contexts through the material they have studied in each of the curricular lenses, allowing these reflections to shape critically contextual recommendations and (where possible) action.

In shaping the modular themes, it was recognized that the school's vision, mission and values addressed the centrality of the *Missio Dei* and the role of both the church and the individual in serving God in the region. Consequently, each year the students engage in a focus on God, on the church and on the individual. In one year, the modules begin with the essential nature of God, community and the individual, moving to an understanding of how that nature might be expressed in life and ministry. In the other year, students examine the manifestation of each, moving to a reflection on how the manifestation speaks of the essential nature of each. The content of these modules is not exclusive: the theme is a matter of emphasis, and as far as possible all elements of the vision, mission and values of ABTS are brought into every module offered at the school.

The goal of curricular integration depends on solid foundations. Consequently, a first year of studies has been developed to build foundations for theological reflection, moving from essential knowledge to understanding, to basic analytical approaches. This shape is built on the recognition mooted in Bloom's taxonomy (Bloom et al. 1956) that foundational knowledge is essential for understanding, and understanding is necessary for the complex thinking associated with analysis, synthesis and evaluation. Entering students are presented with a survey of Bible, history and doctrine to ensure a basic level of assumed shared knowledge. This is followed by modules that provide students with tools for understanding. The goal is to bring students into a high level of analytic and synthetic thinking during the second and third years. Even within these foundational modules we have sought a level of integration, with each module revolving around a theme and culminating in an integrative paper.

In preparation for the February 2008 faculty retreat, a survey of alumni revealed that only about 35 per cent were engaged in pastoral ministry, with large numbers of the remaining alumni involved in church-planting initiatives or a variety of children, youth and family ministries. In response, we developed three specialist tracks that students could choose from in their second and third years of study: pastoral ministries; contextualized church planting; and children, youth and family ministries. Recognizing the variety of student interests and needs, ABTS also preserved a section of the curriculum for elective courses. By 2013 our student body had further diversified, such that our three original specialist tracks were no longer serving the needs of many of our students. In light of the maturity of our student body and the limited faculty capacity at ABTS, we dismantled the specialist-track component, making elective all courses in this component of the curriculum, with recommended courses related to specific ministries. This move greatly simplified our administrative processes.

For more than a decade, the Institute for Middle East Studies at ABTS has conducted a very successful annual Middle East Conference. Speakers and participants come from all over the world, and significant contemporary themes are addressed. In light of the contextual relevance and the outstanding quality of speakers at these conferences, our new curriculum included annual participation in the conference as a compulsory element.

The language of delivery at ABTS is Arabic. Given that theological resources in Arabic are very limited, we have placed a high emphasis on English as the most pressing language need of our students. Because of this, and recognizing the growing number of quality online resources in biblical languages, we have decided not to require extensive study in Greek and Hebrew. Instead, we require students to take an introduction to biblical languages as part of the first-year Interpretation module, in which basic linguistic materials in Greek and Hebrew are provided, along with a thoroughgoing training in using Internet and CD/DVD tools. Greek and Hebrew are offered as a part of the elective component of the curriculum, and suitable students are encouraged to take advanced courses in biblical languages.

In tune with our desire for holistic education, we shifted from our previous use of an American Carnegie counting system to the European Credit Transfer counting system (ECTS credits). Under the European system, a greater number of credits is required for completion of a programme of study, but the expectation is that a large portion of the additional credits will be allocated to non-classroom-based learning activities. In granting credit for such learning experiences, the European approach communicates to students the importance of these elements for their overall education and formation. Some of the compulsory learning activities for which credit is granted at ABTS are as follows:

- A major emphasis is placed on "Theological reflection on life and ministry". A number of different activities require students to reflect both on their engagement in local-church ministry and on such elements of life as their relationship with spouse, children and peers, work experience on or off campus, and the influence of film, media and technology.

- Students are required to be actively involved in the daily chapel time. Several days a week, students lead worship and/or bring a devotional at chapel. Twice a week, the dean of students engages the students in the learning activity of evaluating the leadership and presentation by students.

- All students are provided with a mentor and are expected to meet with the mentor at least seven times during the year.

- Once a week, students , staff and faculty meet together in small groups to study Scripture together.

- In the first month of their time at ABTS, students are required to undertake an induction to theological studies at the school. They are introduced to the faculty and staff, and guided around the campus and community. Library staff introduce the students to available resources. Students have explained to them the vision and educational philosophy of ABTS and they are taken through the student manual to ensure a good level of mutual understanding. They are also given a number of introductory tasks in writing papers, and the meaning of academic integrity is explained to them. Students are also asked to complete a Bible-knowledge examination, personality and spiritual-gift assessments, as well as a self-assessment based on the ABTS profile of the ideal graduate.

- At the beginning of both the second and third years of their studies, students are given a "diagnostic", in which they are asked to repeat the self-assessment based on the profile of the ideal graduate and write a reflective paper on their pilgrimage over the previous twelve months. They are also taken further on the path of research and writing skill development.

- In the second and third years, students are also asked to prepare a contract for independent learning for the academic year ahead. Students are given a large degree of freedom in the shape of the learning contract, and to date these have included such diverse learning activities as studying the history of the Protestant churches in Lebanon, learning to play the guitar and developing greater personal self-discipline.

- For students who have completed a three-year programme of study there is a compulsory capstone course given in the last month of their studies. The purpose of this course is for students to reflect on their pilgrimage at ABTS and to look together to the future. A particular emphasis is placed on the need for continuing lifelong learning and on the means by which students can access relevant learning opportunities in their places of ministry.

A diagrammatic representation of the curriculum is given in figures I.2 and I.3.

Frequently Asked Questions

While we believe that the shape and methodology we have chosen are theologically and educationally sound, we also recognize that they differ significantly from a traditional model, and those who have been educated in the traditional model sometimes have difficulty understanding what we are doing. Consequently, it is important that there is a dialogue between the old and the new, and to respond to some frequently asked questions.

However, before any sort of comparison is attempted, it is important to emphasize that comparing a traditional curriculum with the new ABTS curriculum is like comparing apples and fish. That is because the philosophical roots differ, and so the two types of curriculum must by their very nature look foundationally different. As with any effective programme of study, the concern should not be equivalency of input but whether the outcome is serving the vision, mission and values of the school.

Also, no curriculum can do everything, and there is always a "null" curriculum – what we teach through what we exclude. We have struggled long and hard to select both what to include and what to exclude. The greatest error of curricular formation is to try to please everyone and hence add more and more, the result being a curriculum that has time mainly for content and little for reflection on life and ministry. In examining the curriculum, we invite a study not only of what is missing from our new curriculum that may be common in a traditional curriculum, but even more so the opposite: what is included in the new curriculum that is missing from a traditional curriculum. To do otherwise is to fail to give due credit to the work that lies behind the new curriculum.

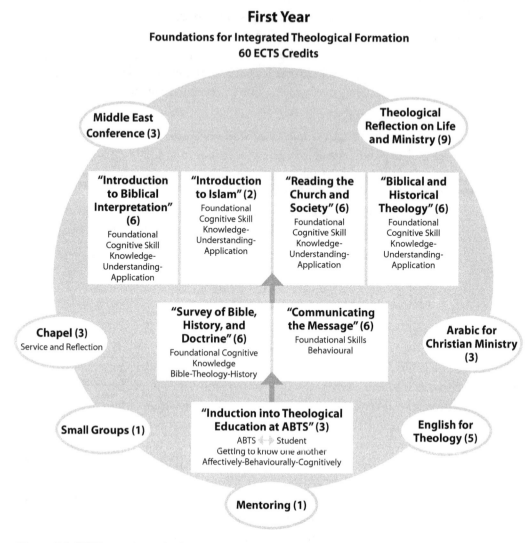

Figure I.2 ABTS year 1 curriculum

Is there enough Bible in the new curriculum?

To respond to this question, it firstly needs to be said that every member of the ABTS faculty has a passionate love of the Scriptures. Consequently, there is a strong biblical component throughout the curriculum – even though it is not always visible. For example, nearly half of the unit on Evangelism in the first year Communication module is devoted to studying biblical models of evangelism; the unit on Cultural Anthropology in the Church and Society module involves dialogue with the model of Jesus and the life of the early church; the unit on Worship in the integrative Nature and Character of God

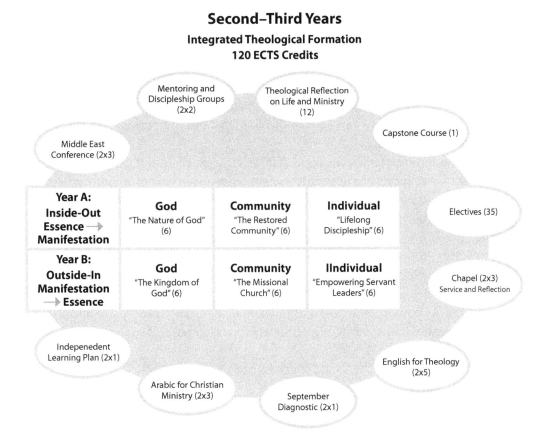

Figure I.3 ABTS years 2–3 curriculum

module is an extended dialogue between worship practices recorded in the Bible and contemporary worship practices; and every exercise in Theological Reflection on Life and Ministry involves an extended reflection on how the Bible instructs the student's life experience. Consequently, the proportion of the curriculum that teaches Bible is far greater than is apparent in the raw figures given below.

In terms of specific courses focusing on the Bible, the first-year academic programme engages the Bible in the following ways: (a) two-thirds of the 6-credit Survey module is a survey of Old Testament and New Testament; (b) the 6-credit Interpretation module is completely devoted to the interpretation of the Scriptures; (3) two-thirds of the 6-credit Theology module focuses on Old and New Testament theology. In other words, approximately 40 per cent of the classroom-based components of the first-year curriculum is devoted solely to the knowledge and interpretation of the Scriptures. In the second–third year curriculum, each of the six 6-credit core modules places the largest emphasis (usually about one-third) specifically on how the theme is addressed in the Scriptures, and a significant proportion of elective courses are on the Bible.

What about systematic theology?

It is important first to recognize that the shape and methodology of modern systematic theology has its roots in the medieval embrace of Greek philosophy, not in the Scriptures. Moreover, all theology is contextual (Bevans 2002), and in light of the missional-ecclesial vision of our programme, we have been reticent about offering an uncritical presentation in the Arab world of an approach to theology that has been profoundly shaped by Western history, culture and worldview.

That said, we are deeply concerned that the central beliefs of the Christian church be faithfully communicated to our students, and a close examination of our curriculum reveals the major themes of traditional systematic theology affirmed and expounded. In the first year, a broad stroke is given in the brief introductory unit, Survey of Christian Doctrine. These broad strokes are expanded in the Theology module held at the end of the first year. In the second–third year core modules we see theology proper in the integrative modules on the Nature and Character of God and the Kingdom of God, soteriology and ecclesiology in the Restored Community and the Missional Church modules, pneumatology in the Empowering Leadership and Lifelong Discipleship modules, theology of the Scriptures in the first-year Interpretation module, and Christology permeating every single module.

What about biblical languages?

At ABTS we affirm that every generation needs biblical scholars and translators who have attained a high level of competence in biblical languages. However, our research has discovered that few of our alumni, most of whom were required to take one year of both Greek and Hebrew, are able to use the languages in any meaningful form five years after graduation, and after ten years very few are even able to write out the alphabet. Many of our graduates cited biblical languages as among the most hated and/or most useless courses they took at seminary. The assessment of our graduates was taken very seriously in the development of our new curriculum.

There is only so much that can be done in a curriculum, and it is difficult to do a good job of learning multiple languages at the same time. While recognizing the subordination of non-Western theological education that tends to be embedded in the universalization of English in theological discourse (Kang 2010), we have nonetheless found from experience the essential value of English for our students, both in terms of accessing resources and for engaging the global Christian community. Hence we have placed our language emphasis on teaching our students English.

With respect to Greek and Hebrew, over the past twenty years outstanding electronic resources in biblical languages have been developed. Rather than burdening students with hours of memorizing vocabulary (which makes up the bulk of most biblical-languages courses), we have chosen to include one first-year compulsory Introduction to Biblical

Languages unit in the Interpretation module, which teaches students the alphabets and basic grammar, then focuses on the use of the available electronic tools. Through the remainder of their studies, students are expected to access and use these computer-based language resources.

Nonetheless, recognizing the need to encourage those who wish to pursue biblical languages at a more advanced level, we provide both Greek and Hebrew as elective courses. Generally, about one-third of our students continue in the biblical languages. While language professors were initially hesitant about making advanced Greek and Hebrew optional, in practice they have found it highly advantageous. Class sizes are smaller, and the students who choose to do advanced language study are generally more adept academically and more motivated in the disciplines of language study. Consequently, substantially more material is covered than was previously the case when half the class or more were unable (or unwilling) to engage with biblical languages at the desired level.

How does Theological Reflection work?

A significant component of our new curriculum is Theological Reflection on Life and Ministry. Students are expected to complete 21 ECTS credits of Theological Reflection prior to graduation, each credit comprising fifteen to twenty hours of experience and five to ten hours of reflection on the experience. A variety of approaches is taken over the three years, the first year focusing on training the student in theological reflection, and the second and third years focusing on practice. In each case, the reflection is at the experiential, attitudinal and theological level. A significant component of the reflection is student discussion of where they have seen God at work in the experience and what they have learned about his character and work through it, as well as theological reflection through the lenses of creation, fall, redemption and consummation. An emphasis is placed on church-ministry experience, but students are also encouraged to do theological reflection on relational experiences, work experiences, service around the ABTS community and the media.

The emphasis on theological reflection is built on the assumption that the Holy Spirit is at work in students' lives and is their ultimate teacher. Through theological reflection, we seek to cooperate with the Holy Spirit's curriculum for our students rather than simply expecting the Holy Spirit to fit in with and bless our agenda.

All of our graduates will be doing ministry among ordinary people such as housewives, businessmen and women, manual labourers, school teachers, youth and children. Central to effective Christian ministry is the ability to help all these diverse types of people to permeate their ordinary lives with the knowledge of God and to see the relevance of their faith for every aspect of their lives. But, as an Arab proverb puts it, "you can't give what you haven't got", and the multiple experience of theological reflection asks students to make these connections for themselves so that in turn they can guide others in the process. Only through repeated practice can students become habituated to seeing the whole of life and ministry through the lenses of the Scriptures and sound theology, and thereby prepare for a future ministry that connects Scripture with the daily experience of ordinary people.

What We Have Learned

As mentioned previously, the implementation of the integrative curriculum has been more straightforward than any of us anticipated and the pattern of integrative education has now become routine to the faculty. However, we have learned a number of important lessons from the process.

Above all else we have learned the importance of faculty buy-in. Ownership of the curriculum has been reached through faculty first being trained in the basics of educational integration and multidimensional learning. A mutual commitment to the vision, mission and values, and to the profile of the ideal graduate, has been foundational. Throughout the process of design and implementation there has been a frequent return to the overall goal of training effective men and women so that the church might be better equipped to fulfil its missional calling. The conceptualization and design of the overall curricular shape and the individual modules emerged through faculty retreats in which faculty members worked in teams to develop the work.

We have also learned that it is crucial to acknowledge and address justifiable fears. At the February 2008 retreat we had two participants closely involved in international accreditation, and their affirmation of our approach allayed concerns about how the changes might affect accreditation. Considerable effort was taken in winning over the more conservative members of the faculty. It was also important to let faculty know that some things would probably go wrong, and that this should not prevent us from moving forward. In retrospect, less went wrong than we originally expected.

The support and advocacy of the president of the school was crucial. We have been fortunate in having a president who has not only been supportive but who has also done all he can to promote the process of integrative education and to be our advocate on the board and in the community.

It is also unlikely that we could have completed the task without a person on faculty with solid background in educational theory and practice, one who could train the faculty and support them in the implementation process. The curriculum-development leader should be a person who believes in the value of what is being attempted and who is somewhat of a risk-taker.

We discovered that you cannot have everything ready before you begin. Not one of the faculty came with experience of this sort of integrative curriculum, and we discovered early on that the best way forward was to sketch the general shape of modules beforehand, but leave the detailing to the individual instructors upon implementation. However, the sketch needed to provide enough "meat" to be meaningful, in terms of both module and unit purpose statements and desired learning outcomes. We have also found it important for module teams to meet before delivery to ensure a level of mutual understanding, and after delivery of the module to review the implementation.

Above all, we have learned that the process demands patience and communication. The development and implementation of the curriculum was the product of several years of preparation and interaction, with weekly faculty meetings and the annual faculty retreats playing a pivotal role. The path could never have been completed if there had been unresolved rivalries among the faculty. While there have been tensions due to differences of perspective, these have been worked through by means of communication and compromise.

Our experience of curricular change has been positive and exciting. Although the process has been demanding and at times fearful, it has drawn us together as a team, and we are proud of the outcome in terms of our graduating students. While not every school has the freedom to carry out the level of curricular shift that has occurred at ABTS, the faculty and students of our school would certainly be advocates for attempting whatever level of integration is possible.

This book was written for those engaged on the ground in theological education, both to encourage comparable transformation in curricula in their own schools, and to provide practical tools for accomplishing that goal. If even a few steps are taken, the implications for furthering the global mission of God are immense.

PART 1

Intentionality in Institutional Language and Culture

Organizational culture shapes every aspect of learning that takes place in a programme of theological education. Consequently, the first step in promoting intentionality in leadership training is developing a shared language and culture. The first part of this book investigates key areas of these issues. Transformative theological education can only take place when these issues are not only fully embraced by the faculty and board, but also understood and applied by the staff, such that a healthy culture permeates every crevice of the organization.

Paul Sanders, former Executive Director of the International Council for Evangelical Theological Education, has observed that "the problem with much of theological education is that it is neither theological nor educational" (Sanders 2009). A missional-ecclesial vision for theological education generates a series of essential educational questions which are investigated in chapter 1. However, a reality check on our capacity and an understanding of the limited role we are playing in the pilgrimage of emerging leaders balances that great vision, leading to another series of essential questions addressed in the second chapter. Accountability is an essential element of intentionality, and this provides the theme for our third chapter.

The next chapters address two key educational concepts that are essential for developing holistic integration in leadership training. Firstly, traditional theological education has tended to focus on the development of the mind as the primary mandate of institutional learning. This emphasis finds its roots in Greek philosophy and the Enlightenment. A more theologically grounded understanding of pedagogy recognizes the holistic nature of learning, embracing not only the cognitive, but also the affective and behavioural domains. Holistic training for leadership in transformative churches necessitates a shared institutional culture and language that embraces these so-called "ABCs" of learning.

Secondly, deep intentionality in shaping emerging leaders for the church of Jesus Christ necessitates a sensitizing of the whole community – board, administration, faculty, students and staff – to the hidden or implicit ways in which learning takes place. Reflection on the hidden curriculum highlights the extent to which students learn about Christian leadership through the way teaching takes place, the model of their teachers' lives and their experience of the school's administration. Likewise, it is rarely acknowledged that what we exclude from our curriculum in both content and methodology – the null curriculum – communicates profound values to all in the learning community. The language of hidden and null curricula is an invaluable element of transformative programmes of theological education.

With shared language and understandings in place, it is possible to begin developing an integrated and holistic curriculum. Some specific suggestions are given in chapters 6 and 7. The section concludes with looking at some of the research on deep learning, the learning that remains five or ten years after completion of studies and that shapes long-term values and practice.

1

Asking the Right Questions (1)

A recent study of over 1,000 churches in thirty-two countries (Schwarz 2000, 23) discovered that there is a direct inverse correlation between denominational growth and educational expectations: the more education a denomination expects of its pastors and educators, the more that denomination evidences decline. More specifically, the research of the Natural Church Development (NCD) team found that only 42 per cent of pastors in high-quality, high-growth churches had seminary training, while in low-quality, low-growth churches 85 per cent had graduated from seminary. While some (Hunter 2004; Van Engen 2004, 138–40) have questioned the NCD research methodology, the widespread dissatisfaction with the product of our theological colleges cannot be ignored.

The classic shape of theological education, with its "silos" of biblical, theological, historical and (subsequently) ministerial studies or applied theology, emerged in a context where the relationship between the church and the wider society was largely in a "Christendom" paradigm – that is, the assumption was that the church could and should have a level of power and influence in society. It is for this reason that missional elements in content and methodology are barely evident in the classic approach to theological education and the emphasis has been on the study of texts from the past (Guder 2010). The "Christendom" paradigm has never been relevant in the non-Western world and is no longer relevant in most of the West. Hence the urging from theological educators such as Robert Banks (1999) and Linda Cannell (2006) for a missional foundation to theological education. As Cannell (2006, 306) puts it, "A structure formalized in the medieval period, modified to suit the theological shifts of the Reformation, influenced by the scientific methodology of the Enlightenment, shaped by the German research university, deeply affected by modernity, and assumed to define true theological education today is likely not adequate for the challenges of contemporary culture and the education of Christians who have been shaped by that culture."

In maintaining the status quo in theological education, we are implicitly affirming a commitment to the Christendom paradigm. Curricular reform is one of the most pressing needs facing theological education in the twenty-first century, and this book is focused on providing tools for curricular review and instructional excellence. In this first section, we examine some foundational curricular questions and their implications for overall curricular design and course development, adapting material from Jane Vella's *On*

Teaching and Learning (2008, 32–47) and Grant Wiggins' (1998) approach to "backward curricular design". In the second section of the book we will look at how a missional-ecclesial vision might be worked out in the classroom.

The development of an integrated and holistic missional curriculum is the ideal. However, even in the delivery of a more classic curriculum, asking the right questions will inevitably lead to perspective shifts which can address some of the widely perceived shortcomings of the current approach to theological education.

The Challenge of Curricular Reform

Fourteen years after penning his seminal work *Theologia* (1983), Edward Farley despairingly wrote the following words: "Are we to conclude, then, that seminaries cannot reform themselves? I am not sure that even a threat to institutional survival is powerful enough to offset a school's structural resistance to reform. Given the way educational institutions conserve themselves, rapid and self-critical reform, accomplished within and by the faculty in cooperation with students and administration, does not seem possible" (Farley 1997).

Change is always difficult, but curricular change is particularly difficult, due to the external and internal factors which are confronted by those who recognize and long for a new standard of excellence in curricular development. As Princeton University President Woodrow Wilson summarized his experience, "It is easier to change the location of a cemetery than to change the school curriculum" (Bailey 2001).

Externally, we have to negotiate the secular education structure, and we have to answer to accrediting agencies – even though these are often more concerned with status and hurdle-jumping than they are with genuine learning. But God help us if our primary consideration is the external reputation and credibility of our institution. Rather, our first concern should be our mandate of training men and women who can lead the church to fulfil its great commission of having Christ acknowledged as Lord throughout the earth.

But internally there are also problems. Most faculty members in higher education have done little if any serious study in educational theory. Frequently, the dominant voices in our theological schools are faculty who are more comfortable in the academy than they are in the local church, and who are theoreticians more than practitioners. As the old adage goes, "Those who can, do. Those who can't, teach." Many academics are fearful of approaches that require them to move outside their specialist areas or that challenge them to emphasize the practice of ministry as well as academic excellence. In addition, theological faculty are generally those who have succeeded in the system and are consequently very reluctant to question the system to which they have devoted so much of their lives. It is therefore difficult for established faculty to initiate curricular reform.

Stakeholder involvement is crucial in any creative path forward, particularly in the initial visioning and conceptualization phase. As far back as 1994 John Woodyard observed,

Within the present paradigm professors – the faculty – have control of their courses, their classes, the curriculum, faculty hiring and tenure decisions. This existing structure is reinforced by tradition, the accrediting associations and bureaucratic government structures. It cannot be changed by trustees, denominations, or administrators and donors. Yet, in many cases, what is needed is a realization by seminary boards, administration and faculty that they will not survive if they continue to look to past successes and old paths rather than deal realistically with the changes needed to assure that their graduates will give leadership to the churches of the next century. (Woodyard 1994, 3)

Another major barrier to curricular reform is the lack of meaningful models. It is difficult for us to break out of traditional patterns with which we are familiar, and we are all prone to teach as we have learned and to develop schools along the models of the schools where we were trained. Consequently, there are scattered across the globe a plethora of little Trinitys, Fullers, Dallases, Princetons, and occasionally Oxfords, Edinburghs and Tübingens – despite the fact that these models are generally irrelevant to the context of the Middle East, Africa, Asia or Latin America. It could even be argued that these classic models are no longer relevant in the contemporary contexts of the Western world.

Asking the right questions is the foundation of curricular reform. The first questions most programmes of ministerial training ask when designing or revising a curriculum are "What?" and "How?" As a result, curricular discussions often devolve into arguments over the fine points of territorial boundaries, each faculty member vehemently defending the allocations to his or her discipline, rather than the faculty together seeing the big picture and working towards the accomplishment of the divine purpose to which we are called. While the questions of "What?" and "How?" are important and must eventually be answered, they are in fact not the beginning but the end of curriculum planning.

What Are We Trying to Do Anyway?

Before beginning curriculum planning, we need to ask ourselves: why exactly do we exist, and what are we trying to accomplish anyway? The Bologna Process for European higher education coined the phrases "Fitness of Purpose" and "Fitness for Purpose" (ENQA 2009). Any effective educational programme must first establish an appropriate self-understanding of why it exists – in other words, a fit purpose. Once this is in place, the institution and its curriculum should then be shaped to best fulfil that purpose.

For theological education we must seek a theological answer to the question of purpose: good theology should drive our pedagogy. The Scriptures make clear that the ultimate goal of all we are and do as individuals and as a church is to participate in the *Missio Dei*: more specifically, to work and serve for the extension of the kingdom of God and the proclamation in word and deed of Christ as Lord. The mission of God comes first and we participate (Gibson 2012). Moreover, throughout the biblical narrative, a strong emphasis is placed on the people of God in the declaration of God's mighty acts (1 Peter 2:9), and for this reason recent discussion has moved beyond Kelsey's (1993) "Athens–Berlin" dichotomy to advocacy for a missional-ecclesial foundation as the integrative basis for theological education (Banks 1999; Cannell 2006; Cronshaw 2012; De Gruchy 2010; Harkness 2013; Hewlett 2010; Kirk 2005; Ott 2011; Penner 2009). As articulated in the Lausanne Movement's Cape Town Commitment (2011, II.F.4), "The mission of the Church on earth is to serve the mission of God, and the mission of theological education is to strengthen and accompany the mission of the Church."

In reality, the church across the globe struggles to fulfil this mandate. Both internal and external challenges to the church blur its vision and stifle its effectiveness. The church is in desperate need of faithful men and women who can guide the people of God to confront and overcome the challenges they face, and courageously and clearly fulfil their missional mandate.

This is where our institutions play a role. Why do theological schools and programmes of ministerial training exist? A missional-ecclesial foundation for theological education suggests that our schools exist in order *to prepare men and women who are capable of guiding the church to be effective in fulfilling the mission of having Christ acknowledged as Lord throughout the earth*. Note that the preparation of men and women is not the ultimate goal, but a significant means towards the accomplishment of the greater goal of seeing empowered churches which significantly impact their communities, such that the marks of the kingdom of God are evident in the world (Fernández 2012).

Although without direct biblical precedent, contemporary education usually expresses the general goal in terms of a "vision and mission" or "purpose" statement. The "vision" is a school's statement of what it believes God is seeking to accomplish within the particular region upon which its ministry is focused; the "mission" is a description of the role that the particular educational programme has within that greater work of God – the specific ways in which the school's programme is seeking to contribute to the *Missio Dei*. A clearly articulated vision–mission or purpose statement can be a valuable foundation by means of which institutional curricular decisions can be measured and evaluated.

While our role as providers of programmes of study is important in preparing faithful men and women for Christian service, in point of fact our time with students is extremely limited, and we do well to acknowledge our limitations. Few of our programmes of study have access to emerging leaders for more than a handful of years, but the divine work of leadership formation continues throughout life. The whole process can be represented diagrammatically as shown in figure 1.1.

There is a tendency in many schools to attempt to deliver in three years everything that an emerging leader might need for the remainder of his or her life. As mentioned in the introduction, the end result is a dense and demanding curriculum that focuses on content, with little time available to train students in reflection on practice and to prepare them for lifelong learning. The curricular implications of the role of learning outside the classroom, the necessity of lifelong learning and the means for nurturing deep learning

**The Pilgrimage of Faithful
Men and Women**

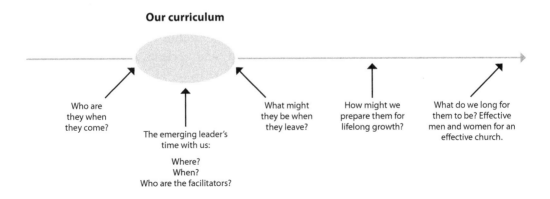

Our curriculum

Who are
they when
they come?

The emerging leader's
time with us:

Where?
When?
Who are the facilitators?

What might
they be when
they leave?

How might we
prepare them for
lifelong growth?

What do we long for
them to be? Effective
men and women for an
effective church.

Figure 1.1 The pilgrimage of a Christian leader

will all be addressed in later chapters of this book. For now, suffice it to emphasize the importance of seeing a student's sojourn with us as simply a part of his or her lifelong pilgrimage of growth towards maturity in servant leadership.

Given a missional-ecclesial foundation of theological education, and a recognition that a student's time with us is limited, a series of significant curricular questions emerges naturally.

Question 1: What Is the Ideal Church in Our Context?

If the reason for our existence is the missional mandate of the church, the first question we need to ask is what an ideal church might look like, a church that serves the *Missio Dei* faithfully and effectively in the local context, particularly in the sort of context where our students are likely to serve. From the outset, it must be acknowledged that we live between the "already" and the "not yet" – that is, while the redemptive work of Christ is complete we have not yet reached consummate glory. Consequently, we must always expect a mix of sinfulness and redemption in our personal lives and in our Christian faith communities. However, as faithful men and women, the mandate to live as the body of Christ necessitates drawing a picture of the ideal to which we can strive by the power of the Holy Spirit.

For this question to have meaning for curriculum development it needs clear and specific responses. Statements like "It is a loving church," while theologically sound, are too general to be meaningful. It is important to give grounded and tangible responses, preferably with specific examples of how theological understandings of the ideal church might be worked out in practice. A good start is to describe every positive aspect of specific local churches served by the theological school; this easily becomes a springboard for other possibilities. In appendix 1.1 at the conclusion of this chapter you can see how participants in a workshop held in Lebanon responded to this question.

One of the major concerns in education is the role of stakeholders, and it is often the stakeholders who are best able to answer this and the following "big picture" questions. Strategic curricular development therefore engages pastors, church members and community leaders, as well as board members, faculty and students, in the initial phases of curriculum conceptualization.

Question 2: What Are the Contextual Challenges?

Every church to a greater or lesser extent reflects something of the ideal of what it means to be the body of Christ. However, it is also true that all our faith communities fall short of the consummate ideal, due to both internal and external challenges that hinder them as an effective agency for the proclamation of Christ. The second question seeks to describe and assess these challenges. It is only as we have a clear articulation of the internal and external challenges to the church that we are in a position to build a curriculum that prepares our students to help the church address these challenges.

In every part of the world there are multiple societal challenges. In the West, the major issues facing the church include both rising secularism, postmodern relativism, family fragmentation and economic downturn, and a new eclectic form of spirituality that has little place for organized religion. In the Middle East and across Asia there is the rise of religious fundamentalism and the reality of being a minority, often oppressed. In Africa, there is intensified poverty and the AIDS crisis. Racial, ethnic or tribal conflict is found in many parts of the world. Violence and corruption are endemic societal challenges across much of the globe, and with this, growing numbers of refugees. Urbanization has brought with it shack housing, human trafficking, drug abuse, and an increasing gap between the rich and the poor. Unless these challenges are clearly understood and in some way brought into our curricular considerations, we can lay little claim to having a meaningful theological education.

Equally, our churches struggle with internal challenges, such as interpersonal conflict, traditionalism, individualism, theological shallowness, lack of vision or inadequate discretionary time. Taking these challenges seriously is essential to a missional-ecclesial vision of curriculum development.

There is a tendency in addressing the question of contextual challenges to devote enormous space to an open attack on the local church. Such an attack accomplishes little. A healthy recognition of both the strengths and the weaknesses of our local churches, alongside a realistic assessment of the local societal challenges, provides the foundation for effective curriculum development.

It is possible that the question of external and internal challenges is the most significant in promoting intentionality in our training of effective men and women.

Consequently, time and space should be given to developing an understanding of contextual challenges, and it is worthwhile to review the list on a regular basis. My own experience is that an initial development of contextual insights demands the better part of a complete day of group work. A sample of how the outcome might look is given in appendix 1.2.

As with the definition of the ideal church, the process of explicating the contextual challenges for effective curricular development needs the involvement of stakeholders (church and community leaders, students and faculty).

Question 3: What Might an Ideal Christian Leader Look Like?

The third major curricular question seeks to draw a picture of the sorts of characteristics needed in leaders in order for them to be able to guide the church through its contextual challenges (question 2) towards the accomplishment of its missional mandate (question 1). It is not that we expect any individual to demonstrate all of these characteristics. Rather, the goal is to have a picture towards which we want to see our students grow, a series of character traits, skills and knowledge that would be needed to best accomplish the task of Christian leadership in our context. More specifically, consideration needs to be given to the following:

- What sorts of knowledge and thinking skills are necessary for the faithful Christian to connect text with context and context with text, and to continue growing and learning throughout the years ahead?

- What sorts of character and attitude traits are needed in the leader so that others will follow?

- What sorts of skills are necessary so that the eternal message can be incarnated in word and deed in the leader and those led?

Answering these questions leads naturally into the formulation of a series of long-term outcome descriptors towards which the learners in our programme should demonstrate growth during their time at our institution. Some schools describe this list of outcomes as a "profile of the ideal graduate". The "profile of the ideal graduate" at ABTS is given in appendix 1.3 as a possible model for your own school.

In too many schools, these descriptors are little more than "ink on paper" to satisfy the requirements of accrediting agencies and stakeholders. For a "profile of the ideal graduate" to have ongoing significance, there need to be means by which students are pre-assessed and post-assessed through the lenses of the descriptors. At ABTS we have developed a self-assessment document based on the profile and which students are asked to complete upon entry to the school; then, at the beginning of every new academic year, they write reflective papers in light of their changing self-perceptions. This becomes the basis for guided mentoring in the students' pilgrimage of growth. A side benefit of this process has been that the students have learned basic skills in lifelong learning, and have come to see the self-assessment document as a tool for continued growth subsequent to graduation.

Conclusion

A missional-ecclesial foundation for theological education necessitates careful consideration of basic curricular questions determining the ideal church, the contextual challenges, and the characteristics of faithful men and women who are capable of guiding the church through the contextual challenges to the fulfilment of its missional mandate. A thoroughgoing reflection on these questions provides the theological institution with a clearer picture of its long-term purpose, and this can become the foundation for designing a curriculum that is contextually meaningful. In the next chapter, consideration is given to the practical questions of the nature of our students and the realities of institutional capacity, limitations which need to be taken seriously as we contemplate what can and cannot feasibly be accomplished on the path towards curricular excellence.

Exercises

1. Consider a theological programme you wish to enhance or develop. If it is an established programme, discuss the theological and philosophical rationale of the "vision and mission" statement. If it is a programme you would like to initiate, formulate a "vision and mission" statement and discuss the theological and philosophical foundations of this statement.

2. Meet with at least two other Christians engaged in ministry in your local context, and working together, develop responses to the first three major curricular questions using the following guidelines:

- Make a list of the characteristics of the "ideal" local church. Begin by describing all the *positive* characteristics of your own local church and of other churches you know of in your region. Be as specific as possible, giving examples. Organize your final list into understandable categories.

- What are some of the challenges that confront the church in your region, that hinder it as an effective agency for the proclamation of Christ? Consider both external challenges (how the societal context hinders proclamation) and internal challenges (particular chronic weaknesses within the Christian faith community). Your response can be in either point or narrative form.

- For your own specific local context, what are the chief characteristics of the ideal Christian leader, the sort of person who would be able to lead the church through its contextual challenges towards the accomplishment of its missional mandate? Take into account character traits, skills and knowledge. Briefly explain why you believe these characteristics are significant. Organize your list of characteristics into a "profile of the ideal graduate", somewhat similar to the example provided in appendix 1.3.

Appendix 1.1

Characteristics of the Ideal Effective Church

(Adapted from workshops held with the Beirut Interschool Consortium March–May 2006)

- **Spiritually oriented**
  - The people love Christ; they wholeheartedly embrace him
  - Christ-centred in a community of love and care – meets members' needs in practical ways
  - Characterized by unity and love
  - Prayer and the worship of God are priorities
  - The members see the church as a dynamic Spirit-led organism, not as an institution
  - Obedient to Christ, demonstrating the fruit of the Spirit
  - Seeks a life that embraces in balance fellowship, witness and service
  - Inclusive, cooperative, kingdom-minded
  - Discipleship is a priority
  - Biblical preaching that is relevant to contemporary society
  - Preaches and teaches the truth of the Scriptures as the foundation for life
  - Seeks to know and live out the Scriptures, taking seriously the hard teachings of the Scriptures (Sermon on the Mount, Matt 25)
  - Values prayer and the worship of God as a lifestyle:
    - i.   Enjoys being in the presence of God
    - ii. Has a sense of awe in God's presence
    - iii. Rom. 12:1–2 → living sacrifice
  - Discipleship happens effectively
  - Renewal as a core value
  - Listens carefully and responds to the Holy Spirit
  - Trusts God for his provisions (faith)

- **Characterized by love**
  - Generous, self-giving, sacrificial
  - Love and unity among believers; love for people not yet believers
  - Accepts and serves unconditionally those who come
  - Commitment to one another (lives and serves together)
  - Characterized by forgiveness

- Accepts differences
- Mourns with those who mourn
- Applies Matthew 18 and other biblical principles in the resolution of conflict

- **Missional: individually and corporately sees self as sent out**
  - Outward-looking – focused on the biblical goal of outreach; everyone is aware of and involved in the mission of the church to the society and the world
  - Culturally relevant
  - Impacts the society
  - Reaches out to the whole community – different ethnic groups, ages, etc.
  - Relevance (people focused, community focused, flexible in form and language)
  - Intentionally addresses the immediate context and touches the immediate neighbourhood meaningfully
  - Self-evaluative of its relevance and effectiveness
  - Focus on holistic ministry (total need)
  - Concerned with social welfare (social, political, economic)
  - Witness in word and deed – through relationships and lifestyle
  - Witnesses of transformation (becoming like Christ)
  - Encouraging, recognizing multiple spheres
  - Concern with outer ministry
  - Striving to be "just like Jesus"
  - Growing and relevant – an organism rather than an organization

- **Multiple Leadership based on spiritual giftedness**
  - Led by servant leaders
  - Priesthood of all believers
  - No one is excluded from the ministry
  - Sacrificial church
  - Encouraging, recognizing multiple spheres
  - Plurality of leadership
  - Self-administrative, self-supportive, self-propagating

- **Creative**
  - Open and responsive to change
  - Reproductive, multiplying
  - Agent of transformation

- **Manages resources well (financial, time, people, etc.)**

Appendix 1.2

Internal and External Challenges to the Church

(Adapted from workshops held with the Beirut Interschool Consortium, March–May 2006)

Internal:

- Spiritually
    - Decrease in spiritual life/disciplines (prayer, fasting, …)
    - Cheap grace
    - Pressure to please people rather than God
    - Inadequate, poor hermeneutics
    - Incorrect concept of church
    - Spiritual abuse
    - Corruption – lack of integrity
- Attitudinally
    - Arrogance – we know it all
    - Exclusiveness (doctrinally)
    - Possessiveness/protection
    - Legalism
    - Poor self-image
    - Spectatorship
    - Social inadequacy
    - Lack of commitment
    - Selfishness
    - People are too busy
- Relationally
    - Lack of trust
    - Lack of transparency
    - Individualism – competition rather than cooperation
    - Social status and hierarchies within the church
    - Poor conflict-resolution processes
    - GFJ – Gossip for Jesus

- Disunity, often leading to church splits and new denominations – denominationalism

- Missionally
  - Resistance to change – bound to traditions – satisfied with stagnation
  - Traditionalist leadership (not teachable; do not want to develop new approaches to ministry, etc.)
  - Blindness to rapidly changing world
  - Insensitivity to social problems
  - Immaturity; West-dependent church/leadership
  - Irrelevant non-practical preaching/teaching
  - Lack of obedience in evangelism out of fear, lack of confidence, enmity and hatred
  - Lack of structure/system for preparation and nurture of Christians to be witnesses of Christ
  - Lack of proper teaching that transforms lives of church members
  - Church moves into development work but for the wrong reasons – to attract financial support

- Organizationally
  - No culturally authentic way of governance
  - Need to control
  - Insecure leaders who feel threatened by younger, better-educated upcoming leaders; pastors are too ambitious or overprotective
  - No mentoring relationship process between leaders and others
  - Lack of role models
  - Traditional, hierarchical and dictatorial – lack of egalitarian relationships
  - Conflict among leaders due to wrong understandings of "success" and "effectiveness"
  - Macho (male chauvinist) leadership
  - Tribal leadership (leaders offended because they have not been given the right honour)
  - Focus on image

External:

- Economic pressure
- Busyness, time constraints
- Political and sociological problems – political instability
- Emigration problem – "brain drain"
- Others' perceptions of the "evangelical church" – fanaticism, Western import, Zionist, "Aren't all Protestants JWs?"

- Social hierarchy and status
- Opposition to Christian mission and evangelism
- Societal and government oppression inhibiting churches' ability to carry out mission
- Religious freedom is actively opposed
- Revival of other faiths
- Secularization of society
- Increase in materialism and consumerism
- Health-and-wealth gospel
- Poverty
- War, conflict
- New challenges like HIV/AIDS

Appendix 1.3

ABTS Profile of the Ideal Graduate

The Arab Baptist Theological Seminary exists to see God glorified, people reconciled and communities restored through the church in the Arab world.

Therefore we seek to equip faithful men and women for effective service who are characterized by ...

Cognitively, a Mind Committed to Reflective Practice

Able to interpret Christian life and ministry through the multiple lenses of Scripture, theology, history and community

To this end, ABTS graduates should have:

- A sound knowledge of the content of the Scriptures and of the way the various pieces fit together in the great metanarrative of God's redemptive work and the acknowledgement of his kingdom.

- A clear understanding of central Christian doctrines and of how theological reflection has engaged these doctrines throughout history. Students should be able to see how theology emerges from context and have taken steps towards developing their own contextual theology.

- An understanding of the flow of Christian history, with a particular focus on the Eastern churches and the distinctive history, doctrine and practices of major Protestant denominations, in light of general events in world and Middle Eastern history.

- An understanding of the nature and impact of culture, and the ability to evaluate culture in light of a genuine Christian worldview. In particular, students should have a thorough knowledge of the history, doctrine and practices of Islam, and the ability to evaluate both positively and negatively the influence of Islam on Middle Eastern society.

- A basic understanding of the social sciences (psychology, sociology, cultural anthropology, politics) and of how these impact theological reflection and the practice of ministry.

- A critical understanding of the psychological and spiritual processes by which people grow in personal and corporate settings.
- The ability to interpret key ministerial issues through the multiple lenses of Bible, history, theology and context: Christian leadership, church planting and church growth, the teaching ministry of the church, Christian nurture and discipleship, Christian counselling, preaching.

Affectively, a Heart of Love for God and Others

Able to be examples of maturing faith in relationship with God,
and in a commitment to reconciled relationships and restored communities

To this end, ABTS graduates should have a commitment to:

- Work personally and corporately for God's global kingdom purposes through the universal and local church. This implies a deep love for God's people and a desire to see the church of Jesus Christ live out its missional calling.
- A vital, daily relationship with Jesus Christ, seen in the discipline of regular practices of worship, spiritual renewal and personal growth, and reflected in the growing evidence of the fruit of the Spirit.
- The cultivation of a deepening ability to hear God's word in stillness and solitude.
- Honour all persons as created in the image of God by appreciating the diversity of cultures, ethnicities and traditions within the church.
- Know and develop their gifts, passions, and calling in ministry.
- A heart of servant leadership that embraces both humility and sober confidence in the calling and direction of God, including the willingness and ability to evaluate their own spiritual development and practices, noting areas of strength and weakness, and seeking lifelong learning and growth in personal life and Christian leadership (a teachable spirit).
- Accountable relationships focused on spiritual growth.
- Stewardship of time, body and finances for effective ministry, including order, discipline, faithfulness, integrity in ministry responsibilities, and wise balance in relationships with God, family, church and society.

Behaviourally, Hands of Servant Leadership for the Empowering of God's People

Able to equip faithful men and women in the church for effective service

To this end, ABTS graduates should have the ability to:

- Create a leadership environment that is characterized by missional strategic vision and direction, team leadership, redemptive action and empowerment.

- Gather and assess demographic, social, economic and cultural information in order to inform a process of planning and development in a particular ministry context.

- Nurture, mentor and train others at both an individual and group level through discipleship, small-group ministry, and/or formal teaching and preaching contexts.

- Study and teach the Scriptures inductively and synthetically, as a basis for responding to contemporary life questions.

- Train others who can train others in holistic Christian growth (2 Tim 2:2).

- Give a clear, personal witness of Jesus Christ and the gospel message to various categories of hearers, ready to defend our faith with gentleness and respect.

- Counsel others in the resolution of life issues and discern when to refer counselees to health professionals for psychological or physical care.

- Speak, read and write clearly the Arabic language, and have a working level of English for access to global theological resources and continuing education.

2

Asking the Right Questions (2)

In the previous chapter you were introduced to some basic curricular questions that emerge from a missional-ecclesial foundation for theological education: (1) the characteristics of the ideal church; (2) the contextual challenges that hinder the church in its missional mandate; and (3) the characteristics of faithful men and women who are capable of guiding the church through the contextual challenges to the fulfilment of its missional mandate. These questions provide a destination towards which we can begin curricular design.

While it is crucial that we keep before us the long-term goal of preparing faithful men and women for service, human and material capacity limit how much we can reasonably hope to accomplish during a student's time in our programme. Further curricular questions help us to acknowledge and define these limitations as a step towards the development of a curriculum that reflects quality stewardship.

Question 4: Who Are the Learners?

Ultimately, the goal of sound curricula is to lead the students from where they are upon entry along a pilgrimage towards the long-term goal of effective Christian leadership. If we don't know our entering students, it is not possible to build a healthy curriculum for transformational learning. Vella (2008, 33) observes: "When this vital question is not asked, learning tasks and materials can be selected that are inappropriate for the learners, the time set may not work for the group, the content is often not immediate or engaging, and the objectives seem to serve the teacher, not the learners. The primary consideration is the learners – their needs and hopes."

Serious consideration should be given to the level of diversity or commonality in the students. If the student body is diverse in terms of background and aspirations, a quality curriculum will provide diverse options. Inasmuch as students come from comparable socio-cultural contexts and/or are anticipating similar future ministry situations, to that extent a set curriculum is acceptable.

Some areas that should be addressed are socio-economic and educational background; the sort of community from which they come (urban, suburban or rural; mono-cultural or multi-cultural); the level and type of religiosity in their upbringing; the sort of churches they come from; and so on. It can be worthwhile to paint word pictures of typical incoming students. Consider the following questions:

- What sorts of homes were your students brought up in? How many people were living together? How large or small were the houses? Were the fathers and mothers strict or lenient? What sort of aspirations did their parents have for their children? To what extent were their families typical of other families in the community?

- In what sorts of communities did your students grow up? Were they urban and cosmopolitan, the secondary cities in the nation, or large or small villages? To what extent did Buddhism, Hinduism, Islam and/or Christianity play a role in the shape of the communities? To what extent has postmodernism and/or secularism played a role in shaping your students' worldviews?

- In what sorts of churches did your students grow up (if any)? How many people came to the churches? What level of education did they have? What role did the pastors play in the churches? How did the people see their own role in the churches? Where did they worship together? If in church buildings, how adequate or inadequate were those buildings for the ministries of the churches? To what extent were the churches outward-looking or inward-looking?

- How much education do your students generally have as they enter your programme? To what extent were there opportunities in their education to develop critical thinking skills, and to what extent was their education focused on the rote learning of information? What were the high schools like? How many students were there in the classes? What were the physical characteristics of the classrooms themselves?

Developing a questionnaire and interviewing a representative sample of your student population, using questions comparable to those shown above, can be an excellent way of assessing the pre-learning capacity, understanding and needs of your entering students. In a world that is changing rapidly, regular reassessment helps ensure that your curricular programme is responsive to the changing learning needs of your students.

Beyond these contextual issues we need to have a general idea of our entering students in three broad areas: (a) What do they already know – and not just about Bible and theology? (b) What do they already know how to do? What skills and abilities do they possess? (c) What kind of people are they? What do we know about their maturity and character? Having the answers to these three questions gives us a starting point from which to develop a curricular plan (Hardy 2007, 134). One of the most valuable exercises we have developed at ABTS is to ask entering students to write a short description of their pilgrimages to date. Through reading these reflections we have gained great insight into the worlds from which they come.

It can also be valuable to create some composite hypothetical entering "students" that reflect some of the key student "types" that you are likely to encounter in your programme of study. As curricular questions arise in faculty discussions, these "personalities" can become lenses that keep our programmes grounded in reality. For example, in a major project seeking to develop online courses for training leaders of the young and rapidly growing church in North Africa, our curriculum development team began by looking at key issues that would probably be confronted by a hypothetically constructed North African man we named Saïd. We began with the picture of Saïd as a believer from a Muslim background who is leading a small house church. He is married, bi-vocational, in his late twenties, and has completed high school. Some of the key issues such a leader might encounter were then tabulated. We also realized that women in the North African context confront unique issues. Consequently, we then drew a picture of a hypothetical North African woman we named Mariam. Mariam is a married believer from a Muslim background whose husband has not yet chosen to follow Christ. She is a homemaker in her early thirties, a university graduate with young children. Mariam is limited in freedom but is seeking to live out her faith meaningfully in her challenging context. What additional issues might she confront? The results of our assessment are given in appendix 2.1. As we struggled and argued over the content and approach of our curriculum, we continually came back to Saïd and Mariam. These representative composite "students" held us accountable, ensuring that our work was both substantial and contextually relevant.

Admissions is a highly significant related issue. Due to financial need, many schools accept virtually anyone who can demonstrate an adequate academic background, irrespective of the student's fitness for leadership in the church. In many parts of the world there is a cultural expectation that children who demonstrate academic and social excellence should go into "respected" professions such as medicine, law or engineering. Only children who are fit for nothing else are permitted by their families to train for Christian ministry. If the purpose and structure of the school is designed for evangelizing and discipling immature young men and women, accepting such students may be reasonable. However, where the curriculum is designed to develop effective transformative leaders, a much more rigorous acceptance process must take place.

Question 5: Where Do the Students Go?

As seen in figure 1.1 in the previous chapter, effective curriculum walks alongside students from where they are when they enter towards the long-term goal of effective life and ministry. We must therefore have a clear picture not only of who students are when they enter our programme, but also where they are likely to go when they leave.

A straightforward starting point is to ask a representative sample of the current student body what sort of ministry contexts they anticipate in the future or to which they aspire. Questions such as the following can be very revealing:

- As your current students look to the future after graduation, in what sort of ministries are they hoping to engage?

- What kind of people are they hoping to serve? Are they wealthy, middle class or poor? What level of education do these people have? Are they literate, illiterate or functionally illiterate (they know how to read but prefer never to read)? If they read, what sorts of materials do they read? Do they own televisions, computers, DVD players or other forms of technology? Where do these people gain information about the world? About the life of faith? How much time do they spend visiting each other? What do they find helpful as they seek to grow spiritually? How important is faith to them?

- What is the nature of the communities in which the students are likely to serve in the future? Are they urban, suburban or rural? To what extent do religious commitments, spirituality or secularism play a role in the shape of these communities?

- To what extent will material resources be available to your students in their future ministries? For example, are they likely to have computers? What about other forms of technology – televisions, DVDs, digital projectors? How will they get around – cars, bicycles, public transport? Will they have easy access to new books?

- What do your students anticipate as being some of the greatest challenges they are likely to face in their future ministries – both within the ministries themselves and from the wider society? What do they fear?

However valuable and significant student responses are to these questions, they are inadequate without a survey of alumni. While students may have aspirations, the reality upon graduation is often far different. While current students may not necessarily follow in the footsteps of those who went before, nonetheless there is generally at least some level of comparability. A survey of the sorts of ministry roles that alumni have today points to the sort of learning needs incoming students are likely to have for long-term future ministry.

It can be beneficial to determine a raw statistic of the percentage of alumni who are now in the following sorts of ministries: local-church pastoral ministry; children's or youth ministry; family ministry; ministry in the marketplace; church planting; counselling; community development and/or advocacy; media; university-campus ministry; cross-cultural mission (and if so, where); academia; and so on. Ranking these from the most common provides suggestive indicators of emphases or specialist tracks that would reflect the needs of the diverse student body.

As a part of the curricular reconceptualization process at ABTS our External Relations Director, who was also responsible for alumni relations, reported to the faculty that only about 35 per cent of graduates were engaged in traditional local-church pastoral leadership. About 15 per cent were involved in creative church-planting endeavours, often in complex contexts in which Christian ministry was largely "underground". About 30 per cent were involved in various forms of church and parachurch children, youth and family ministry. Other significant ministries involved counselling, media and community development. When ABTS was established in 1960 it had the specific mandate of preparing pastors for the Baptist churches of the Middle East, and up until 2008 the structure of the programme reflected the standard paradigm of pastoral-training programmes in the West. It was clear that such a programme had substantial irrelevant components for ABTS students and alumni serving in the twenty-first century. Consequently, a significant element of our curriculum revision was the incorporation of three specialist tracks – pastoral ministry, contextualized church planting, and children-youth-family (CYF) ministry. By 2013, our student body had further diversified, such that our three original specialist tracks were no longer serving the needs of many of our students. Because of limited faculty we were unable to develop further tracks; instead, we dismantled the specialist track component, making elective all courses in this component of the curriculum, moving to recommended courses related to specific ministries. Behind this whole process has been a desire to best exploit the limited time students have through providing the most appropriate courses we can within our capacity constraints.

If contact with alumni is strong, a valuable piece of curricular preparation is to ask alumni what have been some of the greatest challenges they have faced, or are continuing to face. Alumni responses to this question need to be taken seriously in the sort of material that is addressed with current and future students.

It is surprising how few schools take the time to ask appropriate questions about entering and graduating students. The majority of programmes are geared towards the small minority that end up in academic careers, perhaps because it is generally people who have followed this sort of career who have control over programme design. However, a missional-ecclesial vision for theological education necessitates careful research of students and alumni so that our limited resources are utilized with appropriate stewardship in service of God's mission in the world.

Question 6: When? The Time Frame

We need to have the humility to recognize that our role in the lifelong pilgrimage of emerging leaders is very limited. An endemic problem in curriculum design is allocating too much "What?" for the "When?", the end result being a tendency towards the impartation of vast quantities of information at low levels of learning. Educational research (O'Brien, Millis and Cohen 2008, 12) is increasingly discovering that "less is more": when students are asked to engage with a fraction of what is normally covered in a tertiary classroom – but are given the time to go deep – the actual *quantity* that is remembered, valued and applied by students five years later is significantly more than when they are asked to listen, read and digest vast quantities of material.

Faculty have great difficulty embracing the implications of deep-learning research (presented in greater detail in chapter 8). They have spent so much of their lives mastering a field of study – and "it is all so important". However, if education is about learning not teaching, then a reassessment of what is *most* important comes to the forefront. The tendency of most faculties willing to ask the first five questions (examined in this and the previous chapter) is to recognize major areas of neglect in the curriculum and simply try to add on more and more to a programme that is already overloaded. A serious and humble consideration of the "When?" will likely compel us to remove traditionally "sacred" studies in order that more pressing elements can be given their due emphasis.

It is common practice for programmes of ministerial training to attempt to "cover" everything that an emerging leader might "need" in the thirty to forty years after graduation. From the vast quantities of information that inevitably result, students actually remember very little. But worse is that our approach teaches students a dependent approach to learning: graduates are unable to discover the right questions – and the means for answering those questions – after graduation, unless they have an instructor to tell them what and how to do this. An essential element of building intentionality into a programme of ministerial training is to teach students how to self-educate, so that they have the tools to continue to learn and grow continually through the twenty, thirty or more years after they complete their brief three or four years of training. Educating in these processes of "meta-learning" (Meyer and Shanahan 2004; Novak and Gowin 1984) is time consuming but can often be a more valuable gift to our students than most of the information we have traditionally thought we need to transmit.

Choosing between the good and the best is the essence of the null curriculum (Eisner 1994), to be studied in more depth in chapter 5. We cannot teach it all, and the material we include or exclude communicates to our students our understanding of what is or is not valuable. Quality education pays as much attention to what is excluded as to what is included, and chooses strategically that which best serves the purpose within the limited available time.

Having a clear and realistic appreciation of the "When?" can help us best manage the limited precious time available for learning. The "When?" includes all of potential classroom and non-classroom learning contexts, including such significant activities as mentoring, discipleship groups and internships, and informal moments such as general time over meals, trips together, casual encounters and so on.

Question 7: Where? The Learning Environment

Seymour (1993, 145) observes, "It is virtually impossible to create and sustain over time conditions for productive learning for students when they do not exist for teachers." Both teachers and learners are profoundly shaped by the learning environment. Jensen (2008, 17) suggests that the following environmental factors impact the quality of learning: room temperature, plants and flowers, acoustics and sound quality, wall colours and decoration, lighting (natural vs. artificial), room size and crowding, flooring materials, curtains or window shades, furniture and seating mobility, humidity, view to the outside (scenic vs. distracting), the level and kind of external noise, and the existence of positive aromas or toxic smells. Sterile and formal contexts lead to emotional distance between teachers and learners, and among the learners. Closed rooms without natural lighting negatively impact the brain and can hinder learning. Clutter and external noise distract students from focus-on-task.

We cannot always change our location, but simple things such as lighting, the quality of tables and chairs, decorations, and the like, all impact the quality of the curriculum. Outstanding teachers will be highly sensitized to such things as student comfort, lighting and classroom layout. Both tall and short students are particularly susceptible to discomfort using standardized furniture. In general, males see better in bright light, while females prefer more subdued lighting. The environment is a major factor in learning.

Another important consideration is the extent to which the environment serves or undermines the missional-ecclesial goal of theological education. The most effective education occurs when the learning environment reflects the future ministry environment of students.

Question 8: Who Will Facilitate the Learning?

This question addresses our human resources. How many people are involved in facilitating the learning? What is the nature of their training? How much do they know about teaching? Capacity is a highly significant element in curriculum design. The greater the facilitator capacity, the greater the potential for creative curricular design.

As you consider your human resources it will become evident what sort of in-service training might be necessary in order to implement an effective curriculum. In most programmes of theological education, the faculty are well trained in their area of specialization, but have received little in the way of teacher training or orientation in sound educational theory and practice. Sometimes, training in leadership and administration are also needed. Through an intentional process of training you can strengthen your human capacity and increase the possibility of creative and intentional curriculum design that better serves the school's vision and mission.

Question 9: What and How?

Only when all the above questions have been answered are we in a healthy place to build the curriculum. We need to be diligent in keeping "What?" and "How?" as the final questions, as the curriculum must always remain the servant of the fulfilment of our purpose and not the master of our decision-making processes. Our goal is to take men and women along the path towards effective service of an engaged and impacting church, and the courses we teach are simply one of several means to this end.

It is valuable at this stage to begin by trying to put aside all thought of traditional models, and then conceptualizing an ideal curriculum. Imagine that yours will be the first programme of study ever to deliver theological education. How would you design a curriculum to serve your context? What would be the absolutely crucial elements?

The work that has been done in questions 1 to 5 should play a profound role in the conceptualization. Major contextual challenges should be addressed, and the formation of knowledge, character and skills must find its place. Consideration should be given not only to what we want students to learn while they are with us, but also to what they need to learn after they leave us, and how they can continue in lifelong learning. Only after time has been given to dreaming and conceptualizing should the limitations of capacity be brought into curricular design.

The classic curricular shape is like a series of building blocks. Each "brick" is a discrete element, and we lay "brick" upon "brick" until we have (so we believe) a "building", as illustrated in figure 2.1. However, learning does not take place this way, and a "building block" approach reflects an emphasis on teaching rather than on learning. Other models better respond to learning needs.

	Biblical Studies	Historical Studies	Theological Studies	Ministerial Studies
Year 3				
Year 2				
Year 1				

Figure 2.1 "Building block" approach to curriculum

The "layered curriculum" approach (fig. 2.2) begins by determining the absolutely essential elements that every student must engage with; these then become core compulsory elements of the curriculum. Of these, there are elements that form the foundation for everything else in the curriculum. Recognition of diverse future ministry contexts is reflected in the "track" component of the curriculum, and the unique character of each student is respected through providing an elective component. The trap that many schools fall into when using this model is to take current courses and then try to "fit" them into the model, rather than beginning with the research carried out through questions 1 to 5 to determine the essential elements of a curriculum.

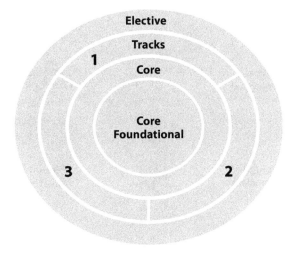

Figure 2.2 "Layered curriculum"

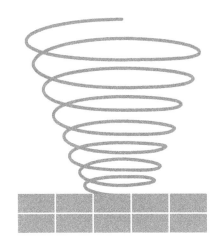

Figure 2.3 "Core foundations – spiral of learning" approach to curriculum

A second model, "core foundational – spiral of learning" (fig. 2.3) is built on the recognition that learning takes place through connecting the unknown with the known, and that consequently review and development lead to deep learning. Within this model a series of core materials begins the curriculum, and then students are taken on a pilgrimage to deeper knowledge through a process of continual review and development. Much of what takes place in more non-formal programmes of learning follows this sort of pattern.

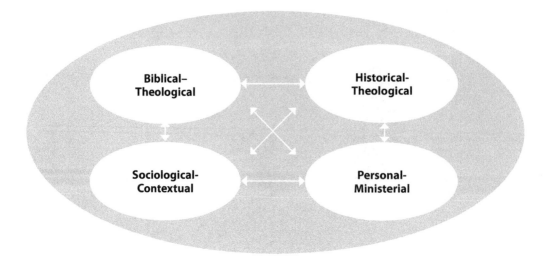

Figure 2.4 "Integrative modular" approach to curriculum

The "integrative modular" approach (fig. 2.4) delivers the core curriculum through modular blocks (four to eight weeks) in which a central theme is addressed through multiple lenses of theological reflection.

There are numerous other models and shapes of curriculum formation. Ultimately, the curricular shape should serve the purpose of the programme, not merely mimic what others have done.

Around the globe, the current focus of accrediting agencies is on outcomes and the need for programmes to be "fit for purpose", with inputs being servants of the outcomes. Consequently, the preservation of traditional models in contexts for which they were not designed is becoming increasingly untenable. Rather, the future of theological education lies in creative and integrative models that have been built on careful consideration of context and capacity.

Conclusion

Brian Tracy has said, "All successful men and women are big dreamers. They imagine what their future could be, ideal in every respect, and then they work every day toward their distant vision, that goal or purpose." So it is with theological education: unless we dream, and then work towards that dream, we can never hope to see the sort of reform in our programmes that is needed in the service of God and his mission in the world. Through asking foundational questions about our vision and mission, the contextual challenges, the nature of our students, and the faithful stewardship of our institutional capacity, we are able to work towards curricular excellence in theological education. To help you along that path, a summary of the nine foundational questions is given in appendix 2.2.

Exercises

1. Meet with at least five students in your programme. Interview the students. What is the background of your typical incoming students, in terms of family, socio-cultural, economic and religious context, education level, and so on? Give at least six major curricular issues that arise from this analysis.

2. Try to determine an approximate statistic that describes the ministry contexts of alumni. To what extent has your current programme adequately or inadequately prepared your alumni for their ministries? Name at least one significant curricular change that you could make that would better serve the probable future ministry contexts of the students engaged in your programme.

3. Describe the time and delivery limitations of your curriculum. How much access time do you have or are you likely to have with your students, and over what period of time? Describe separately the times related to potential engagement in classroom and non-classroom learning activities.

4. Describe in as much detail as possible the context in which the delivery of your curriculum takes place, paying particular attention to room layout, the chairs and tables, lighting – both natural and artificial – heating and/or cooling, teacher resources such as projectors and/or boards, the quality of the paintwork, and so on. If it is an institutional context, also describe in as much detail as possible some of the other learner facilities, such as libraries, lounges and residential dormitories. Draw a map or diagram of the typical learning context you use in your programme.

5. Consider the learning contexts that exist in your programme of study. In light of a missional-ecclesial understanding of theological education, what are some of the relative strengths and weaknesses of the various contexts you use? Recognizing the severe financial limitations of your training programme, give at least three specific ways in which you could enhance the learning environment.

6. If you had total freedom, how would you conceptualize the curriculum for your programme? In light of your responses to curricular questions 1 to 5, what would be absolutely crucial elements? What are the major contextual challenges which need to be addressed? How might the holistic formation (knowledge, character and skills) of students be nurtured? How might you prepare the

students for lifelong learning? Using one of the sample curricular shapes, or ideas of your own, sketch your ideal curriculum.

7. In light of your responses to curricular questions 6 to 8, what are likely to be some of the major capacity limitations to the implementation of your ideal curriculum? What changes do you anticipate need to be made to your curriculum in order for implementation to take place? Give one or two specific suggestions for how you might address some of the major challenges confronting the implementation of your ideal curriculum.

Appendix 2.1

Saïd and Mariam

Saïd				
Individual	*Family*	*Faith community*	*Society*	*Skills*
How to relate to God? Personal worth Authority of Scripture Divine guidance Identity	Marriage & roles Parenting Family communication Extended family relations Sexuality	Worship History/heritage of community Fellowship/ belonging Leadership Structures Mentoring Choosing leaders/ succession Generational development Self-development responsibility	Poverty & economics Violence & insecurity Politics & the Christian Injustice Social change Corruption History Environment Culture	Inductive Bible study & Scripture interpretation Social & cultural analysis Leading small groups Storytelling Teaching: creative, learner-centred, lifelong Facilitating change Mentoring Small groups Discipleship Administration and management

Mariam				
Individual	*Family*	*Faith community*	*Society*	*Skills*
Self-worth in God Discrimination Divorce or second wife	"Submission" Consequences of divorce In-law relations Household management Relationship to other men (not husband, brother, father)	Submission in the church Mentoring other women Biblical examples/ teaching	Social change for women Society's attitude towards women Physical & sexual abuse Female excision	

Appendix 2.2

The Right Questions

1. *What Is the Ideal Church in Our Context?* What would the ideal church look like – one that is sensitive to God's mission and able to empower all of God's people to be significant ambassadors for Christ and his gospel?

2. *What Are the Contextual Challenges?* What are some of the challenges that confront the church, that hinder it as an effective agency for the proclamation of Christ? Consider both external challenges (how the societal context hinders proclamation) and internal challenges (particular chronic weaknesses within the Christian faith community).

3. *What Might an Ideal Christian Leader Look Like?* For your own specific local context, what are the chief characteristics of the ideal Christian leader, the sort of person who would be able to lead the church through its contextual challenges towards the accomplishment of the general goal you have articulated? What sorts of character traits, skills and knowledge would be needed to best accomplish the task of Christian leadership in your context? On the basis of these reflections, develop a "profile of the ideal graduate".

4. *Who Are the Learners?* What arc the sorts of communities from which they come (urban, suburban or rural; mono-cultural or multi-cultural)? The levels and types of religiosity of their upbringings? The sorts of churches they come from?

5. *Where Do the Students Go?* What kinds of roles do your alumni have? What sort of people do they serve? Are they wealthy, middle class or poor? Level of education? Urban, suburban or rural? Individualistic or communal? Religious or a-religious? What do your alumni describe as being some of the greatest challenges they have faced? The greater the diversity in alumni ministry contexts, the greater the need for diversity in the curriculum.

6. *When? The Time Frame.* An endemic problem in curriculum design is allocating too much "What?" for the "When?". The "When?" includes all potential formal times (classroom or equivalent), non-formal times (structured but non-classroom – e.g., mentoring, discipleship groups, internships), and informal times (e.g. general time over meals, trips together and casual encounters that hold potential for informal learning). The "null" curriculum.

7. *Where? The Learning Environment.* What are your material resources? To what extent does the physical context help or hinder learning? How do physical limitations impact the educational possibilities?

8. *Who Will Facilitate the Learning?* Who are your human resources? How many people are involved in facilitating the learning? What is the nature of their training? How much do they know about teaching? Capacity is a highly significant element in curriculum design.

9. *What and How?* Once the initial eight questions have been answered, you will be in an adequate position to consider what the actual curriculum might look like.

3

Implementing and Assessing the Curriculum

Developing and implementing a curriculum is time consuming and demanding. Instructors need to be recruited, course syllabi developed, lessons taught and students' learning evaluated. Schools often function with limited resources. It is therefore not surprising that few schools do more than a cursory assessment of whether the programme of study is actually accomplishing what it claims to exist for. Increasingly, this state of affairs is being challenged, as national governments and accrediting agencies call for a greater level of accountability.

De Gruchy's (2010, 45) comparison of medical and theological education is a sobering challenge to see as imperative a continual process of assessment, review and curricular revision:

> In the former [medical education], the education of the next generation of health professionals is driven by constant attention to clinical practice, drug trials and technical breakthroughs. It makes no sense, and in fact endangers lives, to train students in procedures which are no longer up to date. By contrast, theological education often proceeds on the basis that we have learnt nothing new about the Christian faith in the last centuries, and students can be educated solely on the basis of the wisdom of the ages. Without negating the importance of history and tradition, the truth is that missional practice provides an ongoing contextual laboratory for theological reflection raising new issues and new perspectives on old issues almost daily. Our commitment to life, and to being on the cutting edge of responding to life, should be as profound as that of medical educators.

In this chapter we will investigate the various dimensions of a robust process of assessment. You will be introduced to a variety of practical tools for assessment, as well as to some of the challenges to implementation of quality curricular assessment.

What Exactly Are We Doing?

My colleague at ABTS Rupen Das (Haddad and Das 2012) has sought to adapt the language of community development to theological education by suggesting that there are four levels of process that each needs to have a voice in assessing the curriculum:

- The first level is that of *Activity*: what we are engaged in on a day-to-day basis. Effectively, this is the curriculum we deliver, which includes, among other things, classroom instruction, the work students complete outside the classroom, field education, and formational activities such as mentoring, community worship and discipleship groups. These activities are supported by the administration and take place in learning spaces such as classrooms, online environments or chapel.

- These activities are designed to produce an *Output*: graduates at the end of the programme of study who evidence some sort of quantitative and qualitative growth as Christian leaders.

- However, the purpose of our efforts is not merely the individual growth of students but an *Outcome* of churches that are more effective as a result of the ministry that our graduates bring to their local faith communities. If there is no meaningful change in the churches we are serving, we have failed in our task as schools of ministry formation.

- But this is not the final word. We exist to participate in God's mission of global restoration through the church as the body of Christ, and consequently we seek to see local churches having an *Impact* on their communities. If there is little impact or, worse, if the churches are "invisible" in their local communities, we must raise major questions about the efficacy of what we are doing in our theological programmes. Of course, it is impossible to establish a direct cause–effect relationship between our programmes of study and community impact, as multiple factors contribute to the church's impact on the local community. However, we nonetheless need to attempt to devise tools that will help us assess the contribution of our graduates in transforming the ministries of their churches so that they become more effective in their communities.

These levels can be represented as shown in figure 3.1.

Activity
Theological Education
Curriculum
Output
Change as a result of the activity
Graduates
Outcome
Change as a result of the outcome
Churches
Impact
Longer-term societal change
Society

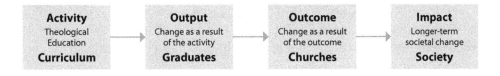

Figure 3.1 The four levels in assessing a curriculum

Quality assessment entails engagement at each level, as shown in figure 3.2.

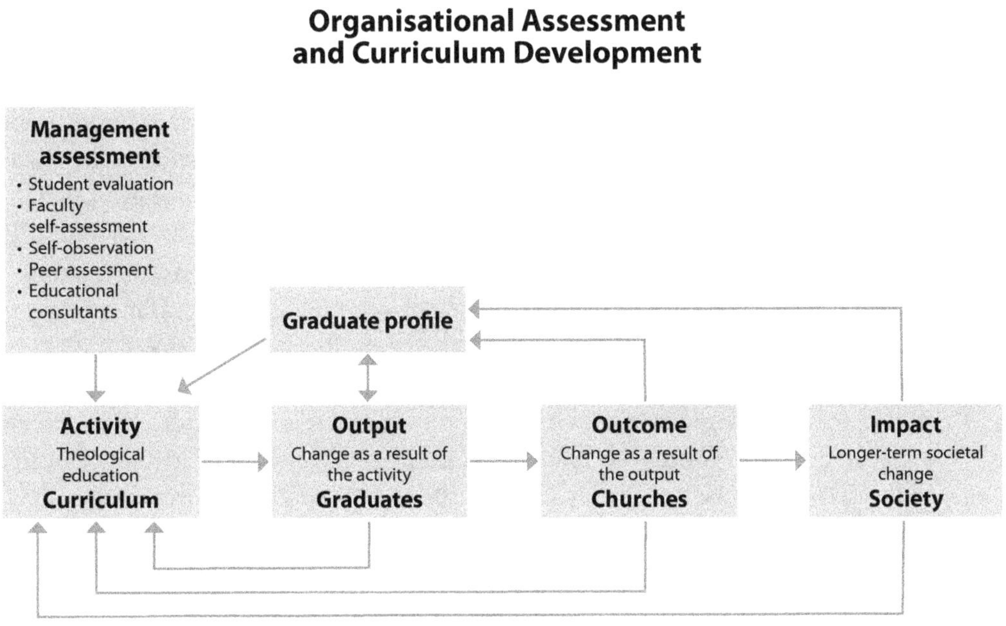

Organisational Assessment and Curriculum Development
Management assessment
• Student evaluation
• Faculty self-assessment
• Self-observation
• Peer assessment
• Educational consultants
Graduate profile
Activity
Theological education
Curriculum
Output
Change as a result of the activity
Graduates
Outcome
Change as a result of the output
Churches
Impact
Longer-term societal change
Society

Figure 3.2 Assessment at the four levels

In the remainder of this chapter we will deal with the various components of this process of thoroughgoing assessment.

Management Assessment

The starting point for ongoing assessment is internal quality management. This includes such processes as student course assessments, peer evaluations and administrative assessment.

The most common form of internal management assessment used in schools is that of *student evaluations of faculty* (SEFs) conducted at the conclusion of courses. These generally comprise a series of questions in which students rate the quality of the content and methodology used in the course, the relevance of the material, and the clarity and fairness of the requirements and their assessment. Usually, space is also provided for free response, particularly suggestions for ways in which the course could be improved in the future. There is an enormous body of literature on SEFs – some positive, some very negative. On the one hand, SEFs have been found to be fairly reliable and consistent, with a high level of agreement among students in their ratings of instructors. No other form of assessment has been found to produce such consistent results (Huemer n.d.).

However, on the other hand, in a number of studies (Rice 1988; Wilson 1998) a significant correlation has been found between SEFs and professorial leniency with grade inflation. In other studies it has been found that high SEFs are linked more to style than to substance: an enthusiastic and authoritative style tends to draw high evaluations even when the content is superficial or even contradictory (Naftulin, Ware and Donnelly 1973; Abrami, Levanthal and Perry 1982). These high evaluations based on style even impact attitudes towards impersonal elements such as textbooks (Williams and Ceci 1997). It seems that a two-item survey would generally suffice for most situations, because students subconsciously treat each of the many items of a typical SEF as a variant of one of the following two questions: (a) Does the professor seem like a nice person? and (b) Is the class well organized?

It is impossible for any course to provide both extensive content and a high degree of creative engagement. Moreover, student needs and expectations vary enormously. Consequently, there can be a tendency for students to focus on the shortcomings of the course and the instructor, rather than acknowledging what was learned through the course. SEFs can therefore be quite devastating for diligent instructors: having exerted substantial effort in preparation within the limited time available, they can be extremely discouraged to receive a string of complaints about the course. It is therefore important for instructors to be trained to read SEFs selectively and constructively.

Recognizing the shortcomings associated with traditional SEFs, several schools have expanded the approach such that student evaluations become more reciprocal: students are asked not only to evaluate the course and the instructor, but also themselves in terms of their personal engagement and interpersonal cooperation. One example of a reciprocal student evaluation form is provided in appendix 3.1.

Student evaluations are less likely to be valid if they are made voluntary. It has been found that women are more likely than men to complete voluntary evaluations, and students who are performing poorly are less likely to complete an evaluation. These factors bring notable bias into the process (Kherfi 2011). It is better either to have student evaluations as compulsory or not to have them at all.

For SEFs to have meaning, there needs to be a conclusion to the feedback loop. Quality schools require instructors to communicate changes they intend to implement on the basis of the evaluations, and these changes are then reported back to the students and the administration. If this process is not undertaken, the student evaluations become a largely meaningless exercise.

Beyond SEFs there are numerous other forms of management assessment that are used to a greater or lesser extent in schools as a means of promoting accountability and enhanced delivery:

- *Faculty self-assessment.* It is generally preferable for faculty self-assessments to be descriptive rather than evaluative. Some of the issues that instructors could be asked to report upon are punctuality at class, types of instructional methodology employed in the classroom, quantity of key themes addressed in the course, methods used for seeking to assess student learning, hours spent with students out of class, time taken to return work, ways in which responses were made to student work and the breadth and depth of these responses. These comments can then be cross-referenced with other evaluative tools, such as SEFs.

- *Self-observation.* Many schools have found it beneficial to require instructors to be videoed from time to time, observe the recording and write a self-evaluative report on what they notice. Most instructors are unaware of idiosyncratic practices that become starkly evident in a recording.

- *Peer assessment.* There can be mutual benefit from peer assessment in that the one evaluating and the one being evaluated can learn from each other. Peer assessment might come through administrative assessment – examining course syllabi, examinations, student work, and so on – or through classroom observation in which modes of delivery, teacher–student interaction and course substance might be assessed. While there is great potential benefit in peer assessment, there are also dangers, especially where there is a spirit of competition between faculty members or tenure is at stake. In many honour–shame societies, peer assessment may be culturally difficult to implement, as peers are reticent about "shaming" a colleague. It also needs to be acknowledged that peer assessment has been found to have poor reliability: colleagues and external observers rarely agree with each other in rating instructors (Marsh and Roche 1997).

- *Educational consultants.* A more costly but potentially beneficial approach is to have an instructional consultant observe faculty members. However, many of the concerns common to peer assessment (mentioned above) are likely to emerge with consultants as well.

Graduate Assessment of the Curriculum

One of the best sources of evaluative information on the curriculum as a whole can be recent graduates. As those who have passed through and completed the whole programme of study, graduates are in the best position to point out redundancy, as well as areas that have played a particularly significant role in their formation to date.

Graduate assessment can sometimes be sobering for institutional faculty, especially those with a book-learning academic bent. A recent major piece of research (VerBerkmoes et al. 2011) conducted in the United States discovered that, while most schools focus their curricula on knowledge acquisition, graduates recorded "integrity" as the most significant issue that needs addressing in the curriculum. While Bible and theological knowledge, and exegetical and homiletic competencies, scored high as crucial elements, of equal value were a love for people, humility, interpersonal skills and resilience. Biblical languages scored lowest of all suggested competencies.

The "profile of the ideal graduate" should play a substantial role in both the shaping and the assessment of the curriculum. An enormous amount of curricular feedback can be generated by the simple process of asking students to undertake a self-assessment based on this profile upon entering the programme of study and then again just prior to leaving. Even better is when the self-assessment is completed at the beginning of each year and then prior to graduation. This material can then become the basis for a level of quantitative analysis of the extent to which the students perceive themselves to be learning and growing through their experience of the programme of study. Interestingly, a piece of research (Wazir 2013) that tracked self-assessments at ABTS over the course of three years discovered a dramatic drop in self-assessment between the beginning of the first year and the beginning of the second year, and then a steady and statistically significant rise in self-assessment over the remaining period in the programme of study.

Alumni can also be significant voices in assessing the curriculum. It often takes several years after graduation to determine (a) what material from the programme of study has been particularly meaningful for effectiveness in life and ministry; (b) what material has been largely irrelevant; and (c) what significant areas of knowledge and skill necessary for effective ministry were missing from the programme. Valuable information for curricular reform can be gleaned through interviewing alumni five to ten years after graduation with appropriate questions addressing these three areas.

A cautionary note: graduate and alumni responses to (a) and (b) above will very often be related more to the quality of the instructor who delivered the material than to the actual substance of the course. Major curricular change should not be made solely on the basis of alumni assessment, but rather in tandem with assessment from other sources.

Engaging the Local Churches in Assessment

In light of the missional-ecclesial vision for theological education, it is important that the voices of local churches be heard in the assessment of our curricula. The rapidly changing context for ministry points to the value of allowing the churches to speak to our curricula in a substantial way at least every three to five years.

While denominational leaders and pastors are important stakeholders in assessment by local churches, they are often not the most valuable voices. As most of these leaders have themselves passed through theological training, it is generally difficult for them to consider creative alternatives for effective curricula. Moreover, for many of these leaders, any substantial change to the curriculum will subconsciously be perceived as discrediting their own training experience. In some cases, denominational leaders and pastors push for more traditional education rather than creative innovation.

The more valuable voices in local-church assessment generally come from lay leaders without formal theological training: elders, youth leaders, children's workers, those gifted in evangelism or mentoring, Christian businesspeople, Christian teachers and so on. These are generally people with a passion for the health and growth of the church. They often have sharp analytical minds and insight into contemporary trends in education and training. They have also been found to be the most vocally critical of traditional ministerial training programmes.

There are a number of ways in which key leaders can be engaged in assessment. Many schools find it valuable to hold periodic one-day events in which these leaders are asked to respond to the second and third questions raised in chapter 1 ("What are the contextual challenges?" "What might an ideal Christian leader look like?"). The responses can readily be incorporated into the "profile of the ideal graduate" of the programme. Often, specific curricular gaps emerge in the discussion.

Where there are committed Christians with expertise in business leadership or secular higher education, these experienced lay leaders can help schools to break out of traditional paradigms and discover new patterns of education that better serve the missional-ecclesial vision of our training programmes.

The Community and Assessment

The ultimate goal of our work is to see missional impact in the community. As Vaughn McLaughlin (2003, 26) astutely puts it, "A local church ought not just drive in on Sunday, have an hour-and-a-half of preaching and singing, and then leave. If you're in the community, then you ought to affect that community. I ask other pastors, 'If your church were to leave the community you're in, what impact would that have? Would they miss you? Would they weep?'" Yet, despite the vision of community impact, it is extremely rare for schools to seek community feedback on the curriculum.

Engaging the community can be challenging for a number of reasons. To begin with, many of the community leaders are not Christian and in some cases are openly hostile to the gospel. Even when they are sympathetic it can be difficult to know whom to consult and how to consult. Politicians often have strong vested interests associated with their voices. Most community leaders are not particularly interested in the training of church leaders. The process of community engagement is often more straightforward in collectivist societies than in individualistic societies, as local "patrons" are significant voices in community decision-making.

Generally, the process of community engagement will come through semi-structured interviews that are in the shape of conversation rather than formal assessment. However, a number of evaluative elements can be gleaned through such interviews:

- To what extent is the church "visible" in the community? In this we are not speaking of physical visibility (a church building), but rather an awareness of activities that are perceived to be restorative in the community.

- What is the general impression the community has of the church, and what lies behind this impression? Of course, simply asking this question in most parts of the world will be an invitation to uninformative flattery rather than honest assessment. More penetrating follow-up questions are needed to move beyond the superficial to the genuine perception of the situation.

- To what extent is the church seen to be both "prophetic" and "priestly" in the community, both outspoken in addressing evil and comforting for the broken and outcast? And how might the church better serve the community?

As responses are gathered to these questions, leaders of training programmes will need to consult with church leaders to determine the implications of these responses for the curriculum.

The Challenges of Assessment

Before concluding our discussion of assessment, it is important to acknowledge some challenges confronting any process of assessment and its implementation.

One of the greatest challenges of assessment is that some of the most important outcomes are intangible. As Eisner (1994, 184–85) has observed, the outcomes of good teaching are multiple and not always measurable. There is something ineffable and hard to define, let alone measure, when good teaching happens (G. Smith 2004). In seeking measurable standards, we can easily prioritize less-significant tangibles and ignore or dismiss highly significant elements simply because they cannot easily be specified and categorized.

Assessment is emotionally difficult for the faculty and administration of a school. Having worked hard to put together the best programme of study that is within the experience and capacity of our faculty and administration, we find that it is still not good enough. We need to recognize that there is no perfect approach, and while continual reassessment and strengthening of the curriculum is healthy and appropriate, we must not seek unattainable perfection. Our goal should rather be to deliver the best that is possible within the limited capacity in our hands.

Faculty ownership is crucial (G. Smith 2004). Ultimately, it is the faculty who deliver the curriculum; consequently, if they do not accept the need for assessment and the results that emerge, the assessment process will be ineffective. Faculty generally resist a process in which they have had little say, especially when they sense that the assessment process is simply an imposition from above (the board and the president) or from without (accrediting agencies). Involvement of faculty in the design and implementation of assessment is more likely to result in faculty ownership of the outcomes.

A careful assessment process inevitably highlights the gaps in the curriculum, and we can easily fall into the trap of trying to fill all these gaps. Particularly with regard to pastoral training programmes, there is the temptation to accept the faulty perspective that a graduate should be an expert at everything related to church life, and to seek to deliver thirty years of knowledge and experience in three years. Such an approach generally ends up focusing on traditional content delivery, with little opportunity for training students in thinking and processing skills. There is also the danger of students seeing the school as the only source of training, and they leave the school ill-prepared to engage in a lifetime of learning. A further concern in many pastoral training programmes is that by seeking to train students to be experts in everything we may be reinforcing a theologically questionable status quo. Far better is to focus on training emerging leaders to be facilitators for the whole people of God to be engaged in ministry.

Wise curricular development will take the comments and observations of key stakeholders as indicators of substantial areas that are lacking in the programme of study. As these areas are incorporated into the curriculum, other areas need to be de-emphasized or removed, such that the overall size of the curriculum remains fairly stable. The challenge is selecting between what is good and important, and what is crucial. As mentioned in chapter 2, educational theorists describe this process as the "null curriculum" – what we teach through what we include or exclude from our curriculum; this will be discussed further in chapter 5. Quality curricular development makes intentional the null curriculum; even better is to make the null curriculum public. Stakeholder feedback into the curriculum can play a significant role in making these hard choices.

A major challenge in stakeholder-informed curricular reform, however, is the specialist backgrounds of faculty members. As people who have devoted long years of study to their particular fields of expertise, they naturally see a vast array of material as crucial to leadership formation. Consequently, in many schools, curricular review becomes a territorial battle rather than a collegial effort. Viewing a curriculum in terms of core, track and elective elements can be helpful in easing these tensions. Even better is a move away from the traditional fragmented curriculum to a greater level of integration. This will be addressed in greater depth in chapter 6.

Those engaged in curricular review also do well to remember that the purpose of ministerial training programmes is to prepare people for ministry – not for higher degrees. In the contemporary global climate of higher education, there are numerous opportunities for students who wish to pursue higher studies to find necessary bridging courses that can provide the tools they need. It is not necessary for all these tools to be delivered in a first theological degree.

Finally, we need continually to keep in mind what we are trying to do in stakeholder assessment: to address unnecessary repetition in the curriculum and to become aware of substantial areas that are absent from the curriculum. We must be careful not to respond too quickly to "We must have more of this or that". We need to make sure that pronouncements of dissatisfaction do not simply express the preferences of more vocal and articulate individuals. It will only be as several voices point to gaps and the need for change that we can allow assessment to be a tool for seeking excellence in what we do.

Conclusion

In light of the missional-ecclesial vision for theological education, curricular change is not optional but imperative. New challenges are continually emerging which confront the church as it seeks to have a meaningful impact on the world, and serious theological educators need to be sensitive and responsive to these challenges in the formulation and review of curricula for ministerial training. Assessment is a key element in this process. Through continual management assessment at multiple levels, and through the contribution of key stakeholders such as alumni and church and community leaders, an informed approach can be taken to curricular review and revision. In this way, our curriculum will be in a better place to develop an effective process of training leaders for local churches as salt-and-light communities of faith.

Exercises

1. Develop your own course evaluation form through the following process: (a) Make a list of key instructional elements that you are seeking to assess. You may find the characteristics of excellence in teaching developed in chapter 16 a good starting point. (b) If it exists, consider your own programme's current assessment form, and make a list of additional items of significance. (c) Add additional items given in the ABTS sample (appendix 3.1). (d) Organize the various issues into between ten and twenty questions. (e) Develop a structure through which some form of numeric analysis could be made. (f) Bring all of the above together into your own evaluative form.

2. For each of the following groups of people, write at least three significant questions that could be addressed to them and through which meaningful assessment of the curriculum could be implemented: (a) alumni who graduated from the school five to ten years previously; (b) lay leaders in local churches; (c) community leaders.

Appendix 3.1

Reciprocal Student Evaluation of Self and Faculty at ABTS

It is very important for us to hear your reflections on classes at ABTS – your perspective on the course itself, the instructor and your own role in learning. To help us as we seek excellence in leadership formation, we ask you to complete the following analysis as honestly as possible. It is helpful for us if you place your name on the evaluation, but this is not compulsory.

Name (optional): _____

Part A

Each of the following pairs of statements represents opposite ends of a spectrum. Consider each pair and make an evaluation by placing a mark at an appropriate position on the spectrum line.

I was unsure in the beginning what the course objectives and expectations were.	3 2 1 0 1 2 3	The course objectives and expectations were clearly communicated from the beginning of the course.
I felt that the course objectives were achieved well	3 2 1 0 1 2 3	I felt that the course failed to achieve its objectives
The course focused on developing complex thinking skills where I was expected to analyse material and develop my own opinions and judgements	3 2 1 0 1 2 3	The course focused on basic information that I was expected to learn so that I could repeat it in pretty much the same form in which it was given
The course methodology was primarily through lecture with opportunities for question and answer	3 2 1 0 1 2 3	The course methodology de-emphasized lecture and used primarily discussion and workshop

| I rarely spoke in class | 3 2 1 0 1 2 3 | I contributed extensively to class discussion |

| The instructor used visual aids | 3 2 1 0 1 2 3 | The instructor focused on verbal communication only |

| The course was primarily practice | 3 2 1 0 1 2 3 | The course was primarily theory |

| The class sessions seemed very well organized to me | 3 2 1 0 1 2 3 | The class sessions seemed rather chaotic to me |

| I found it difficult to understand what the instructor was trying to say | 3 2 1 0 1 2 3 | I found it easy to understand what the instructor was trying to say |

| When I didn't understand, I asked the instructor | 3 2 1 0 1 2 3 | When I didn't understand, I kept my concerns to myself |

| The class mood did not encourage student contribution and participation | 3 2 1 0 1 2 3 | The class mood encouraged student contribution and participation |

| There was too much work in this course | 3 2 1 0 1 2 3 | There was too little work in this course |

| I found I didn't need to work very hard in this course | 3 2 1 0 1 2 3 | I personally worked extremely hard in this course |

| The criteria for assessment were known and understood | 3 2 1 0 1 2 3 | The criteria for assessment seemed arbitrary |

| I saw no need to consult the instructor in the completion of the required assignments | 3 2 1 0 1 2 3 | I prepared draft ideas for required assignments and consulted the instructor to check I was approaching the work correctly |

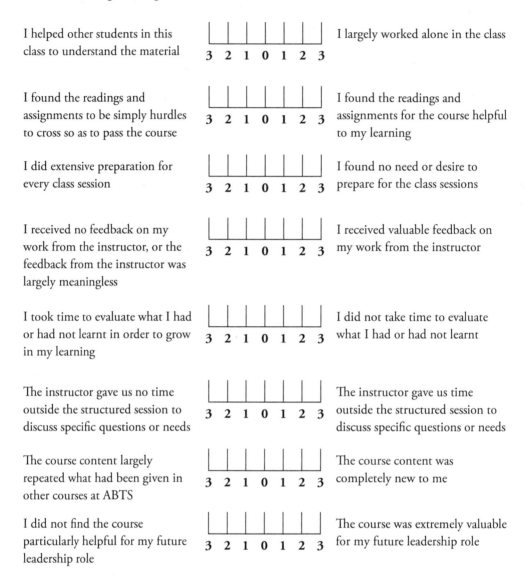

I helped other students in this class to understand the material	3 2 1 0 1 2 3	I largely worked alone in the class
I found the readings and assignments to be simply hurdles to cross so as to pass the course	3 2 1 0 1 2 3	I found the readings and assignments for the course helpful to my learning
I did extensive preparation for every class session	3 2 1 0 1 2 3	I found no need or desire to prepare for the class sessions
I received no feedback on my work from the instructor, or the feedback from the instructor was largely meaningless	3 2 1 0 1 2 3	I received valuable feedback on my work from the instructor
I took time to evaluate what I had or had not learnt in order to grow in my learning	3 2 1 0 1 2 3	I did not take time to evaluate what I had or had not learnt
The instructor gave us no time outside the structured session to discuss specific questions or needs	3 2 1 0 1 2 3	The instructor gave us time outside the structured session to discuss specific questions or needs
The course content largely repeated what had been given in other courses at ABTS	3 2 1 0 1 2 3	The course content was completely new to me
I did not find the course particularly helpful for my future leadership role	3 2 1 0 1 2 3	The course was extremely valuable for my future leadership role

Part B

In the space below, give one or two constructive suggestions for the course.
Please note:

- The purpose of this section is to help improve instructional processes, and not to criticize the person of the instructor. Consequently, negative personal comments will be ignored. However, polite and respectful suggestions for improving the teaching methodology are appreciated.

- The time available for this course is limited. Consequently, if you suggest an addition, you should also suggest what might be removed from the course.

- We particularly appreciate it when students highlight specific elements of the course that are taught elsewhere in the curriculum.

_____

_____

_____

_____

_____

4

Multidimensional Learning in Theological Education

L earning is a complex multidimensional process that goes far beyond cognitive input. A number of models and taxonomies have sought to describe systematically the variety and levels of learning. In this chapter you will be introduced to one of the oldest and most influential of these models, that developed in the 1950s and 1960s by teams led by Benjamin Bloom and David Krathwohl. The fundamental thesis of this chapter is that holistic learning for effective theological education can only be accomplished through the intentional promotion of:

- *Affective learning*, shaping values, attitudes, emotions and motivations.

- *Behavioural learning* through action and experience.

- *Cognitive learning* that moves beyond the mere transmission of knowledge to the development of complex thinking skills.

The ABCD of Learning

Many years ago, Joe Bayly commented that "the only similarity between Jesus' way of training and the seminary's is that each takes three years" (Richards 1975, 163). For too long, theological education has been tied to the university model that runs counter to the foundational patterns of discipleship and leadership formation employed by Jesus and the apostles. The missional-ecclesial mandate of theological schools invites a rediscovery of the patterns of holistic leadership evident in the Scriptures. To accomplish this, we must break out of our fixation with cognitive learning and move beyond mere talk about "head, heart and hands" towards intentional multi-dimensional curricular planning that embraces a broader understanding of learning.

The centrality of the mind and cognitive learning in our theological institutions is based on an understanding of knowledge rooted, not in the Scriptures, but in Greek philosophy and the Enlightenment (Riebe-Estrella 2009; P. Shaw 2010), according to which, knowledge is some sort of object that needs to be acquired. Parker Palmer (1998,

99–108), drawing heavily on the work of Michael Polanyi (1958, 1966), summarizes this faulty understanding as follows:

> [The] mythical but dominant model of truth-knowing and truth-telling has four major elements:
>
> 1. *Objects* of knowledge that reside "out there" somewhere, pristine in physical or conceptual space, as described by the "facts" in a given field.
>
> 2. *Experts*, people trained to know these objects in their pristine form without allowing their own subjectivity to slop over onto the purity of the objects themselves. This training transpires in a far-off place called graduate school, whose purpose is so thoroughly to obliterate one's sense of self that one becomes a secular priest, a safe bearer of the pure objects of knowledge.
>
> 3. *Amateurs*, people without training and full of bias, who depend on the experts for objective or pure knowledge of the pristine objects in question.
>
> 4. *Baffles* at every point of transmission – between objects and experts, between experts and amateurs – that allow objective knowledge to flow downstream while preventing subjectivity from flowing back up.
>
> In the objectivist myth, truth flows from the top down, from experts who are qualified to know truth … to amateurs who are qualified only to receive truth. In this myth, truth is a set of propositions about objects; education is a system for delivering those propositions to students; and an educated person is one who can remember and repeat the experts' propositions. The image is hierarchical, linear, and compulsive-hygienic, as if truth came down an antiseptic conveyer belt to be deposited as pure product at the end.
>
> There are only two problems with this myth: it falsely portrays how we know, and it has profoundly deformed the way we educate. I know a thousand classrooms where the relationships of teacher, students and subject look exactly like this image. But I know of no field – from astronomy to literature to political science to theology – where the continuing quest to know truth even vaguely resembles this mythical objectivism.

A theology of theological education seeks a learning paradigm with biblical roots. Central to such a paradigm is realizing that when the Bible speaks of "knowing", it is not speaking of some sort of objective knowledge, but of a relationship. To "know" in the Scriptures is to have relationship – the relationship between God and a person, between God and the community, between person and person (D. Miller 1987, 271) – a knowing relationship that finds its source in God's self-revelation to us. The affirmation of our need for God's self-revelation is central to theological education (Gillespie 1993): it is not a matter of *us* discovering truth, but of us coming to know *only as we are already known* (1 Cor 13:12; see Palmer 1983). Wright (2008, 239) comments,

We have traditionally thought of knowing in terms of subject and object and have struggled to attain objectivity by detaching our subjectivity. It can't be done, and one of the achievements of postmodernity is to demonstrate that. What we are called to, and what in the resurrection we are equipped for, is a knowing in which we are involved as subjects but as self-giving, not as self-seeking, subjects: in other words, a knowing that is a form of love.

It is significant that in both Old Testament Hebrew and New Testament Greek the term "to know" is used both for sexual intercourse and for the relationship the believer should have with God – pointing to the passionate, personal, relational nature of knowledge. As such, the scriptural call to "know" God is not a call to an objective theological understanding of God's characteristics (even though this can be of great value). Rather, knowing God entails entry into an "intimate personal interactive relationship" (Gorman 2001, 48) as children of a heavenly Father, in relationship with a community of brother and sister believers – a type of knowledge that speaks less of acquiring a masters degree in divinity than of being mastered by Divinity. In short, "knowing" in the Bible speaks not only of cognition, but much more of heart relationship and obedient action. To know God is to be changed by God (McGrath 2002, 139).

Most of our institutions of theological education are anachronistic in their understanding of teaching and learning. While condemning secular rationalism, there is a tacit affirmation of the basic tenets of rationalism through the almost exclusive focus on the cognitive domain. Even courses that are reputedly "skill development", perhaps requiring one or more practical assignments, are largely theoretical in nature. Meanwhile, for over fifty years educationalists have been discussing and analysing what have now become known as the three primary learning domains of affect, behaviour and cognition. Only when these three dimensions are embraced in a holistic concert can fundamental transformation – dispositional learning – take place. Only through a multidimensional approach to education in seminary and church can our learners become increasingly disposed to think, feel and act like Jesus – the ultimate goal of all Christian teaching (Eph 4:1–13).

While the language of "head, heart and hands" is now commonplace in theological schools, the practice continues to focus on the mind. In the remainder of this chapter, each of the affective, behavioural and cognitive dimensions will be examined as a framework for a balanced and holistic approach to curriculum development.

From the outset it needs to be acknowledged that any attempt to categorize learning is doomed to fall short. Learning is complex, and the physical, emotional, relational, cognitive, moral and spiritual aspects of the human person are closely intertwined. It is not surprising, therefore, that so many different models and taxonomies of learning have been suggested (Anderson and Krathwohl 2001; Fink 2003; Harrow 1972; Marzano and Kendall 2006; Shulman 2002; Simpson 1972). As mentioned at the start of this chapter, we will be drawing on the work of Bloom (1956) and Krathwohl (1964), not because their approach is more accurate or fully adequate, but rather due to the relative simplicity and understandability of their model, its widespread influence, and its ready applicability to theological education.

Affective domain

> Human beings are full of emotion, and the teacher who knows how to use it will have dedicated learners. (Leon Lessinger)

> That which does not make one feel, is of no interest; that which is of no interest, is not understood. (Simón Rodriguéz, Simón Bolívar's teacher)

> · Nine-tenths of education is encouragement. (Anatole France)

A serious appropriation of the affective domain is a theological imperative. Values, attitudes, emotions and motivations are matters of serious consideration for the biblical writers. The characteristics of the mature Christian as expressed in the fruit of the Spirit – love, joy, peace, patience, kindness, goodness, faithfulness, gentleness and self-control (Gal 5:22–23) – are all attitudinal in nature. The great commandment (Mark 12:30) does not begin, "Love the Lord your God with all your mind", but "with all your *heart*". Throughout the Scriptures, the heart plays a central role in the process of knowing. According to Paul, justifying belief occurs through the heart, not the mind (Rom 10:10). The broad biblical use of the term "heart" to embrace thinking, feeling and acting both points to the holistic understanding of spiritual growth and is an affirmation of the importance of the affective dimension of the human personality. The word "emotion" itself speaks of "motion": emotions move us (Moreland and Issler 2006, 62). The more we understand our emotional state and that of our students, the better able we will be to channel learning into action.

While right doctrine is certainly important in the Scriptures, right attitudes and right motivations carry equal if not greater significance. As Thomas à Kempis (2003, 1) observed,

> What good does it do to speak learnedly about the Trinity if, lacking humility, you displease the Trinity? Indeed it is not learning that makes a man holy and just, but a virtuous life makes him pleasing to God. I would rather feel contrition than know how to define it. For what would it profit us to know the whole Bible by heart and the principles of all the philosophers if we live without grace and the love of God?

Karen Shaw (2008, 53), in her study of the affective in the Scriptures, observes,

> The Bible is a book of great passion. It presents us with a passionate God who responds to and incites intense human emotions and discerns the noblest and basest of motivations.... [While it] would not be true to claim that

the Bible is *only* affective … [yet] it is *thoroughly* affective…. At times the emotions are dramatically understated, as in the story of Abraham's trip to Mount Moriah (Genesis 22). At other times the affective is highlighted as in the account of the death of Absalom (2 Samuel 18:9)…. If this is how God has disclosed Himself to us, then it follows that our communication of his word is inadequate unless it is thoroughly affective from start to finish.

Although the affective domain is difficult to measure, it plays a critical role in learning – more so than we usually acknowledge. Some fifty years ago, David Krathwohl (1964) and his associates developed a taxonomy of affective learning which continues to guide committed teachers in understanding the role played by values, emotions, attitudes and motivations in learning, and the stages towards full affective embrace.

- The first stage of affective learning is *receiving* – being willing to receive (or attend to) a particular viewpoint. Unless students pay attention to what a teacher says, rather than allowing their minds to wander off to the film they saw on television the previous night or the latest sports results, the effect of the instructional process is negligible or non-existent.

- But passive receiving is a rather poor sort of learning. We want students not simply to pay attention but to move to the level of *responding* – where they move beyond mere listening to actually doing something with the material, entering into classroom discussion, asking intelligent questions, or even discussing key points with the instructor after class.

- But serious instructors are not satisfied even with responding. They long to see their students move towards *valuing* – where the students have wrestled with a perspective and come to express a preference for a particular viewpoint.

- But expression of preference is only meaningful when *organization* takes place – where the students organize what they value into priorities, resolving conflicts between them, and creating a unique value system.

- The final goal is *characterization* – where the students build their lives around the particular viewpoint and its value system.

If we were honest, I think we would agree that the level of affective learning taking place in most of the classes held at our institutions is depressingly poor. Where the goal is characterization, too often students merely survive what they perceive to be fundamentally boring, and the willingness to reach even the level of receiving is largely the product of fear of failure rather than a genuine positive motivation to engage with the material.

The heart of affective learning is the quality of the *teacher–student relationship* (Brookfield 1986, 62–64; Cranton 2006, 112–15). Too often, we have forgotten that "Jesus was not so intent on teaching people religious content as he was on beckoning people into a genuine relationship with him and into compassionate relationships with one another" (Schultz and Schultz 1999, 59–60). In a wide variety of formal studies (Merriam, Caffarella and Baumgartner 2007, 152–53) it has been found that while such qualities as a passionate love for the subject, knowledge of the material and creative teaching styles are common among exceptional teachers, even more so are warmth, genuine concern for the students' learning, even love – all characteristics which speak of relationship and a hospitable classroom environment (P. Shaw 2011).

The rationalist advocacy for divorcing the cognitive from the affective has been found to be contrary to how the human mind is designed to learn. Neurological research has found that the brain does not "naturally separate emotions from cognition, either anatomically or perceptually" (Caine and Caine 1994, vii). Consequently, it should not surprise us that relationships in the classroom have been found to have a powerful impact on student commitment to learning (Rogers and Renard 1999).

Building strong teacher–student relationships is a particular imperative in the seminary. Gibson (2012) has observed, "God is fundamentally relational. Our theological education is therefore most Christian when it is the same." One piece of research (Banks 1999, 227) discovered that "what most people coming into theological institutions desire is the opportunity to get to know their teachers personally, and learn from them in ways that will help them grow spiritually and minister effectively.… While as teachers we regard academic concerns as the most important, students are equally or more interested in the personal and practical implications of what they are learning".

If we are serious about nurturing Christian attitude and character, it is not going to occur through maintaining a formal emotional distance in the classroom but rather through a relationship of love in which we mentor and model a life of quality to those God has called us to develop as future leaders of his church. Quality relationship is one of the foremost characteristics of instructional excellence and is discussed in greater depth in chapter 16.

Behavioural domain

> Knowledge is experience. Everything else is just information. (Albert Einstein)

> Knowing is not enough; we must apply. Willing is not enough; we must do.
> (Johann Wolfgang von Goethe)

Jesus's Great Commission (Matt 28:18–20) is presented by most evangelical theological schools as a significant mandate for every believer. However, the tacit message actually delivered through the emphases and methodologies embraced by our schools is that the Great Commission was to "teach them all things" (a cognitively oriented message), rather than the actual directive "teaching them to obey everything I have commanded you" (an obedience-oriented message).

For a long time, teachers in our seminaries have thought that if they could teach students sound theology, Greek exegesis and church history, these students would begin to function like Christian leaders. We have assumed that students will naturally put into practice what they learn in homiletics, teaching and counselling classes. In short, we have assumed that if we can persuade students to understand and believe the right things, they will act accordingly.

Over the past fifty years, however, social scientists have found much evidence to question that assumption. In 1964 Leon Festinger's research led him to advance the radical notion that the knowledge–behaviour relationship actually works the other way around – that is, people are more likely to behave their way into thinking than think their way into behaving. In the years since Festinger's seminal work, the evidence has continued to accumulate, increasingly pointing to the shocking conclusion that the expressed beliefs of a group of people are almost worthless in predicting how they behave.

This applies even among so-called "active" believers. Studies conducted by a Christian researcher in the early 1990s discovered that conservative Christian students who were orthodox in their beliefs about God and Jesus Christ and active in groups such as Campus Crusade and Navigators were as likely to cheat and as disinclined to volunteer as non-religious and atheist students (McNabb and Mabry 1990, 75). Equally disturbing was the research by the Barna Group (2004) that discovered that the rate of divorce among Americans who claimed to be "born again" was *higher* than that among non-religious Americans. Another researcher (Myers 1978) concluded bluntly, "As far as moral behaviour is concerned [religious belief] appears to have little effect." In the words of the great nineteenth-century educator Horace Bushnell (1979 [1861]), "No truth is taught by words or learned by intellectual means … Truth must be lived into meaning before it can be truly known."

The key to this process of behavioural learning is understanding the principles associated with the lost art of apprenticeship. How did the disciples learn how doctrine impacted life? They served as apprentices to Jesus for three years. While few of our schools are geared towards an apprenticeship model, anything we can do to enhance the behavioural domain in our teaching will have a profound impact on the quality of the education we offer. The European Bologna Process's affirmation of the significance of non-classroom-based learning should increasingly be embraced and emphasized in theological education. Preparation of missional-ecclesial leaders calls for missional-ecclesial experience.

Cognitive domain

Almost everyone has had occasion to look back upon his school days and wonder what became of the information he was supposed to have amassed during his years of schooling. (John Dewey)

The cognitive domain of learning is the prime focus of most schools – from kindergarten to post-graduate. Cognitive learning is attractive in that it is easy to control, easy to plan and easy to measure. However, even in the realm of cognitive learning, our record is mediocre at best, as the focus in too many of our institutions has remained on the acquisition of information – the transmission of vast quantities of data that students are required to learn and then regurgitate in the exams.

The acquisition of information is not enough: if we want to help our students to make an impact on the world for Christ, we need to cultivate more sophisticated thinking skills; we need to help them develop the ability to process and apply facts.

According to Bloom and his associates (1956), there are six different levels of cognitive sophistication, as follows:

- *Knowledge:* the ability to recall facts or information.

- *Comprehension:* the understanding of what is being communicated, and the ability to make use of the material at a simple level.

- *Application:* the ability to use abstractions in particular concrete situations.

- *Analysis:* the ability to break material down into its constituent elements or parts.

- *Synthesis:* the ability to build a structure or pattern from diverse elements, or to put parts together to form a whole, creating a more comprehensive meaning or structure.

- *Evaluation:* the ability to make judgements about the value of ideas or materials.

A simple way to understand these six levels is to consider a variety of questions related to the parable of the Good Samaritan (Luke 10:25–37):

- *Knowledge:* "Who left the man lying half-dead on the edge of the road?" The answer to this question is found in the text: if you *know* the text, you *know* the answer.

- *Comprehension:* "Why did the priest and the Levite pass by on the other side?" The answer is not given in the text, but requires *understanding* of the historical and cultural background to the text.

- *Application:* "Who are your enemies at school or in your neighbourhood? What could you do to be like the good Samaritan with these people?" This question asks that issues and principles be applied to a specific situation.

- *Analysis:* "What is the connection between the actions of the good Samaritan and the ethos of Jesus's own life and ministry?" The answer to this question requires that the elements of both the parable and the life and ministry of Jesus be broken down systematically and *analysed* through comparison.

- *Synthesis:* "*What is the relationship between word and deed in Christian witness? The good Samaritan showed love through action; but surely our love for the world compels us to speak the gospel. What do you think?*" Here there is an apparent contradiction that needs resolution through looking at the broader issues at stake and bringing these together in an overall synthetic understanding.

- *Evaluation:* "*What are the main things which prevent us from doing good to our enemies? Why do you think that Christ sets 'loving enemies' as one of the chief marks of a true disciple of his? Do you seriously think that the Tamils should forgive and show active love towards the Sinhalese, and vice versa? Surely to respond in love will only bring further persecution. What do you think?*" Here, evaluative judgements are solicited through raising questions about the relevance and applicability of the text to real life.

Bloom's Taxonomy of Educational Objectives

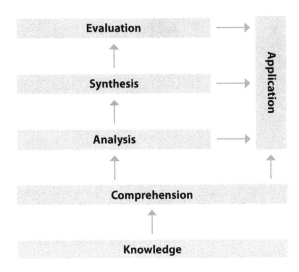

Figure 4.1 Bloom's taxonomy – a possible hierarchy

While it is not completely valid, there is somewhat of a hierarchy in Bloom's taxonomy (fig. 4.1): knowledge is preliminary to comprehension; comprehension is preliminary to analysis; analysis to synthesis; and synthesis to intelligent evaluation. Moreover, the more deeply one grasps the issues related to an idea or question, the more potentially powerful the application. Only when we challenge our students to think more deeply and take steps towards living and leading theologically can we claim to be fulfilling our holy calling of developing effective leaders for God's people.

Forming the disposition

The learning dimensions do not function in isolation but each affects the other (fig. 4.2): positive attitudes motivate students to think more carefully and take risks in action; experience changes beliefs and attitudes; and right thinking provides guidelines for evaluating both emotions and behaviour. The concert of the ABC of learning works together to form the disposition (D) of the student.

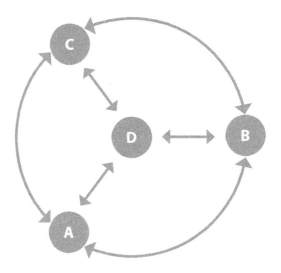

Figure 4.2 The interface of the learning dimensions

An imbalance between the learning dimensions creates distortions in the disposition: a focus on the affective domain leads to ignorant pietism; a focus on the behavioural domain leads to empty technical excellence; a focus on the cognitive domain leads to the pride and irrelevance that are endemic among many theological graduates. Excellence in theological education will recognize the need for a holistic balance which will lead to the healthy dispositional formation of the emerging leaders entrusted to our care.

Conclusion

As responsible theological educators, we can no longer accept the status quo of an imbalanced cognitively oriented education that is founded on the faulty epistemology of modernist objectivism. The challenge is before us to seek a holistic multidimensional approach to learning that alone can lead us on the path to excellence in curricular development.

Exercises

1. Describe two or three ways in which you see Palmer's (1998, 99–108) assessment of Enlightenment learning, quoted at the start of this chapter, at work in your own theological institution. To what extent do you agree or disagree with Palmer's negative assessment of this approach to learning? Why?

2. Riebe-Estrella (2009) and Shaw (2010) suggest that the dominant Enlightenment rationalist paradigm in theological education continues due to the cultural hegemony of white Western males in the academy, and should be a matter of grave concern to women and to those from other cultural contexts. To what extent do you agree or disagree with this assessment? Why?

3. Consider a class with which you are familiar in light of the stages in Krathwohl's taxonomy of affective learning. At what affective stage are the majority of learners? How could you measure whether learners had reached the stage of receiving? Responding? Organization or Characterization? To what extent does the instructor in this class provide opportunity for the learners to express the extent of their affective learning? Name one change which the teacher could make to enhance affective learning in the class.

4. The ABCs of learning permeate the Scriptures. Consider at least two of the following texts, and in a sentence or two explain how the text affirms a holistic interface between "head, heart and hands": Deuteronomy 6:5 (Matt 22:37; Mark 12:30; Luke 10:27); Deuteronomy 10:12–13; Deuteronomy 11:1, 22; Psalm 26:1–3; Psalm 139:23–24; Jeremiah 17:10; Revelation 2:23.

5. In what ways does your school seek to promote a healthy balance between the ABC dimensions? What are some of the main barriers limiting your school's effectiveness in holistic learning?

5

The Hidden and Null Curricula

The final measure of education is the total package of learning that takes place. The intentional instructional component plays only a part of the overall formational experience of students. A good curricular plan recognizes the importance of the environment and the impact of community life in learning. Particularly in theological education, who we are and what we do as a learning community are among the most influential factors in shaping the emerging leaders studying in our programmes (Hardy 2007, 130).

This chapter seeks to address the distinctions between:

- *The explicit curriculum:* those publicly known, stated and planned educational events which are commonly understood by all those who are participating.

- *The hidden or implicit curriculum:* the potent sociological and psychological dimensions of education, which are usually caught rather than intentionally taught.

- *The null curriculum:* what is learned through what is not taught –in terms of both the intellectual processes that are promoted or neglected, and the subject areas that are present or absent.

The fundamental thesis is that theological students learn about Christian leadership not merely through the content taught in the classroom, but also (and often more significantly) through such things as the way classroom teaching takes place, the model of teachers' lives, and the students' experience of the school's administration. An ignorance of the hidden and null curricula at work in theological education can result in the use of methods and structures which subtly undermine the content and intent of our schools. Theological education can only be effective when the hidden and null curricula receive as much attention as the explicit curriculum, and when they are intentionally designed rather than unintentionally accepted.

Gregory

The following is a true story. Only the name of the key character and a few peripheral details have been changed.

> Gregory was an exemplary student at theological college, gaining high grades and known for his keen philosophical mind. Gregory's denomination had provided him with a scholarship through seminary on the condition that he serve the denomination for three years after graduation. His first appointment was to serve as pastor of a small church in a regional city. The church had been without a pastor for over six years. Gregory was very enthusiastic and looked forward to being able to teach all the wonderful new ideas he had learned at seminary.
>
> Shortly after arriving and settling in the city, Gregory announced at the end of one Sunday's worship that the following Friday afternoon an exciting new adult-education programme would begin. Keen to see as many participate as possible, he telephoned key leaders in the church to invite them personally. Gregory was confident that addressing the theological ignorance of this sleepy congregation would transform it into a vibrant church with a powerful impact on the community.
>
> All week long Gregory studied and prepared, and he spent most of Friday setting up the classrooms: one in which he would teach Introduction to Church History from 4–5 p.m., one in which he would teach Introduction to New Testament from 5–6 p.m., and finally the class in which he would teach his pet subject, Introduction to Systematic Theology, from 6–7 p.m. At 4 pm he waited . . . and waited. At 4:30, two of the stalwart old ladies of the church arrived together. About twenty minutes later, an elderly couple arrived. All four stayed for an hour or so and then left. No others came.
>
> Not to be deterred, Gregory focused on the Introduction to New Testament, which seemed to interest these four the most. He again encouraged from the pulpit and by phone, and waited in anticipation for the following Friday. This time, nobody came. Gregory's enthusiasm was shattered, as were his feelings of hope for the church. It was only with reluctance and not a little cynicism that Gregory completed the minimum twelve months at the church, at which point he asked to be appointed to a youth-ministry position in another location. Two years later, he left ministry to study towards a PhD in theology.

When I first wrote down this story, I wondered whether it might be an extreme case in the fairly small world of Middle Eastern evangelical churches. Sadly, as I have presented the story at faculty training events in a wide variety of cultural contexts, I have found it resonating with many seminary faculty and graduates, as well as with lay congregants. Is it any wonder that so many of our congregations refer to seminaries as cemeteries and despise so much of the product of our labour? While many reasons could be posited for the problems illustrated in the story of Gregory, I would suggest that one of the primary factors is our ignorance of the profound impact of the hidden curriculum, and our consequent failure to address its potential negative impact. But what exactly is the "hidden curriculum"?

The Hidden Curriculum: Definition

Most of us, when we think of the word "curriculum", think of the course descriptions included in college catalogues and the syllabi we hand out to students at the beginning of each term. But this is only one form of curriculum, what is technically known as the "explicit" curriculum. The irony is that, while we often devote many long hours to planning our catalogues and syllabi, these are generally far less influential in the education of our students than are the sociological and psychological dimensions of education. These elements are usually caught rather than intentionally taught.

Drawing on the work of Emile Durkheim (1956, 1961), Philip Jackson (1968) first coined the term "hidden curriculum" to describe the sociological and psychological elements of learning. Strong research evidence for the significance of the hidden curriculum was first documented by Bowles and Gintis (1976), and subsequent research has confirmed the powerful influence on learning played by environmental features of education such as the nature of behaviours which are encouraged, the types of relationships modelled and the values emphasized in the learning community. The following simple story may help further illustrate the meaning of the hidden curriculum.

> Mary was a twenty-eight-year-old who taught a Sunday-school class of ten-year-olds. Mary was teaching the children the importance of loving one another. During the class, over half the questions were answered by "good" Christine. When it came time to pray, Christine was asked to do so; when a passage was to be read, Christine read; and on top of all this, the offering was taken up by Christine. Meanwhile, two particularly active and playful boys, George and John, received frequent rebukes, were spoken to harshly, and were finally sent to the Sunday-school superintendent.
>
> Now, while Mary was supposedly teaching on loving one another, the real lesson she taught – the hidden curriculum of her lesson – was "love is conditional on good behaviour", "love has favourites", "there are some who simply cannot be loved".

Here as elsewhere we see the uncomfortable truth that has been well documented by sociologists of education but largely ignored by institutional leaders in higher education: the hidden curriculum generally overrides the explicit curriculum – that is, if the explicit curriculum and the hidden curriculum conflict, the message learned will likely be that embedded within the hidden curriculum, not that taught in the explicit curriculum. Consequently, we ignore the hidden curriculum at our peril.

As with every educational institution, seminaries and Bible schools also have a hidden curriculum. But sadly, this hidden curriculum often trains our students in the exact opposite way to that which we teach in our explicit curriculum and claim in our purpose statements. While every institution approaches its education differently, and consequently provides a different form of hidden curriculum, this chapter will suggest some common hidden messages that many theological institutions communicate to their students. What follows is intentionally negative and provocative. In reality, most theo-logical schools have strong formative components to their institutional life which bring balance to the students' education. Nonetheless, a deliberate consideration of possible negative aspects of your school's hidden curriculum may empower your school to better fulfil its missional-ecclesial calling.

"Schooling" = "Education"

> The mind is not a vessel to be filled, but a fire to be ignited. (Plutarch)

One of the most common lessons that is taught through the hidden curriculum in our ministerial training programmes is this: the best way to help people grow spiritually is for them to be schooled in the Bible and theology. Put more simply, students are taught that "schooling" = "education". In virtually every theological school, grading and other forms of approval hinge on the cognitive mastery of biblical, theological and historical data which can be expressed on papers or in examinations. Illich's critique of school life could equally be applied to the seminary: "In school we are taught that valuable learning is the result of attendance; that the value of learning increases with the amount of input; and, finally, that this value can be measured and documented by grades and certificates" (Illich 1970, 56).

A premium is placed on the accumulation of information, and this prioritizing of head knowledge is subconsciously transferred to ministry, so that those with information rather than those who are examples of a godly life are likely to be selected for leadership roles in the local church (Richards 1975, 159).

The "schooling" model is readily seen in the standard classroom layout used in most theological institutions (fig. 5.1). Even as we enter a class such as this we know the presumed role of the teacher: instructor, director, professional expert authority, an intel-lectual master in the field of study (Lawson 1988, 67). There is a subconscious emotional distance created by the classroom layout that restricts a sense of freedom in opinion and discussion. As Thompson (1995, 134) describes it, "knowledge" is viewed as an external commodity to be digested like lunch, and "learning" is often little more than conforming to a teacher's expectations. It is the instructor who sets the agenda, who determines the syllabus and who is the centre of attention. In more traditional classrooms, most of the class time consists of the teacher lecturing in monologue, as though he or she is the only one who has anything important to say and students will be best served by listening. In this way, emerging leaders are "schooled" to confuse teaching with learning, grade advancement with education, and a diploma with competence (Illich 1970, 9).

The unspoken assumption in formal classroom settings such as these is that the students are ignorant "open receptacles", eagerly awaiting the answers to life's issues. Often the approach reflects the worst of what Freire (1970) has described as the "banking"

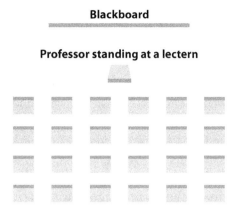

Figure 5.1 Standard classroom layout

system of education, or what Lindeman (1926) called the "additive process", in which the teacher receives from the students exactly what has already been imparted from the teacher's academic repository, while retaining total control over the goals, content and evaluative criteria of the educational activity. Foucault (1977) has suggested that the traditional classroom dynamic is an extremely efficient arrangement for the functioning of the "disciplinary mechanism", which entrenches power and hierarchy at the same time as training those subject to its workings. The very architecture functions to instil discipline, hierarchical relations, and respect for power and authority (Costello 2001, 56).

While this portrayal is perhaps overly negative, it is unfortunately all too common. While inevitably other factors do play a role, nonetheless, the more that the "schooling" approach is a dominant hidden curriculum in Christian training programmes, the more likely it is that graduates will take an emotionally distant "expert authority" pattern into church ministry.

Over the past forty years, Lev Vygotsky's (1962, 1978) work on the social construction of learning has received increasing credence. As we shall see repeatedly throughout this book, the human mind even from birth is not a *tabula rasa* upon which instructors write, and new knowledge cannot simply be transmitted from one person to another. When students are confronted with new information, they must process that information, building upon previous knowledge and experiences, before they can make sense of it, value it and apply it. While this process can take place in isolation, the richest learning experiences are socially constructed in a reflective practising, learning community (Fernández 2012). As dialogue and application are promoted in the context of the theological seminary, students are more likely to bring comparable patterns of significant learning into their subsequent ministries.

An Academic Approach to Ministry

90% of what we do in the Seminary looks backwards. (Manfred Kohl 2010)

The emphasis in most theological training institutions is on the study, analysis and evaluation of texts. While the benefit of this sort of research is enormous, when used exclusively the academic approach to theological education can train emerging leaders to believe that knowledge can only be found in books and an academic approach to ministry. The average age of theological students is growing, and increasingly we are training mature adults more than we are training students straight out of high school. That being so, our schools do well to take seriously the research into how adults learn ("andragogy"). These studies point to contextual relevance as the learning priority among adults: adults are motivated to learn what they need to live life effectively (Knowles, Holton and Swanson 2005, 58–72). The exposition of texts is not enough: the text must be connected to the context. When the connection is not made in the theological school, it is difficult for graduates to make the connections in their ministries.

The academic focus of many theological schools does little to prepare students for future ministry. Sadly, the emphasis all too often is on the delivery of vast quantities of biblical and theological information rather than on modelling the Christian life. As one pastor (Standish 2005, 12–13) described it, "I came out of seminary knowing how to exegete a passage, but I had no idea how to help a person struggling to find a sense of purpose or to feel God's love." While we teach orally "the Word became flesh", too often we teach psychologically and methodologically "the Word became text" (Éla 1988, 181).

This problem is hardly unique to theological seminaries. Brookfield (1986, 201) has observed the same phenomenon across the fields: "One of the most frequently offered criticisms of programs of professional preparation by graduates who subsequently inhabit the 'real world' of practice is that such programs are strong on theory but weak on practical application. It is not unusual to hear practitioners declare that their first few months of practice were spent unlearning the lessons of graduate training programs."

There is no question that the training of seminarians in the disciplines of critical thinking is an important preparation for ministry in an increasingly complex world. The problem is that too often the term "critical thinking" is limited to the comparison and analysis of academic texts. A much more demanding and complex form of critical thinking occurs when we ask students to become "practical Christian thinkers" (Hough 1984; Banks 1999, 34–45) or "reflective practitioners" (Schön 1991; Carr 1997, 113–53) through asking them to analyse, synthesize and evaluate theoretical academic material in the light of practical life situations, and vice versa.

Knowledge-Centred Hierarchy

There is a tendency in many seminary classes to make frequent reference to the original languages and scholarly books, often belittling straightforward interpretations as simplistic and praising complex interpretations as "scholarly". While careful scholarship must be a priority in our training, there is nevertheless a danger that the hidden curriculum might be developing a knowledge-centred arrogance in students, teaching them that only the educated can truly understand the Scriptures, and viewing the simple faith of many believers with disdain.

Goffman's (1959) deconstruction of the academy suggests that we create extensive educational programmes for professionals, not because there is so much to learn, but to gain credibility and status by virtue of academic degrees and specialized training programmes. Members of the public are then led to believe that because their training is woefully inadequate, things should be left to the professionals. While Goffman's analysis is no doubt overly negative, certainly the hidden curriculum in many theological schools teaches that most churchgoers are incapable of coming to the true understanding of the Scriptures and so need us scholars to tell it to them. While paying lip service to the great Reformation teaching of "the priesthood of all believers", the hidden curriculum teaches that there is a new priestly hierarchy, with the academics at the top, followed by the graduates, and with the average Christian in need of the sacerdotal interpretative work of others.

In reality, there is often an ambivalence among lay people towards seminary graduates. On the one hand, they sense that the graduates deserve to be placed on an "ecclesiastical pedestal" because of their theological education. On the other hand, they wonder whether the same graduates fail to understand the realities of life – as if they graduate with the right answers, but addressing the wrong questions (Harkness 2010, 106–8).

Leader Control

The situation is further exacerbated by the tendency of professors to control the syllabus totally. One of the most insidious outcomes of curricular control is the extent to which it undermines the creativity that is essential to our being created in God's image. Illich observes, "Once young people have allowed their imaginations to be formed by curricular instruction, they are conditioned to institutional planning of every sort. 'Instruction' smothers the horizon of their imaginations" (Illich 1970, 56).

If, however, we affirm the value of individuals as created in the image of God, we must provide opportunity for creativity through broadening the variety of instructional methods we employ, enabling our very different students to learn and apply God's truth in very different ways – ways that, while remaining consistent with God's demands, nonetheless reflect their own individual learning styles.

Few instructors consult with the students before delivering the course syllabus as if "from on high". Too often, our classrooms consist of a professor controlling the questions asked and determining the correctness of the answers given by the students. Illich's (1970, 28) description sounds all too familiar when he claims that in educational institutions, "most resources are spent to purchase the time and motivation of a limited number of people to take up predetermined problems in a ritually defined setting". The tragedy is that many students take the same model into their church ministries: inasmuch as our curricula do not connect to the lives of our students, the teaching our graduates take into their churches far too often is irrelevant to the lives of their congregations.

Harkness (2013, 7) observes that,

> In terms of processes for personal transformation, the classical teacher/ student model, with its emphasis on the teacher conveying information for the students to seek to apply by themselves, was readily available in the time of Jesus and the early Church. But the New Testament focuses much more on teaching/learning models which share the connotations of terms like discipleship, spiritual formation, nurture and parenting to enable holistic growth for effective Christian lifestyle and ministry.

Samuel Escobar (2004), reflecting on the contemporary shift of the church to a global-ministry mosaic, suggests that the development of a "participatory pedagogical approach" is no longer optional. As an expression of *koinonia* between faculty and students experiencing both local and global changes, a greater level of listening and learning must take place. If this can be modelled in the seminary classroom, it is more likely to take place in our graduates' subsequent ministries.

One Size Fits Nobody

Too many seminaries take a "one size fits all" approach to theological education, providing little in the way of flexibility and student choice within programme and course requirements. And as with "one size fits all" clothing, so with theological education: the end result is "one size fits nobody". In contrast, contemporary learning styles theory (examined in chapter 14) points to the huge variety in student learning processes, and the imperative of providing variety in both content and methodology to best nurture student growth.

While paying lip service to the gifts of the Holy Spirit, our hidden curriculum, through minimizing student choice in the courses available, bespeaks a commitment to graduate uniformity that simply cannot be justified theologically. The contrast with Jesus's individualized and incidental approach to leadership training is dramatic.

Ministry Is about Competition not Cooperation

The seminary setting, like the secular school, tends to throw individuals into academic competition with one another, which encourages interpersonal distance rather than closeness. Virtually all the assignments are solitary and individualistic, and a premium is placed on grades despite their questionable value in terms of predicting occupational achievement, and overwhelming evidence of their destructive nature (Wlodkowski and Ginsberg 1995) and the ungodly attitudes they promote. Is it any wonder that so many of our students come to see ministry as a matter of individual competition rather than cooperation in community (Hough and Wheeler 1988, 1), and measure success in life and ministry on external bases, often hiding their own internal spiritual poverty?

Interestingly, a study (Cano-Garcia and Hughes 2000) found that those students who achieve the highest grades academically are actually those who prefer to work individually, who show a willingness to conform to existing rules and procedures, and who do not enjoy creating, formulating and planning for problem solution – qualities that are the exact opposite of those found in the creative and visionary leadership so desperately needed today. Goleman (1995, 38) comments, "To know that a person [has succeeded in school] is to know only that he or she is exceedingly good at achievement as measured by grades. It tells you nothing about how they react to the vicissitudes of life."

The question we should ask is not "What grade does this paper deserve?" but "What approach to assessment will best help this student become an effective leader for a missional church?" There are better ways to promote lifelong learning for Christian leadership than that found in traditional tight grading systems.

The Culture of the School

One of the most subtle but influential elements of the hidden curriculum is the culture and structure of the school as a whole. The relationship between the administration, the faculty, the staff and the students communicates potent messages about the nature of Christian leadership and community. Where administrators are distant and authoritarian, students will follow this model, ignoring any classroom instruction about the importance of team leadership. If unresolved interpersonal conflicts exist within the school, students will not take seriously lessons that urge the centrality of reconciliation and peacemaking in the leadership of Christian faith communities. Where "important" members of faculty do minimal preparation and teach the same material year after year, students quickly pick up the message that once you have reached a position of status, you no longer need to grow as a leader (Hardy 2012).

Even the physical layout of a campus teaches our students. If senior administrators have plush offices, while junior faculty are allocated no more than a desk and a bookshelf in a crowded office, students rapidly see the privileges of seniority. Our hidden curriculum undermines all that we may speak and teach about "servant leadership". Likewise, the working conditions of staff model to students the ways in which church staff should be treated.

Students rapidly come to understand power relationships within the theological community, and subconsciously take that model into their ministries. Programmes that seek to address potential negative elements of the hidden curriculum must take seriously the following questions, and measure the responses in light of foundational biblical-theological principles:

- Who has power? To what extent is power centralized or dispersed? How is power exercised?

- How does communication take place? Is it open and bidirectional, or is there a significant level of covert or unidirectional communication?

- Who makes the final decisions, and how? Do decisions descend from above or is there a process of consultation? Are decisions based on careful processes of problem analysis, or do they tend to be arbitrary and impulsive?

The design and application of institutional policy is a particularly significant element of organizational culture that impacts students' implicit learning. Where policies are rigid and impersonal, the school communicates a value of legalism and conformity rather than mature relationships and critical thinking. Where policies are simply "ink on paper" and processes are implemented based on client–patron relationships, students come to model this approach in their practice of Christian leadership (P. Shaw 2013b). Creating a balance between order and relationship in policy design and implementation is not a straightforward process, but effective schools recognize its importance for shaping students' understanding of Christian ministry.

The Null Curriculum

Of profound significance in our education is what is taught through what is not taught – what Eisner (1994) has called the "null curriculum". No school can teach everything, and consequently there are always topics and subjects which are excluded from the explicit curriculum. Eisner observes that "what schools do not teach may be as important as what they do teach. I argue this position because ignorance is not simply a neutral void; it has important effects on the kinds of options one is able to consider, the alternatives that one can examine, and the perspectives from which one can view a situation or problems" (97).

The same applies in theological education: the material we include or exclude, the topics that are emphasized or underplayed – all of this communicates a powerful message to our students as to what is or is not important for Christian life and ministry. For example, in most seminaries the priority is given to biblical, theological and historical studies, while courses addressing spiritual formation and prayer are absent from the curricula, or at best play only a minor role, as though these are peripheral issues unworthy of serious theological reflection and careful training. It should therefore not surprise us that a major survey of theological schools revealed that fewer than 40 per cent of theological students felt their seminary experience helped them grow spiritually (Banks 1999, 200), and another study found numerous graduates complaining of "feeling spiritually cold, theologically confused, biblically uncertain, relationally calloused and professionally unprepared" (Dearborn 1995, 7) as a result of their seminary education.

Similarly, a study of Australian pastors (Burke 2010) found that 45 per cent felt that deficiencies in their theological training caused stress early in their ministries, with the most common complaint being a lack of training in practical, interpersonal and counselling skills. And yet few of our programmes of study emphasize skill development in peacemaking and interpersonal relations. The null curriculum may well communicate to students that conflicts in church and society are insoluble and that we can do nothing about them.

It is noteworthy that in the recent "Global Survey on Theological Education" (Esterline et al. 2013) the four areas which were perceived to need strengthening in theological education – cross-cultural communication, spiritual formation, practical skills related to ministry, and missiology – are often absent or at best weak in our schools' curricula. In ignoring or sidelining these elements, our schools are often out of tune with the needs and concerns of key stakeholders.

Too many of our professors teach without prayer or recognition of the need for the Holy Spirit's direction in theological teaching. By so doing we run the danger of communicating to our students that God does not care about what we are teaching, or even that God is not present in academic classes. Do we subconsciously deliver the message that God is the enemy of truth? Certainly we communicate to our students that prayer is only of secondary importance, and possibly we reinforce the commonly held belief of too many in our congregations that faith is a private matter and should not intrude on other areas of life – academics, social relationships, use of money, lifestyle, and so on. All too easily we can deliver the message to our students that there are aspects of life which are spiritual and others which are not – rather than seeing all that we are and do as intimately related to our identity as spiritual beings.

We cannot teach everything, and traditional emphases may exclude elements that deserve greater prioritization. An open and intentional discussion of the null curriculum can enable our schools to better prepare leaders to serve their communities.

Conclusion

A number of foundational issues have been raised in this chapter on the hidden and null curricula.

- Significant learning is embedded in the hidden curriculum of the sociological and psychological patterns at work in an educational institution. In theological education, students are influenced in their understanding of

Christian leadership by the attitudes and practices of faculty, administration and institutional policies.

- Instructional practices in the classroom create a model to our students for understanding Christian ministry. Intentional design of the hidden curriculum involves serious reflection on the nature of effective discipleship and leadership formation, and incorporating these patterns into the classroom.

- What we do *not* teach communicates values. When we prioritize certain content and learning activities over others, the null curriculum educates students as to how they should interpret life and ministry. Strategic education intentionally selects those elements that have priority significance for the development of missional-ecclesial reflective practitioners.

Exercises:

1. Consider the story of Gregory. To what extent might a "schooling" approach have influenced his understanding of Christian ministry?

2. What do you believe to be some of the major factors that have caused the majority of ministry-training programmes to embrace a "schooling" approach to instruction? To what extent is the "schooling" model dominant in your institution? What are some of the factors that influence your instructional approach? Suggest at least one specific way in which your school could address the potential negative impact of the "schooling" elements of your institution's hidden curriculum.

3. The hidden curriculum has a pervasive influence. Describe two or three other elements of hidden curriculum that you see at work in your theological school. Consider such things as the tendency of the curriculum to be fragmented; the extent to which the curriculum is required or elective for students; the extent to which theological and historical studies are addressed philosophically and/or practically; the shape and application of institutional policy; the way that institutional decisions are made; the relationships that exist between students, faculty and administration.

4. Consider each of the aspects of the hidden curriculum suggested in this chapter: (a) the promotion of a "schooling" or academic approach to ministry; (b) the affirmation of a knowledge-centred hierarchy; (c) the encouragement of leader control; (d) a competitive rather than cooperative understanding of ministry; (e) the administrative and institutional culture of the school. Describe at least three ways in which you see elements of these patterns at work in your school. To what extent do you agree or disagree that the patterns are as destructive as are described in this chapter? Give reasons for your response.

5. In what ways does your school counter negative patterns of hidden curriculum through its community life or otherwise?

6. In light of what we examined in chapters 1 and 2, which two or three aspects of the null curriculum do you believe most need addressing at your school? Why do you believe that these aspects are particularly important? If you had the choice, what elements in your current explicit curriculum would you remove to make space for your higher-priority content? Why?

7. Suggest at least one specific way in which your school could address and shape the hidden and null curricula by design, rather than simply accepting an accidental or unintentional form of hidden curriculum.

6

Beyond Fragmentation in the Curriculum

Concerns about curricular fragmentation in theological education have been voiced for over a hundred years. However, it is with the passing of the modernist hegemony of educational theory and the shift of Christianity to the Global South that the call for integration in theological education has become an urgent imperative. In this chapter you will be introduced to a very brief historical sketch of how curricular fragmentation has emerged in theological education, and to some of the main reasons for promoting curricular integration. We will conclude with a series of practical suggestions, some relatively straightforward and others more far-reaching and substantial.

The Roots of Curricular Fragmentation

Linda Cannell, in her seminal *Theological Education Matters* (2006, 126–237), gives a detailed narrative of the history of Western theological education and how we have reached the current globalized model. The roots of curricular fragmentation in theological education are largely found in the Western embrace of Greek philosophical schemata, and more particularly in Thomas Aquinas's application of Aristotelian philosophy to theological reflection, the first attempt to systematize distinct categories in theology. With the dawning of the Enlightenment and the development of the scientific method, it was increasingly perceived that truth could only be apprehended through a process of "rational reflection".

It needs to be acknowledged that the scientific method has brought great benefits to the development of knowledge, particularly in the physical sciences. The careful disciplines associated with studying the elements of knowledge have helped the scientific world move from a speculative understanding of reality to approaches that are carefully tested with clear supportive evidence. Because of the great benefits that Western society experienced through this form of analytical reasoning, particularly during and after the Industrial Revolution, the scientific method was applied to all fields of study in the modernist era as the only means of discovering sure knowledge (Ziolkowski 1990).

Rationalist approaches to theological reflection became standard following the establishment of the department of theology in the University of Berlin (1810). The tendency in the scientific method to focus on the parts as a means to understanding the whole contributed further to the institutionalized fragmentation of theological study, and the three main "disciplines" of biblical, historical and systematic theological studies became increasingly discrete.

European structures of higher education were admired across the Atlantic, and when seminaries began to be established in North America from the beginning of the nineteenth century, the model of distinct biblical, historical and systematic theological studies was retained, with the addition of a fourth area of ministerial or liturgical studies. Ironically, within these disciplines, ministerial studies or "practical theology" has generally been seen as lowest in rank, with biblical or systematic theological studies occupying the pre-eminent position. While the seminary curriculum purports to exist for the preparation of men and women for Christian ministry, through the hidden curriculum the training component of ministerial studies is communicated as being of secondary importance (Madueme and Cannell 2007). The lack of any integrating paradigm has served to reinforce this sense of hierarchy.

In each of these areas, studies were further compartmentalized into, for example, Old Testament and New Testament, and then within these disciplines, Pentateuch, Wisdom Literature or Prophetic Literature. The predominant expectation became, and continues to be, that scholars will be highly focused on a small field – for example, becoming an expert on "Johannine literature", "early medieval European church history" or "Pentecostal pneumatology". Moreover, over the past hundred years, the leadership of theological training has increasingly been transferred from scholar-pastors to academics, most of whom have completed advanced studies in highly specialized fields using an adapted form of the scientific method, and culminating in a dissertation addressing a highly limited research question. This whole process has led to a high level of professorial specialization, and the fragmentation of the curriculum has consequently become endemic.

As the modern missionary movement spread the gospel around the globe, it was predominantly North American missionaries who established theological colleges, European and British missionaries focusing more on medical, schooling and evangelistic ministries. It is not surprising, therefore, that in most parts of the world the theological curricula resemble the patterns of Princeton, Dallas or Fuller seminaries more than British or European patterns of ministerial training. The American Carnegie credit system predominates, with most schools delivering courses of 2- or 3-credit hours. The four foundational disciplines drive the curriculum, and it is normal for students to take concurrently a series of distinct courses often with little connection, moving without apparent reason from a class on Exodus to one on Reformation History, and then to a class on Pastoral Care and Counselling. Rarely are students asked to "join the dots" and see how the pieces fit together.

Towards Integration

A holistic understanding of human personality is essential to biblical anthropology. As we have seen in chapter 4, effective learning requires interconnection between the cognitive, affective and behavioural dimensions. Such interconnection is an essential element in the thinking and learning patterns of women in general and of learners from most non-Western contexts.

While the Enlightenment advocacy of theoretical speculation and claims of dispassionate objectivity has lost some of its credibility in the postmodern world, it still tends to dominate the *shape* of higher education, even among those who pay lip service to the demise of modernism. However, the challenges embedded in the work of non-Western scholars such as Paulo Freire (1970) have increasingly gained ground in secular higher education, particularly in terms of promoting field-engaged learning, prophetic transformational emphases, and the value of *emic* (from within) as against *etic* (from without) approaches to understanding and engaging the world.

In light of our missional-ecclesial calling, the endeavour of theological education does well to embrace many of these trends. Priest (2000) has suggested that there might be greater significance for the church if the emphasis on "reflective practice" was more on the practice than on the reflection, and the basis of assessment was the student's ability to lead a church reflectively in evangelism, the pursuit of justice, discipleship and spiritual growth, rather than simply to sit in a classroom or library. Andrew Kirk (2005, 33) has reinforced the potential of this: "It is now a commonplace of much theological endeavour in the church of the global South that the verification of genuine theology is determined not so much by criteria formulated within the parameters of the academic community, as by its ability to liberate people for effective involvement in society. If it does not have this effect, it is considered an alienated and alienating force."

The traditional disconnect between theory and practice (the "ivory tower" phenomenon) has very often led to theory that is irrelevant or out of touch with reality, and practice that is uninformed and driven by culture more than by careful theological reflection. In contrast, the "Global Survey on Theological Education" (Esterline et al. 2013) cited the integration of practical learning with traditional academic studies as a key perceived need for effective theological education. In the accomplishment of meaningful training for reflective ministry practice, a greater integration between theory and practice must take place. Ideally, this should be bidirectional: classroom studies connected to life realities, and field experience reflected upon through the multiple lenses of biblical, historical, theological, social-contextual, ministerial, and other classroom-based studies.

Paul describes Christian ministry as a "ministry of reconciliation" (2 Cor 5:18–20), which entails at its source the ability to work with and for people. Consequently, for effective holistic theological education to take place, space must also be made in the curriculum for nurturing the affective dimension of the human personality. Such a concern is not unique to theological education: Goleman's (1995, 2006) seminal work on emotional and social intelligence suggests that a person's intelligence quotient (IQ) contributes at best about 20 per cent to life success. Of far greater significance is one's emotional and social intelligence (EQ and SQ), including such factors as emotional stability, social skills, positive attitudes and self-motivation (see Salovey and Mayer 1990; Banks and Ledbetter

2004, 50). These elements are foundational to effective Christian ministry but are at their best when informed by biblical and theological reflection.

Some Practical Suggestions

Numerous possibilities exist for promoting greater or lesser levels of integration in theological training programmes. The following are some suggestions:

Embrace the social sciences and other fields of knowledge

Particularly since the Enlightenment, the study of theology has largely been understood as a separate academic discipline with only minimal interaction with other fields of knowledge. As a result, many seminary graduates look to biblical, theological and ecclesiastical studies as the main source of information for church ministry, with perhaps a few aids from skill-based material in homiletics, leadership and counselling.

The process of Christian ministry training is not unique: in the same way, most Christian professionals, businesspeople, teachers, and in fact the majority of church members resort only to knowledge provided by their field of expertise when confronted with concrete challenges in life. Because of their experience of fragmentation, these believers struggle to connect the Scriptures with their own life contexts, and rarely interact with the biblical text when responding to social, professional or personal demands (Fernández 2012).

Theological schools have the potential for modelling a more integrative approach to learning that utilizes knowledge, skills and strategies derived from different disciplines and fields of research. The first step is the demystification of social sciences and a healthy integration of theology and the truth found in other disciplines of human knowledge (Fernández 2012).

Engaging studies beyond the traditional disciplines can be costly, both in terms of time and finances. However, for a curriculum to be both integrative and missional, it must continuously affirm the truth that God is at work in a world characterized by diverse occupations and fields of knowledge (de Gruchy 2010). The more we help our students to see points of connection between social, scientific, aesthetic and theological studies, the better prepared will be our graduates to help the church engage the world around it. Dialoguing between the classic disciplines and the emerging social sciences will contribute substantially to missional practice.

Give behavioural emphases in the classroom

If we are serious about preparing leaders who can be agents of transformation, we must help them relate theory to practice. Many professors deliver their material in such a dispassionate and specialized fashion that it is no wonder that students see the content as disconnected from the realities of life and ministry. Substantial progress towards integrated learning can take place when professors are required to provide a practical component to their courses, discussing the implications of the content for daily life, and developing assignments that require students to carry out critical reflection on real-life situations. If professors are unable to connect theory with practice, it is highly improbable that students will be able to make these connections.

For effective integration between theory and practice to take place in the classroom it will be necessary to reduce the content and give more time to discussion of key themes that are of significance to contemporary daily life. However, by relating the field of study synthetically with the practicalities of ministry and the implications for our daily lives, not only will students be better empowered as reflective practitioners, but also they will be more likely to see the substance of the course as relevant and significant. The implications of positive student perceptions for long-term or deep learning will be discussed in greater depth in chapter 8.

Nurture spirituality in the classroom

Special events such as retreats, days of prayer, or a week of special spiritual emphasis are important means of developing the spiritual tenor of the community, the faculty and the students. However, unless these activities are interfaced with formal classroom experiences they can become counterproductive, promoting a fragmented perspective on learning whereby the classroom is seen to be for academics and the chapel for nurturing spirituality. For too long the classroom has been severed from personal spirituality. Pilli (2007) has noted that academic work can and should be a spiritual exercise. Throughout church history, theological reflection has been at its best when it is connected with daily realities and culminates in prayer. When instructors teach in a spirit of prayer and humility, they become models of teaching and learning under the guidance of the Holy Spirit, and acknowledge that God is present in the classroom and is concerned about what happens there. Banks (1999, 202–3) has observed that while some may perceive this approach to be "unacademic", it is certainly not untheological. Rather than isolating academia from faith, we should welcome their healthy interaction, respecting the student as a whole person and seeking integration between mind and spirit.

Change the learning context

One of the best ways of helping students see the connection between theory and practice is to take students out of the campus and into the workplace, meeting and reflecting with practitioners and discussing how the theory might be applied in practice (see Banks 1999, 177–79). Such a process need not be confined to "practical" subjects: for example, holding a course in the central business district on the Prophetic Writings of the Old Testament will elicit foundationally different discussions from those that would occur in the "hallowed halls" of the theological college – simply because of the intensity of the context in which learning is taking place.

Require integrative papers

Some schools have found it beneficial to require students to do one or more integrative papers as capstone pieces to their studies, perhaps one at the conclusion of the second year of study and another at the end of the third year. These may or may not be granted credit but are a compulsory element of the student's studies. Such papers address a significant theme through multiple lenses, drawing together the material into concluding recommendations and responding to such questions as the following:

Biblical-Theological

- How is the issue addressed in the Scriptures? What principles might be gleaned from the example of godly leaders of biblical times? Of particular significance are elements of Jesus's life and teaching that bear on the issue.

- How is the issue addressed in the Torah? In the Prophetic writings? In the Psalms? In the teaching of Jesus? In the Epistles? Through careful exegetical reflection on key passages, what biblical principles are relevant to the issue being studied?

Historical-Theological

- How has the issue been dealt with at other times in church history?

- How has the key issue been addressed by significant Christian thinkers throughout history – particularly those from the region in which the student serves?

Ministerial-Contextual

- What missiological issues are at stake in the issue? How might different responses to the issue help or hinder the proclamation of the gospel in word and deed?

- What educational and pastoral issues need to be taken into account when considering a response to the issue?

Alternatively, it may be beneficial to be more directive, guiding the student on a step-by-step journey through the process of integration. This is particularly helpful in cultural contexts in which students are less attuned to research design. Consider, for example, the following model:

1. Choose a specific group of believers with which you are intimately involved. This may be a local church, a ministry team, a house group or a discipleship group. Reflect in depth on *one* major aspect of God's nature and character (e.g. justice, love, goodness, faithfulness, holiness, wisdom, creator, redeemer, sustainer, king) and explain to what extent this characteristic is or is not manifest in clear ways in this group.

2. Choose *two* key biblical passages (*one* each from the Old *and* New Testament) that address the aspect of God's nature and character mentioned in point 1 above. Taking into account the literary and historical context of each passage, do a detailed and careful exegesis, and develop key principles evident in the passage which are particularly applicable in your own local context. Discuss some of the practical implications of these principles for your chosen group.

3. Choose *one or more* great Christian theologian from history who has reflected seriously on the aspect of God's nature and character mentioned in point 1 above. What key theological insights did this theologian bring to understanding this aspect of God's nature and character? In what ways did the theologian's historical context impact the development of his or her thinking about God?

4. Consider the local social and cultural context in which your chosen group serves. Describe in detail at least *two* contextual factors that contribute to the strengths and/or weaknesses of the group in terms of reflecting the attribute of God that you have been discussing. How has the broader society both correctly and incorrectly communicated and represented this aspect of God's nature and character? Give at least *three* recommendations as to how the group could overcome local cultural challenges in order to better be the "face of God" to the community in which they serve.

5. For your chosen group, give a series of *three to six* specific strategic steps that will help the group better make manifest God's attributes in their lives. Include in your discussion elements that promote right worship of God.

6. Describe one specific, tangible step that you personally could take before the conclusion of this module to better manifest in your own life the attribute of God you have been discussing above.

In most cases, integrative papers such as these are suggestive rather than comprehensive, as time and space are limited. The purpose is not so much for the student to have conclusive answers to complex questions, but to see how the various elements of theological study can work together to inform ministry practice. Even when the bulk of the curriculum remains fragmented, one or two experiences of this sort of integrative work can be transformative in the student's growth as a reflective practitioner.

Include problem-based learning (PBL)

Because those involved in the professions need to learn to deal with real-world problems, the methodology of problem-based learning (PBL) has become common in virtually all fields of professional education. Howard Barrows (1996, 1), who has been instrumental in seeing the use of PBL become an essential element in many North American schools of medicine, describes the process of PBL as follows: "The basic outline of the problem based learning process is: encountering the problem first, problem solving with clinical reasoning skills and identifying learning needs in an interactive process, self-study, applying newly gained knowledge to the problem, and summarizing what has been learned. "

PBL finds its theoretical roots in Vygotsky's (1978) notion of social constructivism: some of the most effective and long-lasting learning occurs through social interaction around a central idea or question. Through group engagement with appropriate challenges, and with assistance from teachers or more capable peers, students are moved forward into new areas of learning (Arends 2007, 386). Formal PBL entails an extensive and detailed work of multidisciplinary reflection, generally in teams of students with a faculty supervisor. This sort of grounded team learning is a powerful learning experience at the level of both the explicit and the implicit curricula.

The strength of PBL lies in its demand for students to integrate material from multiple disciplines in addressing specific and real-life situations. Students are thus better empowered to develop skills in reflective practice. PBL also opens the possibility for engaging knowledge that ordinarily "falls through the cracks" of the traditional disciplines. Problems and life issues inevitably raise questions that a traditional curriculum ignores, taking students into areas that are highly significant for effective practice, but which don't naturally fit traditional boundaries. For example, in a recent PBL activity held at my school (see appendix 6.1), students found themselves wrestling with the leadership dynamics of local-church life, how these dynamics had emerged from wider cultural patterns, and the question of how we might evaluate these patterns in light of biblical, historical and theological principles. This sort of dialogue rarely finds a place in traditional theological curricula. In light of the missional-ecclesial vision we have examined in chapters 1 and 2, the relevance of PBL for theological education can readily be seen.

The key to effective PBL is the significance and quality of the case study or problem upon which the group research is based. Well-designed problems have the following characteristics (Madueme and Cannell 2007):

- The problem is realistic and close to the probable future ministry context of the students.

- There are multiple possible perspectives on the problem, and the potential for different responses to the problem to result in different outcomes.

- The problem fosters strong personal response in the students, generating a desire to work together in investigating the case through multiple lenses.

- Response to the case needs investigation through multiple primary and secondary sources. Students recognize immediately that appropriate analysis and response needs theoretical material from multiple subjects and disciplines, and counsel from a variety of resource people.

- The problem delves into areas in which students' prior knowledge may be limited, such that the investigation of the problem introduces new areas of insight and learning.

Quality case studies are a potent form of education; chapter 13 is therefore specifically focused on the development and application of case studies in theological education.

An institutional embrace of PBL as a substantial element in the curriculum holds great promise for formative growth in students. However, even when the school is reticent to make substantial change towards PBL, many of the integrative benefits of PBL can ensue from simple classroom exercises which use case studies as a springboard for integrative discussion, in integrative seminars or as the basis for integrative papers.

Incorporate theological reflection on life and ministry

Most theological programmes incorporate elements of field ministry in their curricula, including some sort of report from the student and supervisor. However, such reporting tends to focus on what practical lessons have been learned from the experience, rather than on substantive theological reflection. Consequently, the existing fragmentation between theory and practice is generally reinforced rather than reduced. For field ministry to be a means of meaningful integration, the reporting process needs to incorporate elements of theological reflection and not merely practical reflection. Students can be encouraged to make connections between theory and practice through questions related to such aspects as the evidence of God's presence in the experience, the extent to which the ministry context reflected sound ecclesiology, endemic patterns that have been seen elsewhere in history, as well as the extent to which material presented in courses in ministerial studies was evident in the experience.

While theological reflection on ministry experience is important, equally if not more significant can be exercises in which students are asked to reflect theologically on life experiences. Fragmentation is not merely an issue in the theological school: for many lay Christians there is a profound fragmentation between the church-centred spiritual component and the routine daily business of life. After all, how does the Christian faith relate to cooking, cleaning and changing dirty diapers? What connection is there between the Bible and the rut of a routine and boring job? Most of our graduates are ill-prepared to respond to such questions. One step towards integration between theology and daily life can be to ask students to carry out theologically reflective exercises on such things as their relationships with other students, working in the college cafeteria or in the gardens of the school, or the struggles of raising one's children while engaged in theological studies. Through connecting theological studies with the routines of life, students are better placed to serve in churches, given that daily life for many believers is profoundly dull and tedious.

Quality theological reflection incorporates all of what Cranton (2006, 34) describes as content, process and premise reflection. Content reflection seeks to analyse the problem itself: what is happening, and what are the issues at stake? Process reflection examines the development of the situation: what factors have contributed to the current status, what problem-solving strategies have been applied, and where do these processes appear to be leading? Premise reflection asks the question, Why is this important? Why should I care about this problem in the first place? To a certain extent, these three levels are comparable to cognitive (content reflection), behavioural (process reflection), and affective (premise reflection) elements. Some specifics of how the process of theological reflection can be strengthened will be discussed in the next chapter.

Cluster courses

Why do students have to take five 3-credit courses a semester? What prevents us from doing three 5-credit integrated and team-taught courses, or even providing one 15-credit course that involves total integration of the material? This concept is not new: when I first studied education many years ago at the University of New South Wales (Australia), the one-year programme entailed three elements: Theory of Education; Curriculum and Practice; Practice Teaching. The last was on a pass/fail basis, while the first two "courses" were team taught and multi-faceted; for example, Theory of Education involved studies in developmental psychology, educational psychology, sociology of education and philosophy of education, but only one final integrated grade was given. This sort of team-taught clustered education is increasingly being advocated in higher education, and it needs to find its place in theological education. There is no reason why, instead of separate courses in Old Testament 1 and 2, New Testament 1 and 2, Biblical Hermeneutics, Hebrew, Greek, and so on, we cannot have one combined team-taught 15–20-credit course on Bible. Such a process could be implemented with minimal change to a traditional delivery process. However, at the level of the hidden curriculum, multiple lessons on integration and team ministry would emerge.

"Sandwich" education

Following the common pattern in many teacher-education, surveying and engineering programmes of study, some theological schools have restructured their programmes towards "sandwich" delivery: following a year of foundational studies, the student is sent into a field context for six months, and then returns for six months, then goes back to the field, and so on. The repeated movement from school to field ministry and back again helps the student make continual connections between theory and practice. Sandwich delivery is more suitable for schools which are intimately connected with a particular denomination, as effective sandwich ministry and study requires close cooperation between church and seminary. Sandwich delivery is more difficult to implement in inter-denominational schools, although it may be valuable for such schools to consider ways in which it could be offered as an option.

Balance "text to context" with "context to text"

The classic curriculum is dominated by the study of texts – whether the Bible, or history, theology, social science and practical-ministry textbooks – with the hope that students will then be able to apply the material to their own contexts. In reality this rarely happens – because the instructors themselves have rarely made this step. A curriculum that develops a significant number of courses that begin with contextual challenges (poverty, religious discrimination, changing technologies), and then investigates how the texts address these issues, will better prepare students for the ministry challenges they will face upon graduation. Only through taking context seriously can we hope to develop an integrative curriculum that touches our changing world.

Reconceptualize the shape of the curriculum

To a certain extent, all the above suggestions are somewhat cosmetic, in that they assume retention of the traditional fragmented structure of theological education. A serious embrace of integration demands more. For genuine integration to take place there needs to be a thoroughgoing reconceptualization of the curriculum as a whole, in which integration is part of the "warp and woof" of theological education. A handful of schools have moved in this direction. Most have found that while the initial reconceptualization requires a high level of trust and team commitment, and generally needs someone comfortable with educational theory and its practical implications, the actual implementation is less challenging than was originally feared.

Conclusion

In light of the missional-ecclesial vision for theological education, we can no longer remain satisfied with the status quo of curricular fragmentation that is inadequate for the task of preparing effective reflective practitioners for Christian ministry. Particularly in light of the growth of the church in the Global South, new paradigms for integrative theological education need to be sought. Possibilities include simple classroom-based steps, such as the promotion of spirituality and behavioural emphases in the classroom, or basic institutional changes, such as the incorporation of integrative seminars and projects into the curriculum. However, far better is to move to a reconceptualization of the curricular paradigm for theological education in which multiple layers of integration are at the core, and students are continually challenged towards effectiveness in well-informed reflective practice.

Exercises

1. Compare the programme of study at your school with the patterns described in the earlier parts of this chapter. What system of credit-counting do you use, and how does it work? How are credits allocated? To what extent does your programme of study employ the classic divisions of biblical, historical, theological and ministerial studies? To what extent are curricular decisions driven by a "battle" between specialists in the various disciplines? What do you see as some of the major barriers to integration in your programme of study? What efforts (if any) has your school made at encouraging some level of integration among the disciplines?

2. Of the "Practical Suggestions" given in this chapter, which two or three do you already do particularly well at your institution? Which two or three do you think are the most challenging to implement in your institution? What are the main barriers to implementing these suggestions? Have you ever seen other schools or individuals implement these suggestions better than is done in your institution? How was it done?

Appendix 6.1

2065 Empowering Servant Leaders Integrative Project

The project will be delivered through an adapted problem-based learning approach:

- Students will work in teams of three to four students.

- An initial compulsory three-hour workshop will be held early in the Module in which the students will begin work on the project, sketching the key areas that they wish to address, and delegating responsibilities.

- Each group will be expected to present a 300–500-word progress report by 9 a.m. on Monday, 18 November.

- On Friday, 29 November, beginning in the morning and continuing into the afternoon, each group will be asked to bring to the rest of the class a 20–30-minute presentation of the findings of their project. Each member of the group should participate in this presentation. Groups that exceed 30 minutes will be penalized.

- The final written work for the project must be presented prior to 9 a.m. on Monday, 2 December. The final project should include the elements described below, as well as a final page that details the contributions of each member of the group.

1. The project will revolve around a focus group, which is a group that one of the members of your team has led or (preferably) is currently leading. The situation may be pastoring an established church; leading a new church plant; leadership of a church group (teenagers' group; young adults' group; women's group; a team of Sunday-school teachers); leadership of an evangelistic team; leadership in a parachurch organization; etc.

- Describe in detail the leadership patterns functioning in this group: how many leaders; how the leaders relate to one another; how decision-making takes place; how new leaders are incorporated into leadership.

- Visit a comparable group here in Lebanon, and through observation and questioning, analyse the leadership patterns at work in this other group, and compare its strengths and weaknesses with the patterns evident in your own focus group.

2. *Biblical-theological lens.* How does the Bible speak to your case study? You should make extensive biblical reflection, which may involve the careful exegesis of specific texts or reflection upon broader biblical-theological themes. There should be engagement with the material presented in the Leadership Insights from the Bible course, but outstanding presentations will go beyond this course and dig deeper into foundational biblical principles for leadership as they relate to the specific case study you have presented in section 1.

3. *Historical-theological lens.* How does our great heritage speak to your case study? You are encouraged to look at comparable situations in history, and how the church failed or succeeded in those situations. An outstanding presentation would examine the work of great theologians in their historical contexts as they relate to the situation you have described in section 1. There should be evidence of engagement with the material presented in the course Living Leadership Lessons from Church History.

4. *Social-contextual lens.* How do the social sciences (psychology, sociology, social psychology, cultural anthropology, politics, etc.) speak to the situation you are studying? You may wish to draw on material from the first-year Church and Society Module, but there should also be engagement with the Biblical Leaders Engaging Culture course.

5. *Personal-ministerial lens.* How do you see your own role in being a transformative agent in this situation? In light of the material given in the Personal Journeys in Leadership course, what should you be and do as a leader in this context?

6. *Integration.* How do these lenses come together? What shared principles do you see here? How can you nurture multiple lenses for looking at situations such as this?

7. *Recommendations.* What would you recommend in terms of growth? How might the focus group better become the face of Christ to their communities? How might genuine impact on the world be nurtured? Your recommendations should be (a) grounded in Scripture and sound theology; (b) specific, attainable and measurable; (c) holistic – looking at the members of the group as whole people; (d) comprehensive, dealing with multiple aspects of the situation; (e) personal, explaining how you personally will think, relate and act differently in order to facilitate appropriate change.

One Final Requirement

Quality leaders seek good work while retaining balance in life. You will be expected to commit yourselves to the 30 hours per team member, but not more. I expect that you will do outstanding work in some areas and only acceptable work in others. I expect to see that while you are working on this project you are also giving appropriate time to body, heart and relationships.

Hours in class: 6. Hours out of class: 24
Total hours: 30

7

Curricular Elements Outside the Classroom

There is no question that traditional structured classroom experiences are a significant element in the formational learning of emerging Christian leaders. However, meaningful preparation for Christian ministry must also entail curricular elements which take place outside the classroom. In this chapter you will be challenged to consider ways in which these elements can be better affirmed institutionally. You will then be introduced to a variety of possible out-of-class curricular activities, and means by which integrated learning can be intentionally designed and implemented through these activities.

Definitions

Increasing evidence points to the learning efficacy of activities such as field education, mentoring and community worship. In some parts of the world these activities are classified as the non-formal or informal components of the curriculum, but this terminology is confusing in contexts where the terms "non-formal" and "informal" are used prescriptively for particular kinds of non-institutional learning, rather than as a description of certain forms of learning that could take place in virtually any educational context (Rogers 2004; M. Smith 2012). The term "extra-curricular" is even more problematic, in that it implies that the only meaningful curricular elements are those which take place in the classroom.

Even though it can be highly beneficial to include a classroom reflective component to field education, mentoring and so on, the associated learning activities are primarily realized in contexts which are less formal than the traditional classroom. Consequently, perhaps the least unsatisfactory option is to refer to these educational activities as "curricular elements outside the classroom" or "non-classroom curricular elements", and these terms will be used in this chapter.

Bringing Meaning and Intention to the Non-Classroom Curricular Elements

The American Carnegie credit-counting system that has dominated theological education in much of the world is based on the number of classroom hours devoted to various
elements of the curriculum. Consequently, the forms of learning that occur outside the
classroom generally receive little or no credit allocation, despite the significant formative
nature of such learning and the hours that students devote to these elements in many
schools. There are multiple shortcomings of the Carnegie system, especially at the level
of the hidden curriculum. In granting credit almost exclusively to the classroom-centred
component of the curriculum, we communicate to students a hierarchy of values: what
is most important is the classroom, and the formative learning of curricular elements
outside the classroom is of little or no real value. Also, in granting credit based on classroom hours we may be communicating that education is about teaching more than it is
about learning.

The European Bologna Process that began in the late 1990s provides affirmation
and substantial space for a much wider variety of curricular elements within its flexible
European Credit Transfer System (ECTS). ECTS credits are based not on hours spent in
the classroom but on total hours of "learning activity", at the first degree level (BTh or
MDiv) each credit comprising a total package of twenty-five to thirty hours of learning
activity. This is comparable to what is generally expected within Carnegie-based schools,
but the difference lies in the total annual expectation in Europe of 60 ECTS credits as
against the 30–40 credits expected in American-system schools. In theological education, the 20-credits difference is generally applied to curricular elements offered outside
the classroom. In that the European approach focuses on "hours of learning" rather than
"hours in the classroom", and affirms with credit the substantial formative value of the
non-classroom-based elements, it holds potential for positive steps forward in quality
theological education.

Of course, the reality is that schools do not need to feel bound either to the
American or to the European system. The whole system of credits is not "the law of
the Medes and Persians", but simply a convenient device for maintaining accountability
and for providing an understandable approach to the wider world of higher education.
Indeed, some schools have sought a hybrid approach in which substantial credit is granted
for educational elements outside the classroom without the constraints of either system.
What is important is that your school's processes be understandable to all stakeholders.

Within the European system, credit can be granted whenever the following three
elements are in place:

- *Predetermined learning outcomes.* These will be discussed in greater depth
  in chapter 9, when we discuss course-syllabus design. Essentially, learning
  outcomes are a description of what kind of learning is being sought through
  the course or activity, and are preferably prefaced by a general-purpose

statement that describes why the course or activity is important in the student's growth towards the "profile of the ideal graduate".

- *Predetermined learning tasks and activities.* This component describes in detail what sorts of tasks and activities the student will be asked to complete. Within the European system, these tasks and activities should be carefully quantified so that the "twenty-five to thirty hours per credit" can be explained and justified.

- *Predetermined means of assessment.* There needs to be some form of tangible evidence that meaningful learning has taken place. This need not be extensive, but it must be substantive. For many educational activities that take place outside the classroom, assessment will be on a pass/fail basis, and will be documented through such means as logging of times, journals, evaluative reports and short written reflections.

As we examine various common forms of curricular elements outside the classroom in theological education, some examples will be provided of how this process of documentation and credit allocation might work in practice.

Field Education

The field experiences that students are asked to undertake as a part of their course of study form perhaps the most common educational element in the typical theological curriculum that takes place substantially out of the classroom. The value of these experiences has been widely recognized, and most theological accrediting agencies require evidence of field education as a compulsory component of the BTh or MDiv courses of study.

Most schools have recognized not only the value of field education in itself, but also the importance of student reflection on their experience. However, in most cases this reflection tends to be primarily at the affective and behavioural levels, with students being asked to comment on practical lessons learned and the extent to which their field work was a positive or negative experience. In order to move towards a more substantive level of reflection it is necessary to consider some of the potential learning benefits that might be acquired during and after the field-education experience. The following are some possibilities at each of the affective, behavioural and cognitive levels.

Affective learning

Perhaps the greatest affective potential in field education lies in the possibility of students growing in their understanding of themselves and their sense of vocation. Often, students come to theological education with an overall desire to serve God more extensively and effectively, but the sense of vocation is general rather than specific. Field education can be an ideal context in which students can explore and discover their gifts, and gain a greater insight into how those gifts might best be used in the service of God's kingdom. Field education can also highlight areas of personal weakness which need attention in the pilgrimage of growth towards the ideal described in the "profile of the ideal graduate". Possible questions that might guide students on the path to reflection in the affective domain include:

- What did you feel before you began the placement? Fear? Excitement? Or some other emotion? What was the source of these feelings? In retrospect, were these feelings justified or unjustified? Why?

- What was the most exciting thing that happened during your time on placement? Why was it exciting for you?

- Was there anything during your placement that discouraged you or concerned you? What, and why?

- What was the most important lesson you learned about yourself during this placement? Why?

- To what extent was your sense of calling strengthened or weakened during your placement? Why?

Behavioural learning

Field education can be a key opportunity for students to test in the field theoretical material they have studied in class. Of course, the extent to which this can be accomplished is dependent upon the level of freedom granted by the supervisor. But when possible, the dialogue between theory and practice can be a significant means of promoting a greater level of integration in learning. Consider the following examples of reflective questions in the behavioural domain:

- Reflect on some of the courses you have taken in communication, psychology, sociology, preaching, teaching, counselling, evangelism and so on. Describe at least two ways in which the material from these courses was helpful. Why did you find these particular elements helpful?

- Describe any situations you experienced that you didn't expect or that were contrary to what you were taught in class.

- Name at least two areas in which you need to develop greater skill as you further pursue your studies.

Cognitive learning

In most theological programmes, the greatest emphasis in field education is placed on behavioural and (possibly) affective learning, and theory–practice dialogue focuses on the ministerial studies courses that the student has taken. Rarely are students asked to engage in substantial dialogue between their field experience and their biblical, historical and theological studies. However, only when reflection is carried out between field experience and every area of their studies are students genuinely challenged to see all of ministry as a profoundly theological process. As De Gruchy (2010) observes, "Missional practice is precisely that: engagement, doing, action. There is enough written to suggest that such action without on-going reflection is bound to degenerate into activism that soon loses its way. Theological education provides an important sphere in which missional activity has to answer for the content and process of its engagement, sharpen its perspectives, and emerge chastened and more able to engage the world."

Examples of possible integrative reflective questions include:

- Where did you see God at work in your placement? What aspects of his character were revealed as you served?

- To what extent did your placement context reflect the missionary heart of God? Explain.

- Reflect on the church context where you served. Name at least two ways in which the church demonstrated sound biblical ecclesiology. Were there any ways in which the church context differed from what you see as the biblical ideal of the church? Explain your response.

- A central theological lens is that of salvation history – creation, fall, redemption, consummation. Humans are created in God's image but fallen, and consequently, we can expect to see something of God's character and something of the fall in those we serve. Without mentioning names, describe a situation where you saw this in action. The work of Christ has opened the way for redemptive responses to negative situations as we strive towards the consummate ideal. Consider at least one negative situation you observed. How might this situation have been approached in a more redemptive way? What could you personally, as a cross-bearing servant, have done to promote redemption?

- Describe at least one pattern evident in your placement that you have also observed in church history. How might a dialogue between the historic and contemporary patterns guide you to more effective ministry?

In order for students to engage in dialogue with questions such as those above, a part of the field-education exercise needs to be a substantive concluding reflective paper. Calculation of the total hours of learning activity will therefore need to include both the hours of ministry engagement and the hours that students are expected to work on the final integrative reflection. Additional elements that can further facilitate the process include journaling during the field experience and/or a debriefing of the experience following the placement.

Before concluding this section on field education, it is worth issuing some important notes of caution:

- Sadly, in many contexts the level of supervision is poor or exploitative. Students may find themselves in contexts where the supervisor is unwilling to give substantial time to orientation, guidance and debriefing. In some situations the supervisor uses the student to do the "dirty" work that he or she does not want to do. Those responsible for field education need to take care in selecting and monitoring placements and supervision.

- In honour–shame societies, leaders are reticent about putting evaluative comments in print. If forced to do so, they will tend to portray the student as "a new Billy Graham" or similar, or, on some occasions, the opposite. Consequently, the standard Western requirement of a written supervisory evaluation is probably inappropriate in most parts of the non-Western world. In such contexts it may be necessary for the institutional field-education director to make personal contact with the supervisor and discuss the student's performance conversationally.

- Students can have unrealistically high expectations of their placements. It may be that the classroom material has inspired a new vision for effective Christian ministry, but the reality falls far short of the ideal. There is a long history of students in ministry placements being openly critical of the local-church leadership, leading to resentment on both sides. In other cases, leaders severely restrict what students are permitted to do, and this can be a highly frustrating experience for the intern. It is important to prepare students for disappointment, and also to encourage them to be gracious and patient with those whom they serve.

- While the above barriers to the effective integration of theory and practice are significant, Argyris and Schön (1974, 187) suggest that the greatest hurdle is the faculty: "Faculty tend to resist the intrusion of field work into the curriculum, or, at any rate, tend to carry on the academic programme parallel to field work as though the latter did not exist." For field education to become an effective element in developing integrated formation, the faculty must be committed to the process and attuned to the students' field experiences.

Mentoring

Jesus's primary mode of leadership training was to mentor a small group of disciples. This intimate and personalized approach to learning can be among the most significant and life-changing educational experiences a student has while engaged in theological studies. However, if poorly designed and managed, it can equally be perceived as a waste of time. Definitions of "mentoring" abound, but generally in theological education the practice is a one-on-one relationship between the student and a more mature leader. The goal is a relationship of encouragement and direction in the student's holistic formation.

The greatest challenge in implementation of a mentoring programme is the recruiting and training of mentors, as quality mentoring can be time consuming. Many leaders with already busy schedules are unwilling to make the necessary sacrifices of time. Other leaders are better talkers than listeners, or may have hidden agendas that they seek to impose on the students. Where there is a need to challenge ministerial stereotypes such as the "one-man-show" approach to pastoral leadership, recruiting local pastors may be counterproductive if they simply reinforce the traditional model.

In some schools the process of mentoring is seen as a training opportunity in which more senior students are asked to mentor more junior students. This can be logistically easier than recruiting mentors from outside. However, where the senior students are unproven or still somewhat immature, the result can be less than satisfying. There may also be the lost opportunity of hearing a substantially different voice.

Another major challenge is where the mentor and the student are a bad match. Processes need to be established for students to request a change of mentor, although this can be delicate, as the first mentor may see the request as a slight on his or her character or leadership. The school's coordinator for mentoring needs to have good personal relationships with mentors, and the wisdom to know when the student is justified in his or her request for a change.

A further challenge is the documentation necessary for affirming mentoring as a credited component of the curriculum. For mentoring to be at its most effective there needs to be a high level of trust between the mentor and the protégé, which can only be built through preserving confidentiality. In most cases it is not necessary to give detailed records of mentoring sessions; it is enough to demonstrate that the process has taken place and that appropriate learning has ensued. A log of meetings together with a brief evaluative report from the mentor and a final reflective paper from the student is often sufficient evidence.

Irrespective of the context or approach, in order for mentoring to be an effective curricular element it is essential that mentors be given training in the process. In particular, where mentors are recruited from outside the school they need to understand the purpose of the relationship and how it fits into the overall vision and mission of the training programme as a whole. Mentors also need to be sensitized to the need to listen as well as to the means by which they might facilitate honesty and quality self-reflection in the protégé. Providing mentors with sample questions and approaches is often greatly appreciated.

A final word needs to be said about the unique challenges associated with mentoring in honour–shame societies. While most of these societies have a long heritage of gurus, pundits, rabbis and other types of spiritual leaders, the shape of their mentoring relationships is very different from the Western conception of mentoring. The culture is also such that many students may be unwilling to be made vulnerable in mentoring relationships with more senior people, and they are sometimes untrained in self-reflection. Consequently, mentoring processes in non-Western contexts may need to be adapted appropriately.

Small Groups

Small-group ministry is becoming an increasingly fruitful element of many growing churches around the world. As a part of their training it can be highly beneficial for students to experience the value of being part of a small group. Residential programmes are particularly conducive to bringing this element into the curriculum, but even for non-residential programmes, processes can be established for allowing or requiring small-group ministry to be a part of the students' experiential learning.

It is important that the purpose and learning outcomes of small-group experiences are clearly delineated, as the outcomes should shape the process. Where the emphasis is on the spiritual pilgrimage of the students, the process may need to have substantial direction from faculty members. Where the focus is more on the skills of preparing and facilitating small-group Bible study, students will generally need to play a more hands-on role in the process.

Community Worship

Particularly in residential programmes, the norm is for there to be a regular time of community worship. While many schools prefer to keep these times as extra-curricular, it can also be beneficial to structure elements of community worship as intentional learning experiences for students. This may be done in a variety of ways, including the following:

- Following training in the basics of quality public speaking, students are asked to journal their reflections on, say, two to three of the messages delivered each week. These assessments would look at elements of both content and methodology, and are best done through focusing on the positives rather than the negatives – what the student learnt from how the message was done well rather than the opposite.

- Each student is required to lead the community worship and/or bring a message a fixed number of times each year. The leading and message are then evaluated as means of skill development. In some schools this evaluation is done privately by a speech or preaching instructor. In other schools the focus is more on peer assessment, where students evaluate one another. In either case the emphasis should be positive and forward looking rather than negative and critical.

As with other curricular elements outside the classroom there needs to be appropriate documentation of the process, including a description of the purpose, learning outcomes and activities associated with the student learning and the sort of growth that is sought through community worship. An example of how this might be worked out in practice is given in appendix 7.1.

Theological Reflection on Life Experience

Effective theological training should not prepare for mere ministerial professionalism, but for intelligent, committed, creative and faithful service to God, and for training others in right thinking about the right thing to do (Hoeckman 1994). Many Christian believers struggle to make connections between their faith and the routines of daily life. While they may be faithful at Sunday worship, there is minimal application of the faith to the workplace, studies, parenting and leisure. Consequently, a very valuable curricular element outside the classroom can be to require students to engage in activities that require theological reflection on life experiences.

Employing questions similar to those described in the section "Field Education" above, students carry out journaling and theologically reflective exercises on a wide variety of life experiences, such as their relationships with their peers, their family life, working on or off campus, even sporting activities. As students learn how to look at all of life as a theological activity, they are better prepared to help others do likewise. The overall approach to theological reflection that we have taken at ABTS is summarized in appendix 7.2.

Independent Learning Contracts

Repeatedly through this book I have urged you to recognize the limitations in what can be expected from a programme of theological education. We need to have the humility to recognize that some of the students' most valuable learning experiences will take place not in the short period they are under our care, but in the years following graduation. In serving this broader vision we do well to reduce the content in our curricula and train students in how to plan and design their own learning. One of the most helpful approaches to training students in this process is independent learning contracts.

As with all curricular elements outside the classroom, quality learning contracts entail careful planning in which students detail what they desire to learn, why they perceive this learning to be significant for their future ministries, in what activities they intend to engage themselves towards accomplishing the learning, and how their learning might be assessed. As a point of reference, the approach taken at ABTS is given in appendix 7.3.

While those of us who have received a traditional theological education are inclined to restrict independent learning to cognitive exercises, sometimes the more substantial need may be in the affective or behavioural domains. For some students, among the best means of preparation for future ministry, both in content and in process, may be to engage in an independent learning contract that focuses on such life skills as time management or self-discipline, or practical skills such as playing the guitar or using a sewing machine. Guiding students through a self-education learning contract towards personalized learning goals can be a major contribution to their long-term education, a process that may be the foundation for intentional lifelong learning.

Exploring Intentionality in Incidental Theological Learning

Jonathan Bonk (2008) has observed that Jesus's ministry was largely "incidental"; that is, most of his ministry both in word and action came in response to incidents that occurred as he walked through the land. In many cases, the people Jesus met were in crisis, and the ways in which he acted and spoke led to a paradigm shift in thinking and behaviour, both for the direct recipients of his care and for those listening and observing. In the same way, transformational learning in theological education often occurs incidentally. Serious educators do well to seek ways to respond to these "learning moments" with intentionality and possibly with some sort of structure.

While the language used by the dominant voices in transformational learning theory (Brookfield 1987; Cranton 2006; Loder 1982, 1998; Mezirow 1991, 2000; Piaget 1970, 1985) varies, the description of the processes involved is fairly consistent. The key is to see life crises and experiences of personal disequilibrium as potential opportunities for qualitative growth. Brookfield (1987, 26–28) has suggested five stages of transformational learning:

- *Trigger event* that causes perplexity or discomfort.
- *Appraisal phase* – clarification of the issue and self-examination of what is going on.
- *Exploration* of explanations or of new ways of responding.
- *Developing alternative perspectives*, through which new ways are tried and tested.
- *Integration* of the new with other aspects of our lives.

Most students experience multiple stressors on their lives. Even in the ordinary flow of life, seeking balance between study demands, ministry involvement, and personal relationships with God and others can leave an individual feeling overwhelmed. The additional stress of personal or family emergencies or political unrest can cause a major crisis. These crises can be highly destructive for the individual or, if handled wisely, can become a catalyst for transformational growth. Debbie Kramlich (2013) relates her husband's approach to leadership at a Bible college:

> We had so many conflicts and issues that arose, and rather than seeing them as distracting from what we wanted the students to be learning in the classroom, these struggles became opportunities to flesh out what the

students were learning. My husband burned the rule book and came up with guiding principles for the students to follow in learning to live together as a community that reflected multiple cultures and age groups. There were not hard and fast rules, but rather guiding principles to help the students evaluate how they lived together…. Our principles were fluid and adapted to the community. This process resulted in our students graduating and ready to face a world that was not black and white, having learned how to live together and respect each other.

Life crises are the most prominent forms of "trigger events" and hold the potential for the greatest level of transformative learning. However, for most people in crisis, the last thing they want is someone telling them what to think or do. How then can we become more intentional in incidental theological education? The following are a few suggestions:

- *Anticipate.* Certain crises are somewhat predictable. For example, it is common for students to experience personal or family health crises, and on occasions the death of a loved one. For married students, pregnancy should not be surprising. In some parts of the world, political crises and violence are common either in the country in which the school is located or in the students' home countries. In other parts of the world, the persecution of Christians is to be expected. Addressing these issues theologically and pastorally before they occur can give students the tools they need to carry out effective and positive reflection during the "appraisal and exploration" phases.

- *Respond to the moments.* Instructors devote long hours to lesson preparation and can become so fixated on the substance of the lessons that they miss substantial teaching moments. Knowing your students personally and being aware of their life situations can open the door to facilitating transformational life learning. Wisdom is needed, however, to ensure that we do not err on the side of the incidental and underplay the value of more structured elements of the curriculum.

- *Take a "parakletic" stance with students.* The Greek word *paraklesis* alludes to a relationship in which a more mature person comes alongside another and points the way forward. This process is bathed in comfort and encouragement, although it may also on occasion involve rebuke and warning; but always it is from alongside, not from above. Engaging in *paraklesis* with students in their times of crisis can have a positive impact on them that lasts far longer than the content we teach in classes.

Conclusion

This chapter is a very brief introduction to a growing number of non-classroom curricular elements being used in the formation of students in programmes of theological education. The learning efficacy of these educational elements has been known for many years. With the growing global influence of the European ECTS approach to credit based on hours of learning activity, it is now acceptable not only to incorporate these elements into the curriculum, but also to allocate significant credit for the learning that takes place.

Common non-classroom elements include field education, mentoring and small-group experiences. However, the curriculum need not be limited to these. With appropriate processes in place, community worship, independent learning, theological reflection on life experiences, and other elements can be affirmed and promoted as substantial components of the curriculum.

Although more difficult to document, incidental learning is also a significant element of students' formation, and schools do well to be sensitized to the potential embedded in these "learning moments", and to seek to respond wisely and appropriately.

Exercises

1. In which of the various non-classroom curricular elements described in this chapter do you feel your own programme is most successful? Why? From your own experience in your programme or from what you know of other programmes in your context, give at least two suggestions for how non-classroom elements of the curriculum might be strengthened. Your response may be in terms of other creative types of non-classroom learning or specific processes for implementing these elements more effectively.

2. Read the following case studies and respond to the following questions: (a) What are some possible lessons that might have been learned through the crises and responses? (b) Describe at least two specific ways in which the "learning moments" described here might contribute to the formation of emerging leaders. (c) Give at least one suggestion as to how you believe one or more of these "learning moments" might have been handled better. (d) Describe a "learning moment" you have experienced personally or have observed. What were some of the significant lessons learned or potentially learned through this experience?

- It was to be a routine class on the book of Acts. As the time approached for the beginning of the class, the students came in as usual and found their seats. However, Kamil was standing near the door in intense conversation with one of the other students. Suddenly, Kamil picked up his books and left the class. I was tempted to ignore what had happened and launch into the lesson, but the situation was so unusual that I asked one of the other students if he knew what was wrong with Kamil. "He has just heard that his brother [a leader in one of the underground churches in Kamil's country] has been arrested for apostasy." Instead of immediately starting on the lesson, we spent ten minutes praying for Kamil and his brother, and for the church in his country. We then began our study of Acts by looking at the experiences of Peter in Acts 12 and Paul in Acts 21.

- It was a class in Social Psychology, and as a means of introducing issues of conflict and perspective I asked two students to do a role play about Dr Philip, a professor who had lost patience with the poor attitude and work of his class, and Miriam, a student who was dissatisfied with her grade and had come to Dr Philip to plead for a higher grade. In the role play, Dr Philip responds sharply and in a demeaning tone towards Miriam. Suddenly, in the middle of the role play, Sarah, the student playing the role of Miriam, burst into tears. It transpired that she had experienced an almost identical treatment from a professor that same week. We stopped our lesson and spent time praying for Sarah before continuing the lesson – which took on new intensity as a result of what had happened. I was not in a position to advocate on her behalf, but after the class she and I had a cup of tea together.

- We arrived at the morning worship time to discover that during the night a bomb had exploded in the neighbourhood of Michael's family in their civil-war-torn country. A rapid consultation was held between the college chaplain and the students who were scheduled to lead and speak. Instead of us following the schedule, the chaplain gave a short devotional, and the community broke into small groups and prayed for Michael and his country, as well as for other neighbouring countries suffering from conflict and instability.

Appendix 7.1

Public Speaking at ABTS Chapel: Syllabus

Purpose and Description

The mission of ABTS is to serve the church in our region as it realizes its biblical mission of having Christ acknowledged as Lord by offering specialized learning resources and equipping faithful men and women for effective service. Part of the equipping process involves providing formational contexts in which students develop into effective communicators within a range of settings. Chapel at ABTS provides a significant context by means of which students may grow in their communication skills, in terms of both public speaking and presentation, and interpersonal communication.

Each student will bring a message to the ABTS community. Facilitated informal feedback sessions will follow chapel, involving all the students and some members of faculty. Students will also be asked to participate in self-evaluation. The process of giving and receiving constructive feedback also develops interpersonal skills, crucial for effective Christian service. This process will contribute towards the overall evaluation of students, completed each year by the ABTS faculty.

Learning Outcomes

Cognitive

- Students will grow in their understanding of the elements of effective content and methodology in public communication in Christian ministry.

- Students will grow in their understanding of the principles of effective edifying evaluation.

Affective

- Through this process, students will demonstrate vulnerability, transparency and accountability, within a supervised context.

- Students will value the process of giving and receiving constructive criticism in a gracious and loving manner.
- Core ABTS values such as *community cohesion*, *reflective practice* and *servant leadership* will be developed through this process.

Behavioural

- Students will improve their ability to communicate clearly in a public setting.
- Students will improve their ability to give constructive feedback to their peers.

Process of Evaluation and Logistics

- The elements upon which the students will be evaluated are included in a separate attached document and will be used by students and evaluators as guidelines.
- The students will go through *self-evaluation* as they share their thoughts with faculty or the student body.
- Receiving feedback: first-year students will be evaluated privately after chapel by two faculty members. They will be given one or two items only to work on, other than the positive reinforcement given. After the first year they will be evaluated by the student body led by a faculty member.
- Giving feedback: first-semester students will be observers of this process. Only after they have taken courses in communication skills will they be allowed to participate.
- A pass/fail grade will be awarded to students based on both their public communication skills demonstrated through their regular sharing during chapel, and their interpersonal feedback skills and attitudes demonstrated during the feedback meetings.
- Every student will be evaluated twice per semester.
- Not more than two chapels per week should be considered for evaluation, in order to keep a relaxed atmosphere.

Appendix 7.2

ABTS Theological Reflection on Life and Ministry

Certificate of Theology: 9 credits total
Bachelor of Theology and Master of Divinity: 21 credits total

Purpose and Description

ABTS exists for the purpose of "equipping faithful men and women for effective service". For this to occur, the learning that takes place in the classroom must be applied in the context of life and ministry. The process of theological reflection on life and ministry is a major component of the student's preparation for effective Christian leadership.

Given that all of life is a theological act, students are asked during the course of the theological reflection component of the curriculum to reflect upon: (a) various forms of church and parachurch ministry engagement; (b) elements of daily life such as family relationships, relationships with others in the ABTS community, and on-campus employment; (c) current affairs in the wider society.

Learning Outcomes

Affective

- Identify and further explore personal and ministerial calling within the context of ministry practice and life experience.

- Deepen commitment to integrated and missional ministry within the context of their future ministry.

- Value the role of self-assessment and the assessment of others, in relation to ministry.

Behavioural

- Learn and practise skills relevant for current and future ministry within their context of ministry.

- Further develop reflective skills and self-analysis.

Cognitive

- Deepen their understanding of the social, political, religious and economic settings in which they will be involved in ministry in the future, and make connections between these and their ministry activities.

- Develop theological understanding in relation to practical ministry settings.

Format

Phase one: First year (CertTh, BTh, and MDiv students)

Training in theological reflection (4 credits)

During the course of the first year, students will be trained in the dialogue of theory and practice through two extended reflective papers. Through a spiral of increasing depth and breadth, students will take what they are learning in class and apply the principles to their life and ministry prior to arrival at ABTS. [An element of credit is hence granted for prior experiential learning.]

- In the first week of the Interpretation Module, a session will be held in which students will be asked to discuss their previous life and ministry experience in light of each of the units from both the Survey and the Communication Modules. These reflections will then be documented in an extended and guided reflective paper.

- In the first week of the Theology Module, a session will be held in which students will be asked to discuss their previous life and ministry experience in light of each of the units from each of the Survey, Communication, Interpretation, Introduction to Islam, and Church and Society Modules. These reflections will then be documented in an extended and guided reflective paper.

Upon satisfactory completion of these two papers, students will be granted 4 credits for Theological Reflection on Life and Ministry.

Independent theological reflection (5 x 1 = 5 credits)

Booklets have been prepared that students must complete – 1 booklet for each ECTS credit. In order to be granted credit, the student must complete the following:

1. A description of the nature of the reflective practice and an explanation of why this activity is significant in preparation for future ministry.

2. At least 8 one-page written reflections. These can be reflections on specific events or on the overall experience over a period of time.

3. An extended reflection either on a significant event within the framework of the reflective practice exercise, or on the experience as a whole, that addresses the following:

- A reflection at the affective level on the feelings and attitudes felt during the event or the experience, a discussion of possible sources of these feelings and attitudes, and reflection on the extent to which these feelings and attitudes were a help or a hindrance in the situation.

- An analysis of the event or experience through biblical, historical, cultural-contextual and personal-ministerial lenses.

- A discussion of recommendations for personal or ministerial growth in light of the event or experience.

The total length of this extended reflection should be 600–1,000 words.

4. A chart of dates and times documenting both the experience and reflections on the experience.

Considerable flexibility is offered students in terms of the focus of their reflective practice: while reflection on Christian ministry is a significant component, students are also expected to engage in theological reflection on other life experiences such as with spouses, parents, or peers sharing accommodation at ABTS; the routine of manual labour on campus; living at a distance from families. The latter are all experiences common to the people our students/emerging leaders will be serving subsequent to their time at ABTS, and if they are to be effective in serving these people, it is essential that they have experience in seeing all of life through theological lenses.

Total for Year One: 9 ECTS credits

Phase two: Second and third year (BTh and MDiv students)

Ministry and reflection (2 x 3 credits)

- During the summer between the first and second years and between the second and third years, students are expected to keep a detailed record of life and ministry experience, giving the number of hours of engagement and a brief description of each kind of engagement. The total number of hours should be at least 70.

- During the period of the September Diagnostic, students will be expected to complete an extended reflection on the summer experience that addresses the following:
  - At the affective level, the feelings and attitudes that were experienced through the event or experience, a discussion of possible sources of these

feelings and attitudes, and reflection on the extent to which these feelings and attitudes were a help or a hindrance in the situation.

- An analysis of the event or experience through biblical, historical, cultural-contextual and personal-ministerial lenses.
- A discussion of recommendations for personal or ministerial growth in light of the event or experience.

- The total length of this extended reflection should be 1500–2000 words.

Advanced theological reflection (2 credits)

During each of the second and third years, a number of sessions will be held in which current societal issues are discussed in light of foundational theological principles. Students will be asked to write brief reflective papers after each session.

Independent theological reflection (4 credits)

Students are expected to complete 4 booklets for theological reflection on life and ministry as for the first year above. Other booklets, with certain focuses, may also be added to this process.

Total for Years Two and Three: 12 ECTS credits

Appendix 7.3

Independent Learning Plan

1. Purpose Statement

A crucial part of the mission of ABTS is to equip faithful men and women for effective service. Assisting students to become lifelong learners is an essential component in leadership development. Consequently, during each of the second and third years, students are asked to design and complete a 1-credit independent learning contract. The student is free to choose the nature of the learning that he or she wishes to undertake, and it may be cognitive (for example, learning the basics of Latin, investigating the life of al-Ghazali, learning the basics of elementary statistics), skills-based (for example, learning a ministry-related computer programme such as Microsoft PowerPoint or Microsoft Publisher, learning how to design and evaluate questionnaires, learning how to share one's faith with Jehovah's Witnesses) or personal (for example, learning how to be better disciplined, learning how to gain better control of one's anger). However, the student must be able to explain why the particular learning is important for him or her. The Independent Learning Project is introduced each year during the September Diagnostic.

2. Learning Outcomes

By the end of this course, the student should have demonstrated growth in the following areas:

- *Cognitively:* understanding self, recognizing areas of weakness, and knowing how to address these areas in meaningful and tangible ways.
- *Affectively:* valuing lifelong learning, and developing a commitment to continual self-evaluation and self-enhancement.
- *Behaviourally:* developing and implementing a plan for self-directed learning.

3. Learning Tasks

By the end of the September Diagnostic, students should have chosen their learning project and laid out the learning plan for the coming year. This plan should encompass the following elements:

- *My learning needs:* a brief explanation of what the student would like to learn, and why it is important for him or her to learn this.

- *My study plan:* a brief summary of how the student plans to go about learning what he or she wishes to learn, followed by a detailed study plan, explaining what will be worked on during each phase, what resources are planned to be used, when the work will be done, and how much time is planned to be spent on the learning. The total hours should be in the range of 25–30. The student will also be asked to list resources recommended by an advisor.

- *Evidence of learning:* a brief description of the evidence the student plans to bring that learning has taken place. This could be in the form of a written report, presentation, lesson plan, journal, etc., but needs to demonstrate that significant effort has been made and that appropriate learning has taken place.

On the completion of the learning plan, the student will be asked to present the contracted evidence to the supervising instructor.

Total time in class: 0 hours
Total time out of class: 25–30 hours
TOTAL: 25–30 hours = 1 ECTS credit

8

Deep Learning

Education is about learning – not teaching. While most teachers pay lip service to this principle, few actually take it seriously in the way they teach. Even fewer consider what kind of learning, and how the right kind of learning can be nurtured and developed. For ministerial formation, the real learning is not what is remembered at the end of a course, but what is remembered five or ten years after taking the course, and even more what shapes in the long term the character and actions of the learner. In this chapter you will be introduced to the concept of "deep learning" – learning that lasts and that impacts life.

An understanding of the nature of memory is the foundation for promoting deep learning. Consequently, you will be introduced to Atkinson and Shiffrin's (1968) widely used model of memory, and some of the associated research. In the process you will be presented with the central discovery that the primary factor in deep learning is whether the student considers the material to have significance for life. A discussion of the implications of deep learning for curriculum, course and lesson design will conclude the chapter.

The Nature of Memory

The brain is a highly complex organ, and a number of theories and models have been suggested to explain how we remember and recall knowledge and skills, and what factors shape the remembering process. Some influential but fairly complex models have been proposed by Baddeley (2000, 2003) and Tulving (2000). However, as an introductory entry into discussing memory and deep learning we will use in this chapter an earlier and simpler model developed by Richard Atkinson and Richard Shiffrin (1968), as it is relatively straightforward to understand and has become a foundational model for the more complex models that have followed.

Atkinson and Shiffrin suggested that there are three fundamental components to human memory (see fig. 8.1): sensory memory, short-term or working memory, and long-term memory. Of course, the key to deep learning is to understand how best to guide students to the last phase of long-term memory and recall.

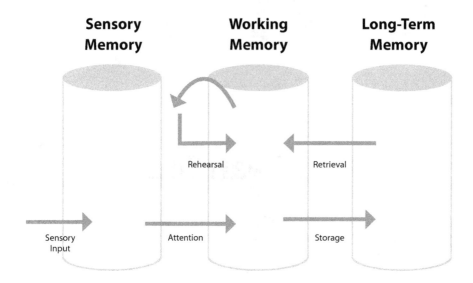

Figure 8.1 Atkinson and Shiffrin's Theory of Memory

Sensory Memory

According to Atkinson and Shiffrin, sensory memory is what arrives at the brain as stimuli directly from the five senses. If you were to quickly stand up where you are, rapidly turn around and then sit down, an enormous amount of sensory information would be recorded in your brain – primarily what you saw, but also what you heard and what you felt physically. However, if you were asked to write down what you saw, heard and felt, you would have difficulty remembering more than a minute proportion of the sensory input. Sensory memory is very rich and detailed, but the information is quickly lost unless it is transferred into short-term memory.

Every day, literally millions of sensory stimuli come into your fields of sight, hearing, touch, smell and taste: spring buds on the trees, trains rumbling underground, the heat coming out of a vent, the smell of coffee drifting from a local café. Although you do not process all these stimuli, a lot more of these sensory stimuli remain longer than you consciously notice. Even now, if you were asked to describe what is behind you in the room where you are sitting, while you would be able to describe a few things well, you would also have a number of vague memory "flashes" that are present but indistinct. We simply experience too much sensory stimuli to process it all for more than a brief moment, and consequently it is lost to memory. In short, most of the information that touches our brains goes no further than the stage of sensory memory of sight, sound, smell, taste and touch. Within moments it is lost for ever.

Working Memory

For sensory memories to go further and be processed in short-term or working memory, somehow a person must have a reason to pay attention. Say the following string of numbers out loud once, and then look away and attempt to write down as many as you can from memory:

61749581507240631 4603

It has been found that after a brief exposure, the majority of people are able to remember only five to nine digits – what has been called the 7 ± 2 phenomenon (G. Miller 1956). There is simply too much material for most people to heed, and most is lost. But even our short-term memory is limited in capacity and retains information for no longer than thirty seconds unless strategies are exercised to retain it for longer. While most people could recall several of the above digits for five to ten seconds, few would be able to recall even the first two digits the next day. The material entered working memory, but went no further.

Most people pay limited attention to what is said or seen, and in order for material to be absorbed more deeply – the next step towards deep learning – some form of retention technique needs to be applied. Of the numerous retention techniques that have been researched over the years, two have been found to be particularly significant: "chunking" and "rehearsal".

Chunking involves grouping, or "packing", information into groups that can be remembered as single units. It works by making large amounts of information more manageable.

Say out loud the following list of words, and then look away and attempt to write down as many as you can from memory:

Curriculum, programme, Bible, training, church, mission, theology

No doubt you found it easier to remember these words than the string of numbers because they are somewhat interrelated – they are "chunked" around a central theme, and more specifically the theme of missional theological education that is at the heart of this book.

The most significant implication of "chunking" is the need we have as instructors and curriculum developers to group information around central themes and concepts which become "hooks" for student learning. For example, in this chapter a number of key concepts and terms have been introduced as hooks for learning: "Education is about learning – not teaching", "Sensory memory" and "Short-term or working memory". The fewer of these "chunks" you include in a learning session, the more likely the core idea of the "chunk" will be remembered. In chapter 10, when we look at lesson planning, considerable attention will be given to the formulation of "main points", key truths around which lesson content revolves. By chunking the learning around "main points", there is the potential that, while students may not remember every detail from the lesson, they will be able to remember the central concepts, and recall of details will be facilitated through their connectedness to the main points.

Another way to improve short-term memory involves *rehearsal*, the conscious repetition of information, what communication theorists describe as "appropriate redundancy". Let's go back to the list of numbers:

617495815072406314603

This time, say the string of numbers *three times* out loud, and then look away and try to write down as many as you can from memory. It is probable that the repetition helped you remember more than you did at the first attempt. It is even possible that you may be able to remember the first two or three digits tomorrow. The rehearsal, or repetition, has aided retention.

Of course, the time available for learning is limited and we need to be highly selective about what we choose to repeat. The list of numbers given above is largely meaningless, but hopefully the core concepts being presented in your classroom are of far greater relevance. Repetition of key concepts and ideas is essential to memory and learning. Without such repetition, deep learning is unlikely to take place.

Rehearsal is best when it involves multiple senses. It is more likely that learners will absorb in their memories a main concept when it is both spoken and shown on a PowerPoint slide than when it is only spoken.

The Primacy–Recency Effect in Learning

A feature of working memory that also needs to be noted is what is called the primacy–recency effect. Stated simply, it has been found that we remember best that which comes first, second best that which comes last, and least that which comes in the middle. In other words, a person's ability to pay attention and transfer material into the working memory is strongest at the beginning, next best at the end, and minimal in the middle. After the first few minutes of a learning period, the information that follows exceeds the capacity and is lost (Craik and Tulving 1975).

Figure 8.2 gives an approximate picture of how the primacy–recency effect works during a forty-minute learning episode (Sousa 2006, 89–94). As you can see, there are two prime times for learning: the best period at the beginning and a lesser stretch at the end of a learning period. In the middle is a time period when not much is retained.

There are important implications of the primacy–recency effect for teaching. Important information or skills should be taught first, during the first prime time. Students are most likely to remember information coming at this time – whether important or not. In one observed class (Sousa 2006, 90), the teacher began by putting on the board the literary term "onomatopoeia", and asked students to guess its meaning. Many of the students' *wrong* guesses appeared in the follow-up test. In another class, the

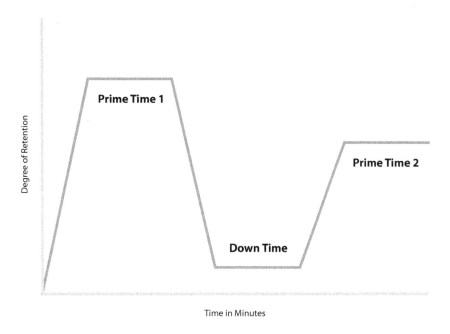

Figure 8.2 Retention during a learning episode (adapted from Sousa 2006, 90)

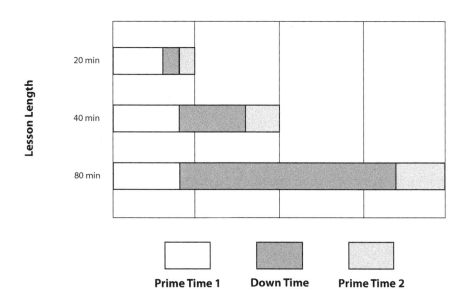

Figure 8.3 Approximate ratio of prime times to down time (adapted from Sousa 2006, 92)

teacher began by calling the attendance. In interviews after the class, the *only* thing many students remembered from the class was who was and who was not present in class! How do you usually begin your classes? How you begin will largely influence what is learned.

Table 8.1 Retention varies with length of teaching episode (adapted from Sousa 2006, 93)

Length of Lesson	Two Prime Times (approximate)	%	Down Time (approximate)	%
20 minutes	18 minutes	90%	2 minutes	10%
40 minutes	25 minutes	60%	15 minutes	40%
80 minutes	30 minutes	35%	50 minutes	65%

The proportion of prime time to down time changes with the length of the teaching episode (fig. 8.3, table 8.1). In a high-quality forty-minute lesson, the two prime times total about twenty-five minutes, or 60 per cent of the teaching time. The down time is about fifteen minutes, or 40 per cent of the lesson time. If we double the length of the learning episode to eighty minutes, even if the lesson is high quality, the down time increases to fifty minutes or more, or 65 per cent of the total time period. As the lesson time lengthens, the percentage of down time increases faster than that of the prime times. The information is entering working memory faster than it can be sorted or checked, and it accumulates. This cluttering interferes with the sorting and chunking processes and reduces the learner's ability to attach sense and meaning, thereby decreasing retention.

This pattern urges shorter learning episodes for greater learning. Short is sweet. Teachers who are concerned about education for learning will break their classes up into twenty-to-thirty-minute packages to help students better retain important material. These short packages of learning can be created by shifting into a new activity that engages the students, such as a case study, role play or forum discussion. Even showing a short video clip accompanied by a few short reflection questions can create the opportunity for a new learning episode.

Remember: education is about learning, not teaching. Education for deep and significant learning must grab the attention of learners, moving from fleeting sensory memory to working memory, and then must give a reason for learners to process the material into long-term learning.

Long-Term Memory

Long-term memory is a relatively permanent type of memory that stores huge amounts of information for a long time. Long-term memory is complex. However, research suggests that long-term memory comprises two foundational substructures which have been termed "explicit memory" (remembering who, what, where, when and why) and "implicit memory" (remembering how).

Explicit memory is the conscious recollection of information such as specific facts or events. Examples might include recounting the events of a movie you have seen, or describing salvation history or the meaning of the kingdom of God to someone.

Implicit memory is memory we don't think about but which affects our actions – skills and perceptions that enable us to do such things as play tennis, drive a car, speak our own language using correct grammar, or even recite the Lord's Prayer without thinking about the words. Implicit memory comprises habitual actions and attitudes, and includes such things as complex synthetic and evaluative thinking skills, as well as empathetic and aesthetic responses.

The key to effective Christian teaching and training is the deep-learning goal of developing significant long-term *explicit* memories that are a continuous resource for life, and, even more importantly, substantial and theologically sound *implicit* memories that have come so much to shape the person that life decisions are habitually formed by healthy reflective practice. It is the retrieval of these long-term explicit and implicit memories that forms the basis of life decisions and actions.

Criteria for Long-Term Storage

But the big question is, "How?" How might we develop teaching, such that what is genuinely important does not simply drop out of the short-term working memory but is stored for future recall and use – or even better, becomes a habitual practice of implicit memory? On what bases does the working memory make that decision?

It has been found (Sousa 2006, 48–49) that what we need to survive is readily recorded in long-term memory. For example, you do not need to relearn every day that walking in front of a moving bus or touching a hot stove can injure you. Strong emotional experiences also have a high likelihood of being permanently stored (Willingham 2009, 44–45). We tend to remember the best and (even more) the worst things that have happened to us. It has been said that the worst experiences make for the best retelling, and if you were asked to recount your worst teaching or travel incidents, you would have little difficulty remembering. You would have greater difficulty recalling positive life experiences. If a teacher can elicit strong emotions in learners, those learners are certainly more likely to remember. Hence the value of experiential learning activities such as field trips, case studies and role plays. But the danger is that the learner will remember only that which is connected to the strong emotion, not necessarily the key learning concepts being presented.

Beyond survival and emotional elements, it seems that the working memory asks just two questions to determine whether an item is saved or rejected (Sousa 2006, 48–49): "Does this make sense?" and "Does this have meaning?" These two questions are the keys to deep learning; these are the keys to education that is not mere teaching but which promotes genuine life change.

Does this make sense?

This first question refers to whether the learner can understand what is being said and can connect it to past experience. Where strong foreign or dialect accents make it difficult to understand a teacher, it is likely that learning will be deficient. But the use of technical or theological jargon can equally create a barrier to learning. Explaining concepts in simple terms is essential to learning. When a student says, "I don't understand", it means the student is having a problem making sense of the learning and is unlikely to process it beyond working memory. A significant part of understanding is the ability to connect new material with previous concepts and ideas. Does it "fit" into what the learner knows about how the world works? Students are more likely to engage with new learning when it is presented either as an extension of or even an antithesis to previous learning, as they feel a sense of mastery in the face of new challenges.

Does it have meaning?

This second question refers to whether the learner finds the material relevant and significant for life. It is the fundamental question of "Why should I even bother remembering this item?" While the question "Does it make sense?" is important, ultimately students will only make an effort to remember material if they believe that it is important enough to do so.

Fink (2003, 7) describes two characteristics of significant learning: (a) the material results in significant changes in the students, changes that continue after the course is over and even after the students have graduated; (b) what the students learn has a high potential for being of value in their lives after the course is over, by enhancing their individual lives, preparing them to participate in multiple communities or preparing them for the world of work. Unfortunately for most students, the only level of significance they are ever given is "It's going to be in the exam". And so they make the effort to engage with the material for as long as it is significant – which is until the end of the course. As soon as the examination is over, the material is no longer significant, and what has been learned quickly drops out of memory. But as serious Christian educators with a calling to stewardship of what God has given us, this cannot be enough. We must seek deep learning in students, and deep learning will only take place if the student considers the material to have significance for life.

Why should you pay attention to this chapter on deep learning? Why should you remember what is being presented? If you don't see this material on deep learning as important, if you don't see it as being able to help you become a more effective teacher or ministry leader, you will finish this chapter and within a few days you will forget most of what has been presented. And even if you remember some of the material in this chapter, it is only those elements that you find meaningful and valuable for your life and ministry that have any chance of being remembered and used five years from now.

Implications for Learning in Leadership Training

So how do we deal with this in practice? How do we develop and present material so that those who participate in our leadership training programmes actually engage with them at a deep level of learning that impacts life? There are three basic areas that must be taken seriously.

The curriculum: "context to text"

The first is the curriculum. Most of us, irrespective of where or whom we teach, begin shaping our curriculum based on what we are familiar with – and that is the classic theological curriculum with divisions of Bible, theology, history, and applied or pastoral theology. It is a shape that is overwhelmingly "text to context" – that is, beginning with the set texts and moving (hopefully) to the context of the student (although in practice the last step often does not take place). It is a shape that assumes young students with minimal life experience. It is a shape that assumes a compulsory audience of full-time students. It is a profoundly fragmented shape that gives a lot of information but little in the way of tools for filtering life through biblical and theological lenses. In short, the deep learning value of the traditional curriculum is questionable.

In reality, the average age of learners in theological schools and training programmes has been steadily increasing, and no longer are they predominantly fresh out of high school or college. Most are adults who bring to the classroom significant life experience and major life questions. Many have only minimal spare time, who given any choice will study only the material that they see helps them answer their questions or gives them tools for effective service and living – in short, the material they consider to be useful.

Consider, for example, the true case of a theological college in the Middle East where two community courses were offered simultaneously – one in background to the New Testament, and one in child development and Christian parenting. The first drew an initial attendance of six, which dropped to two by the end of the course; the latter drew an initial attendance of fourteen, which grew to eighteen by the end of the course. Those who came had little spare time and were looking for tools for life, not only interesting information.

A serious appreciation of the nature of deep learning calls for a greater emphasis in the curriculum on "context to text" than now exists. For deep learning to be promoted, curriculum development must begin not with the shape that has always been used in the past, but by asking ourselves, "What are the major life concerns and questions that our potential learners have?" and "What are the life and ministry skills our potential learners need?", and then developing courses that seek to answer these questions through the texts of Scripture, history, theology and the social sciences.

How is your curriculum? Is it predominantly "text to context", or have you taken seriously the questions, needs and contexts of the learners in building a strong "context to text" component? If you are serious about deep learning, the latter must be a priority.

Course syllabi: why even bother?

The second area that must be taken seriously is how we shape our courses. Too often, learners enter courses because they want the diploma – not because they want to learn. Too often, students are not really sure why they are studying a particular course, but do so simply because it is a part of the required curriculum. Too often, students see what they are studying as fundamentally a waste of time. But then again, instructors also are often not sure why they are teaching what they are teaching! Roland Barth (2001, 4) has commented that "Most of what teachers teach is of no real interest to them; it is only what teachers think someone wants students to know".

By way of example, one of the greatest tragedies of theological education is the high proportion of students who find church history to be one of the most boring and useless subjects in the curriculum (VerBerkmoes et al. 2011). What a loss! But then again, how many church history instructors have ever themselves thought through why students should care about church history – beyond that you cannot have a theological programme without it? There are profound and significant reasons for teaching church history: (a) so that we can better see God's sovereign hand through good and evil, and so deepen our trust in him; (b) so that we can better understand how we have come to be who we are – that is, identity formation; (c) so that we can better understand how others have come to think and behave differently from us and hence appreciate diversity in the people of God; (d) so that we (hopefully) can learn from the lives and the mistakes and successes of those who went before us. There are other reasons that could be suggested. But do students understand these reasons – and even more importantly, is the material taught as though these reasons are actually important?

Research has revealed that courses that tend to result in a surface approach to learning have the following characteristics (Rhem 1995):

- An excessive amount of content. The instructor is so focused on delivering the body of information that little time is left for the complex reflection necessary for deep learning. Students learn the material that is required to pass the course, but there is little personal ownership.

- Relatively high class-contact hours. The education paradigm is teacher-oriented rather than learner-oriented, with the focus being on what the instructor delivers rather than on the learning the student personally generates.

- An emphasis on passive rather than active learning. Students spend most of the time listening and watching rather than actively engaging with the material.

- A lack of choice over subjects and a lack of choice over the method of study. The learners see themselves as disempowered and consequently as recipients rather than active agents in the learning process.

- A threatening and anxiety-provoking assessment system. Our commitment to grades serves to undermine intrinsic motivation in students. Deep learning is better served through multidimensional rubrics that both affirm areas of strength and challenge areas of weakness in students.

A serious commitment to deep learning will present less content, challenge students to reflect deeply, empower students through providing a variety of appropriate learning options, and defuse anxiety through learning-oriented assessment practices.

Lesson plans: why even bother?

Knowing why a course is important to a learner is highly strategic – but not enough. *Every time we engage in teaching* we must understand and communicate why the material is important and significant for the life of the learner.

Why should students study the "we and you" patterns of Ephesians 1–3? Why should they study the development of the creeds? Why should they study the contemporary faces of postmodern philosophy? Why should they wrestle with Maslow's hierarchy of needs? If you as a teacher cannot answer this sort of question, you can be pretty sure that your learners will not be able to. And unless the answer is speaking to real-life questions and real-life concerns, it is probable that deep learning will not take place.

The starting point for promoting deep learning is to know the deep concerns of the learners. This is one of the reasons why the teacher–student relationship is an essential element in quality education. If a teacher wants students not merely to complete the course but to be transformed by the material being presented, that teacher must know the learners well and must repeatedly ask him- or herself the fundamental question: "How will this material help my learners to live well in the face of their daily concerns and needs? How will this material help my students not only to know their faith but also to live their faith?" Only when students consider that the material has significance for life is deep learning likely to take place.

Conclusion

Research into how the brain receives, processes, stores and recalls material suggests that much of our current educational methodology is ineffectual. Serious educators must appropriate patterns that best facilitate deep learning – learning that lasts, learning that impacts life. Whether it is in the curriculum as a whole, in the design of a course or in the delivery of a specific lesson, deep learning can only occur if students value the material as significant for life. The search for meaning and purpose in our teaching is the key to transformative learning.

Exercises

1. Take a sixty-second stretch break. Stand up, rub your body, get your blood circulating and, if possible, tell another person in your building/household something about this chapter. When we sit for more than twenty minutes, our blood pools in our seat and in our feet. By getting up and moving, we recirculate that blood. Within a minute, there is about 15 per cent more blood in our brains (Sousa 2006, 34).

2. Try to do an approximate analysis of your overall curriculum. What percentage of your curriculum comprises "text to context" courses, and what percentage is "context to text"? Describe at least one specific step that you personally could take during the next month to help your school better promote deep learning through a greater emphasis on "context to text" education.

3. Consider a course that you have taught recently or that you are teaching now and try to build a purpose statement that explains why the course is significant for the students. Why should your learners take any interest in this course? How might this course connect with the felt needs, concerns and questions of adult learners in your context? How is this course going to help your learners be more effective in Christian living and Christian ministry? If you cannot adequately answer this question, you can be guaranteed that your learners will not be able to answer it either, and while they may go through the motions and pass the course, deep learning will not take place. In order to develop such a purpose statement, imagine that you have a group of students in front of you who have the choice of whether or not to take this course. Your task is to convince these students that the content of this course is absolutely crucial for their future life and ministry. What would you say to convince them? Present the reasons you have developed to a lay person in your church who has never taken a formal theological course. Ask them what they think about your proposed course and the reasons you have offered for studying this course. To what extent are they convinced by your reasons? Why or why not?

4. Think about a lesson you taught recently and about the learners in the class. To what extent was the material speaking to the deep concerns of the learners? On what basis did you make this judgement? How can you know whether your lesson is connecting with the learners in significant ways that might promote deep learning?

Part 2

Intentionality in Class Instruction

The institutional vision for integrated and missional theological education that has been addressed in the first part of this book is essential to meaningful curricular conceptualization. However, the best curricular structure in the world will fail if the ethos of integration and missional relevance is not understood and embraced by the faculty in their classroom practices. For many faculty, their own educational experiences have left them with a limited and fairly traditional "toolbox" of instructional approaches. The second part of this book is devoted to providing guidelines for strengthening classroom practice and expanding the possible repertoire of instructional methods that can be employed in teaching. The goal of this material is to develop instructional approaches that take seriously the missional mandate of the church and which are focused more on learning than on teaching.

Creative intentionality in class instruction begins with how we shape a course. Chapter 9 guides teachers through a "backward design" approach to course development. The starting point is an articulation of how the course might contribute to the development of leaders who are equipped to help the church fulfil its missional mandate. With this purpose in place, more specific outcomes are developed, then learning tasks that might measure student growth towards these outcomes, the learning activities that are needed to provide students with the desired knowledge, attitudes and skills, and then learning resources and logistical details. When faculty members enter their classes with a long-term view in mind, their approach inevitably shifts from a focus on teaching to a focus on significant learning.

The prevalent model of lesson delivery is modelled more on the shape of a research paper than on what is known of how people learn. The tendency is to develop a "logical" rather than a "psychological" approach, moving through introduction, points one, two, three, and so on, with sub-points. A learning-oriented approach has a totally different shape: in tune with what is known of deep learning, effective lessons develop clear concept statements, and each learning episode dialogues between text and context. Key guidelines for a learning-oriented approach to lesson planning are given in chapter 10.

Chapters 11 through 13 are devoted to filling the teacher's "toolbox" with methodological possibilities. A particular focus is given to question design, beginning with the sort of divergent questions that challenge students to think deeply about issues at the analytic, synthetic and evaluative levels. Instruction at the purely cognitive level will rarely lead to holistic, transformative learning, and consequently guidelines will also be given on the design of questions that bring the affective and behavioural dimensions of learning into classroom dialogue. Story is valued around the world, particularly in the Global South and East. It should not surprise us, therefore, that case studies are a particularly potent approach to classroom instruction in theological education. The design and implementation of case studies is the focus of chapter 13.

Theological education was first developed in the West and for centuries was an almost exclusively male domain. It is therefore not surprising that much of the educational methodology employed in theological education better suits white Western males than it does those from the Global South and East, or women in general. Meanwhile, the global centre of theological education is shifting away from the West, and the proportion of female theological students is growing in every denomination and in every region of the world (Esterline et al. 2013). Chapter 14 surveys some of the recent theories of learning styles, as well as some of the research on gender and cultural preference in learning. For the accomplishment of the missional mandate of theological education, instructors need to take seriously the diversity of learning patterns and respond to the different learning needs of their students.

The grading and assessment of students is pervasive in education. In chapter 15 the prominent role of grades is challenged – particularly in theological education. A variety of alternative assessment structures are proposed; these are more likely to promote an intrinsic commitment to learning and hence better serve the missional vision for theological education.

The final chapter of the book is a word of encouragement and challenge. Much research has been undertaken to investigate the characteristics of outstanding teachers, and this chapter summarizes some of the key contours of this research. A key implication of living between the "already" and the "not yet" is the need for continual self-assessment in light of the ideal (P. Shaw 2006b), and these characteristics can provide helpful lenses as together we strive towards excellence in theological education.

9

Course Design for Multidimensional Learning

For many teachers, the writing of a course syllabus is a burdensome task, with relatively little meaning. However, effective syllabi provide a basis for intentional learning-centred education, with parameters for mutual accountability between the instructor and the students. In this chapter you will be introduced to the notion of "backward design" of courses, and you will be guided step by step through the following process of course design for multidimensional learning:

- Define the *purpose* of the course.

- Establish long-term (deep learning) desired *learning outcomes* at the cognitive, affective and behavioural levels.

- Create appropriate *learning tasks* that seek to measure the extent to which students have made progress towards the learning outcomes.

- Design *learning activities* that will provide the students with the knowledge, skills and opportunities for holistic growth that are necessary to complete the learning tasks.

- List relevant *learning resources* that the students can access to support their learning.

- Provide *mutual accountability* elements, such as time allocations for work requested, class policies and teacher commitments.

Backward Design

As educationalists increasingly take seriously the notion that education is about learning not teaching, and as research grows about the nature of learning and the means by which learning can be promoted, new models of educational design are emerging. One of the most influential course-design models is what Grant Wiggins (1998) has described as "backward design". Rather than beginning with the content, the instructor begins by asking the question, "What is it I hope that students will have learned, that will still be there and have value, several years after the course is over?" The answer to this question forms the basis of the "learning outcomes" for the course. The course designer then moves backwards in time to the end of the course and asks the question, "What would the students have to do to convince me that they have made progress on their pilgrimage towards the desired long-term learning outcomes?" This then becomes the basis for what is described as the "learning tasks", through which students give evidence of the extent to which learning has taken place. And finally, the instructor moves back into the course itself and asks, "What would the students need to do during the course to be able to make progress in the learning sufficiently to master the learning tasks?" The answer to this question forces the instructor to shape instructional design for learning and not simply teaching.

"Backward design" can be a challenge for instructors educated in a traditional paradigm. However, the process is quite straightforward, and in the remainder of this chapter a step-by-step process of course design will be presented. Each step has its place in the process, and the whole works together to promote intentionality in instruction, an important element in enhancing student motivation to learn. An example of what the final syllabus might look like is given in appendix 9.1; you may find it helpful to refer to this sample syllabus as we work through each step.

Step 1: Purpose Statement

Every meaningful course seeks to address a fundamental lack – either in the church or in the students. While we as instructors tend to focus on cognitive needs, the most significant lacks are more often behavioural or affective. The starting point for every meaningful and significant course is to think through why this course is important. How might this course help emerging leaders in their preparation for future ministry? Why should the students care about this course enough to engage with us in significant learning? The challenge of quality theological education is to transform our instructional design from the mere transfer of information to the holistic training of a generation of theologically reflective practitioners. As we discussed in the previous chapter on deep learning, students' long-term embrace of learning is directly related to the extent to which they perceive meaning and value in the material they are studying. The purpose statement explains to the students why this course is of significance as they prepare for their future ministry contexts.

A good purpose statement has the following structure:

- A short summary of the vision and mission statement of the programme or institution where the course is being offered.

- A description of some of the specific contextual challenges that this course is seeking to address.

- A description of how the content and methodology of this course might help the learners to be better able to address these challenges, and to help others to address these challenges.

The purpose statement should lead naturally into the "learning outcomes".

Step 2: Learning Outcomes

As with many educational terms, the expression "learning outcomes" has been used in a variety of ways. For many years it was almost synonymous with "behavioural objectives" – specific and measurable outcomes of a learning "package", whether it be a lesson, a course or a complete programme of study. This highly directive understanding has been widely criticized as undermining intellectual creativity, experimentation and discovery, fostering a climate that inhibits the capacity of teachers and students to welcome and engage uncertainty, and ultimately leading to the trivialization of learning (Furedi 2012).

The problem with equating "learning outcomes" with "behavioural objectives" is that the most important learning is not that demonstrated in examinations and term papers at the conclusion of a course, but rather what remains five years or more later. Consequently, a more meaningful approach to learning outcomes seeks to answer the question, "What is it I hope that students will have learned, that will still be there and have value several years after the course is over, and be impacting the thinking, character and behaviour of the students?" The goal of your course is to take your students on a pilgrimage towards these significant learning objectives. The focus of the learning outcomes should be on holistic growth, and consequently an appropriate framework is as follows:

By the end of this course you should have demonstrated growth in the following areas:

- *Cognitively* [With what significant knowledge and thinking skills does this course intend to provide the students?]

- *Affectively* [What attitudes, motivations and character traits does this course seek to develop in students?]

- *Behaviourally* [What personal and/or ministry skills does this course seek to develop in students, and/or what actions do you hope to see your students take during or following the course?]

A recognition of the importance of learning outcomes is nearly a century old and was formalized through the taxonomies developed by Bloom's (1956) and Krathwohl's (1964) teams (discussed in chapter 4) following an informal meeting of college examiners attending the 1948 American Psychological Association Convention in Boston. In the years since the publication of the original learning taxonomies, numerous educators have devised lists of verbs that are detailed tools for designing learning outcomes. A selection of learning verbs is given in appendix 9.3.

More recently, concern has been expressed about the need to develop metacognitive skills, through which students not only learn, but also learn *how to learn*, and how to manage their learning by understanding how learning takes place. This then becomes the foundation for lifelong learning. Suskie (2009, 123–24) observes, "Because knowledge is growing at an exponential pace, there is increasing recognition that we must prepare students for a lifetime of learning, often on their own, making metacognition an increasingly valued skill."

Metacognition includes cognitive traits such as discussing and evaluating one's own problem-solving strategies; the ability to critically examine and evaluate the bases for one's own arguments; and the development and evaluation of learning plans. In the same way, quality affective learning goes beyond the goals of appreciation, character development and valuing, to an awareness of how one's values, attitudes and opinions can continue to be nurtured and developed throughout life (Suskie 2009, 123). Theological education for lifelong growth entails the development of self-monitoring and self-evaluative learning skills that should play a role in the learning outcomes of our courses.

Step 3: Learning Tasks

The learning tasks are what the students need to do in order to demonstrate that they have grown in the areas described in the section above on learning outcomes. Good learning tasks are not merely busy work but promote genuine learning. The learning tasks seek to answer the question, "What would the students have to do to convince me that they have made progress towards the learning goals?" Excellence in course design involves linking each learning task directly to one or more of the learning outcomes, and equally ensures that each learning outcome is in some way addressed through one or more of the learning tasks. This procedure provides accountability for the instructor in the process of ensuring that the course, not merely in word but in practice, is designed for intentional holistic growth.

Good learning tasks give students clear direction, as well as an estimate of the amount of time the task is likely to take. In many cases, the final destination of the course is behavioural (obedience), in which case learning tasks should embrace something practical.

Quality learning tasks set challenging but realistic expectations. Often, when students know exactly what they need to do to achieve a high score, they will rise to meet that standard, even if it means accomplishing things to which they never thought they could aspire. While the claim of Jaime Escalante (as portrayed in the 1988 film *Stand and Deliver*) that "students will rise to the level of their teacher's expectations" may not always work out in practice, and high expectations do not guarantee effectiveness, they do play a major role in student achievement. This is seen most clearly in what is now known as "the self-fulfilling prophecy", first observed by Rosenthal and Jacobson (1992) in their famous experiment through which they demonstrated a link between teacher expectations and student performance. In the original experiment, students in eighteen classes were set a standard test of verbal intelligence. Their teachers were led to believe that this test would help identify those students who were about to bloom academically. The experimenters labelled 20 per cent of the students as potential bloomers. These students, however, were selected at random and with no regard to the test scores – a fact of which the teachers were unaware. A re-administration of the same test some eight months later showed marked differences in intellectual growth between the supposed bloomers and the rest of the students.

Similar experimental evidence, including research among mature-age students (Avolio et al. 2009; Etherington 2011), strongly supports the notion that achievement is highly related to the expectations and attitudes of the teacher. Teachers who expect great things often act to fulfil their "prophecy". Consequently, in your learning tasks, you do well to ask students to demonstrate not just simple understanding but also thinking skills such as analysis, evaluation and creativity. If you set out clear and detailed parameters for a learning task, and a clear description of what is expected in order to achieve well, together with an enthusiastic affirmation of the students' ability to accomplish the task, your students are more likely to respond positively to the learning tasks before them.

The time available for students out of class is limited, and the quality design of learning tasks considers carefully whether the time students put into an assignment will yield an appropriate payoff in terms of their learning. There is a tendency to give extended research papers to students, with little consideration of whether they will really learn twice as much from an assignment that takes twenty hours of out-of-class time as from one that takes ten hours. Will students learn significantly more from a thirty-page paper than from a five-page paper (which may take the instructor one-sixth of the time to evaluate)? Sometimes, cognitive learning outcomes may not demand a traditional term paper or research project. Students may achieve progress towards the learning outcomes just as effectively by completing a research proposal or an annotated bibliography (Suskie 2009, 159).

Affective tasks are generally assessed through journaling or forms of creative expression such as poetry, music, painting or dance. Behavioural tasks look for experiential means of learning, such as peer mentoring, community research, or a service activity with reflection.

Designing quality learning tasks is one of the most time-consuming elements of quality course design. The creative element of task design is only the first step. There also needs to be a clear step-by-step description of what is required, clarification of what needs to be done in order to attain excellence in the task, a just estimation of the time required for the student to do a good piece of work, and a clear connection with the relevant learning outcomes that have been defined previously.

A final important element of the learning tasks is to ensure that the total amount of work (reading, writing and practice) being asked of students is within the parameters allowed by the school. For example, under both the American Carnegie System and the European Credit Transfer System, each credit of work is expected to represent a total of twenty-five to thirty hours of learning. The normal practice at undergraduate level is for about half of this to take place in class and half out of class. A 3-credit course would therefore entail a total of, say, ninety hours of learning, of which forty-five would be in class and forty-five out of class. The total of all learning tasks (including time allocated for reading) should then be approximately forty-five hours.

Most schools require students to do substantial reading as a part of the learning tasks. It is important for schools to develop a realistic understanding of student reading speeds. In general, native English speakers at the bachelor level of study should be able to read fifteen to twenty-five pages per hour, depending on the nature of the text. Complex theological texts may take longer to read than more practical books. If students are reading in English as their second language, lower reading speeds should be expected. If faculty give unrealistic reading expectations, it is probable that the students will either not complete the reading or resent the work given by the instructor.

Institutional monitoring of learning-task hours is important for ensuring that comparable amounts of work are expected for comparable credit allocations. It can also defuse some of the tensions that ensue when one instructor places such high demands on students that their work for other faculty members is detrimentally affected.

Step 4: Learning Activities

The learning activities are what the instructor (or better, the "learning facilitator") carries out to enable students to learn and grow. Learning activities embrace both the content and methodology through which the instructor plans to facilitate multidimensional student learning. To paraphrase Grant Wiggins (1998), the learning activities are designed to answer the question "What would the students need to do during the course to be able to do well on the learning tasks?"

The content and methodology should always remain servants to the curricular purpose and learning outcomes, not be masters of the course curriculum. The following are some basic principles of excellence in design of learning activities:

- The focus should be on multidimensional learning rather than on teaching.

- While there will always be the need for engaging students in new content, the mere presentation of material rarely produces formational change.

- Learning is directly proportional to contextual significance and student involvement in the process of learning.

- A diversity of learning activities that includes elements of content presentation and reading, discussion and creative teaching methodologies is most likely to result in effective formational learning (cognitive, affective and behavioural).

It is inevitable that in the first presentation of course material an instructor will need to spend many hours mastering the content and ensuring that appropriate knowledge and understanding is provided for students. However, a focus on learning necessitates more than mere content mastery. Effective learning emerges when the instructional methodologies are designed to help students to engage with the material at a deep level. Outstanding teachers not only read and grow in their fields, but also thoroughly revise course methodology each time they teach. In the long run, instructional methodology should consume at least as much of our attention as does the content we present. In the following chapters, a variety of educational methodologies will be presented, which should help you on the path to excellence in learning facilitation.

Step 5: Learning Resources

The learning resources support the learning activities and the learning tasks. Traditionally, this part has comprised a list of texts available in the library, often on reserve. However, instructors are increasingly supplementing texts with online resources, including links to significant databases. It may also be valuable to include human resources, people on or off campus whom students might consult in the process of completing the learning tasks. The more varied the learning resources, the greater the potential for training students in processes of lifelong learning.

Step 6: Mutual Accountability

The final element in quality course development is the establishment of mutual accountability between student and instructor. This should be two-way:

- With respect to the students, classroom policies that clarify the instructor's expectations for professional engagement. These expectations may include such things as preparation for class sessions and active participation in the sessions, respect of other students in and out of class, arrival at class on time, adherence to submission deadlines, academic integrity and appropriate feedback to the instructor regarding his or her performance.

- With respect to the instructor, commitments towards the students. At a basic level these include the provision of contact information (email address, office telephone, etc.) and details of out-of-class availability (office hours). However, it is highly significant for students if an instructor is willing to make commitments to such things as time on task (using class time effectively and well), prompt feedback, a positive attitude towards students and a respect of diversity.

Conclusion

Quality course design takes time and effort but pays enormous rewards. When we work backwards from the purpose and long-term learning outcomes, through tasks that measure progress on the learning pilgrimage, and only then develop the activities that might serve that learning, we are able to gain perspective as to what is genuinely crucial and what is of secondary value. Teachers who commit themselves to this process inevitably develop a contagious passion for their material, and students are more likely to see their educational experience as valuable and transformative rather than merely a means to attain a diploma.

Three Foundational Questions in Backward Design of Courses

1. "What is it I hope that students will have learned, that will still be there and have value, several years after the course is over?" The answer to this question forms the basis of the learning outcomes for the course.

2. "What would the students have to do to convince me that they have made progress on their pilgrimage towards the desired long-term learning outcomes?" This then becomes the basis for what is described as the "learning tasks", through which students give evidence of the extent to which learning has taken place.

3. "What would the students need to do during the course to be able to make progress in the learning sufficiently to master the learning tasks?" The answer to this question forces the instructor to shape instructional design for learning and not simply teaching.

Steps in Course Syllabus Design

Consider a course that you intend to teach in the near future.

1. *Purpose statement.* In the exercises at the conclusion of the previous chapter on deep learning you were asked to develop a purpose statement that was understandable and meaningful for the learners. Review what you did in that exercise and rework the purpose statement into the following shape: (a) "The … [programme /college /school] exists in order to … ; (b) "However, … [cite contextual challenges]; (c) "This course seeks to serve this purpose by …" You may like to consider the approach taken in Sample Syllabus 1 (appendix 9.1).

2. *Learning outcomes.* Looking five or ten years into the future, from this course, (a) *cognitively:* What is it essential for students to know? What thinking skills would you like students to be able to develop through this course? (b) *affectively:* How do you want your students to change in attitude, motivations or emotions through studying this course? (c) *behaviourally:* What ministry skills do you want students to develop through this course? On the basis of these reflections, establish learning outcomes in the form: "By the end of this course you should have demonstrated growth in the following areas: cognitively …; affectively …; behaviourally …" In formulating your learning outcomes, you may find it helpful to consult the model given in Sample Syllabus 1 (appendix 9.1) and the list of verbs given in appendix 9.3.

3. *Learning tasks.* Suggest tasks that would both facilitate the learning outcomes and measure the extent to which they have been accomplished. Be creative! Consider such things as guided journaling, a sermon or Bible lesson, chapel, a faith statement, poetry, drama, painting, a piece of music, a mentoring relationship, trips with reflection, prayer groups with reflective work, case studies written and discussed by students, group presentations in class and interviews with reflection; even a research paper could include affective and behavioural components. Give appropriate details on the learning tasks, checking that the following are all in place:

- sufficient detail to avoid ambiguity;
- an explanation of what needs to be done to achieve excellence in the task;
- a realistic time estimate for accomplishing a good level of work;
- the total amount of work being asked of students (including all reading, writing and practical work) is within the parameters allocated for the course by the school;

- each task includes an explanation of the learning outcome being addressed;

- every learning outcome is in some way addressed by one or more of the learning tasks.

4. *Learning activities, learning resources and mutual accountability.* For the course syllabus you have been working on, (a) Sketch the main content you wish to address in each session of the course; (b) Make a list of possible methodologies that you might employ in your class sessions as a means of enhancing the learning process; (c) Develop a list of learning resources, including texts, online resources, and human resources available in your context; (d) Write up a series of commitments you expect from your students, and commitments you would be willing to make to your students. You may find it helpful to review and adapt the policies given in the sample syllabus in appendix 9.1.

Exercises

1. Read the two sample syllabi given in appendices 9.1 and 9.2 and answer the following questions:

- With which of the two syllabi do you feel most comfortable? Why?

- What do you like best about the alternative syllabus (appendix 9.1)? Why? What do you most dislike? Why?

- The traditional syllabus (appendix 9.2) begins with content and then gives assignments, while the alternative syllabus moves from course description to goals, to learning tasks. Give two or three reasons why the latter approach might be considered more sound educationally.

- In what ways does the alternative syllabus attempt to embrace the ABCD of learning, (a) in terms of the goals for the course; (b) through the learning tasks; (c) through the instructional methodology?

- Describe one or two negative aspects of the hidden curriculum that are embedded within the traditional approach and which the alternative approach is seeking to address positively and intentionally.

- The traditional approach is fairly risk free for the instructor. What possible pitfalls do you see in the alternative approach? Describe some specific steps that could be taken to overcome these pitfalls.

- From the alternative syllabus, name at least one aspect that you are not currently using but which you believe you could incorporate into your own teaching.

2. Kennedy, Hyland and Ryan (2007) distinguish between "learning aims" and "learning outcomes" – the former being more general, the latter more specific. In this chapter this distinction has not been made, due to the emphasis on deep learning and backward design. Instead in this chapter, what Kennedy, Hyland and Ryan call "learning outcomes" are embedded within the "learning tasks". What do you see as the strengths and weaknesses of making a distinction between "aims" and "outcomes" in the actual implementation of course design?

3. Fink (2003, 24–25) describes several common problems faced by teachers: (a) getting students to prepare before class – hence the students are unprepared for working on challenging problems and questions; (2) student boredom, either with the teacher's lectures or with the whole course; (3) poor retention of knowledge, particularly as students move on to other courses. In what ways might a backward-design approach to course development serve to address some or all of these challenges?

Appendix 9.1

Sample Syllabus 1
ST 201 Introduction to
Systematic Theology

Spring 2007
Learning Facilitator: David Kouri
4 credit hours (60 hours in class + 60 hours out of class = 120 hours)

Course Description

"A survey of major Christian doctrines, following the method of systematic theology and including a study of creedal and doctrinal statements, and their implications for life and ministry."

Purpose

The central purpose of your theological studies is to strengthen your knowledge, attitudes and skills as a person who can help the church in its missional task of having Christ acknowledged as Lord throughout the earth. The church cannot be effective in fulfilling its missional mandate without a clear understanding of who God is and how he works his purposes out in the world. For this reason, the effectiveness of any person in Christian service is based on an ever-deepening relationship with God. Knowledge about God – his character and his ways – is essential to knowing him and serving him. The purpose of this course is to lead you into a deeper understanding of God on the path to a deeper personal knowledge of him and to living the Christian life in the light of a personal relationship with him. As you grow in your knowledge of God, you will be able to help the people of God grow in their knowledge of him. It is also important for you to realize that your pilgrimage of faith in God is not solitary, but we share in the reflection on experience of two millennia of Christian thinkers. Consequently, the course will guide you to an understanding of theology in historical perspective.

Learning Outcomes

By the end of this course, you should have demonstrated growth in the following areas:

- *Affective:* a deeper personal relationship with God through reflection on the great theological themes seen in the Scriptures and discussed through history.

- *Cognitive:* a greater grasp of some of the great theological themes discussed throughout church history, and their significance for personal spirituality, church life, and mission to the surrounding society.

- *Behavioural:* the taking of practical steps towards being able to reflect theologically on personal and ministerial issues and/or issues confronted in the secular world, and hence act as a theologically reflective practitioner.

Learning Tasks

1. Your first learning task is to *read through the set learning tasks* given below (1 hour). You will be provided with a "contract" in which you affirm that you have read carefully through the learning tasks and commit yourself to completing them.

As the purpose of the learning tasks is for you to provide evidence that you have made tangible progress towards the learning outcomes, I encourage your creativity and ownership by *suggesting alternative tasks* that better suit your learning style. However, your suggested task(s) must involve a comparable amount of out-of-class effort and must serve the learning outcomes. If you are interested in designing an alternative learning task or tasks, I encourage you to speak with me, and I will assist you in the process.

2. You will be required to keep *a personal journal* of reflections. For each of the readings (14 x 2 hours = 28 hours) and class sessions (14 x ½ hour = 7 hours) the journals should include at least the following:

- A brief summary of some of the key issues raised in the reading or class session.

- Strong feelings – either positive or negative – that were elicited by the material, with a brief statement as to the possible source of these feelings.

- Response to the question "If this is true, so what?" – the practical implications of the key issues in ministry and life.

Journals might also include such things as prayers, sermon outlines and hymns, in response to the readings and lectures.

You will be asked to form accountability groups of 3 or 4, and a half hour of class time will be allocated every second week for these groups to meet and discuss your journals and pray for one another. (8 x ½ hour = 4 hours)

The purpose of this learning task is to nurture your deeper personal knowledge of God through reflection on the great theological themes seen in the Scriptures and discussed through history.

(Total of 39 hours = 50% of course assessment)

3. You will be asked to work cooperatively in groups of 3 to present key issues around a great doctrine of the church. For each group *a forum* will be held, which I will moderate, in which each member will take on the *personality* of one of the great thinkers of church history and give a 20–30-minute presentation on the context in which that person lived, why the issue was important to him or her and a brief outline of that person's ideas on the doctrine. (For example, one triad may choose to present a forum on ecclesiology, with participants representing St Ignatius of Antioch, Augustine and Calvin.) During these presentations, each participant must act out the person they are presenting, even to the point of dressing in a style appropriate to the time and context in which the person lived. Consequently, the student should have a thorough mastery of the person they are presenting. In addition, the student should provide each member of the class with at least two pages of information on the life and theology of the person – in essay, note or tabular form. Following the presentations, opportunity will be given for the rest of the class to ask the participants questions, and the participants will be able to interact with one another. (Total of 10 hours preparation = 20% of course assessment)

The purpose of this learning task is to assess the extent to which you have grasped some of the great theological themes discussed throughout church history within their historical context.

4. You should complete **one** of the following learning tasks:

Either

(a) Without mentioning precise names and places, describe carefully a situation you have observed from ministry or the secular world, and provide (i) a theological reflection on the situation; and (ii) specific steps that should be taken in response to this situation in light of the theological reflection.

Or

(b) Prepare *and* present in *a local-church context* **one** of the following:

- A *sermon* addressing a great doctrine of the church, helping those listening to understand the practical implications of the doctrine for their daily lives and challenging them to take appropriate action in response. Please don't give another tedious academic treatise!

or

- A *topical lesson* for either a teenagers' or young-adults' group addressing a great doctrine of the church, actively engaging the learners, encouraging them to a deeper understanding of the practical implications of the doctrine for their daily lives, and challenging them to take appropriate action in response. Be aware that young people get bored easily. This lesson should live!

or

- An *article* for a popular magazine addressing a great doctrine of the church, helping those reading to understand the practical implications of the doctrine for their daily lives, and challenging them to take appropriate action in response. As it will appear in a popular magazine, the writing style and approach should be simple, winsome and non-technical. Examples of this style of writing can be obtained by emailing me a request.

In each case you should be able to demonstrate the ability to connect something of the great doctrines of the church with the practicalities of daily life. (Total of 10 hours' preparation = 20% of course assessment)

The purpose of this learning task is to assess your grasp of the significance of key theological themes for personal spirituality, church life, and mission to the surrounding society, and your ability to take practical steps towards being able to reflect theologically on personal and ministerial issues and/or issues confronted in the secular world.

5. You will be expected to prepare for class, and participate in discussions, debates and case-study reflections, as directed. 10%

6. At the conclusion of the course you will have a private interview with me to discuss what has been learned, and to consider implications for personal spiritual formation and behavioural change.

Learning Activities

Weeks 1–3: The Doctrine of God
Required Readings: …

Weeks 4–5: Theological Anthropology

Required Readings:…

Weeks 6–8: Christology
Required Readings: …

Weeks 9–10: Salvation History
Required Readings: …

Week 11: Pneumatology
Required Readings: …

Week 12: Divine Revelation
Required Readings: …

Weeks 13–14: Ecclesiology
Required Readings: …

Week 15: Eschatology
Required Readings: …

Professorial notes will be delivered to students a week in advance of each class session. Students will be expected to have read this material prior to the class time. As appropriate, class sessions will comprise a selection of the following:

- Opportunities for prayer – both improvised and through published liturgies – public, small group and private

- Hymn singing

- Personal testimonies, in which students will seek to connect great doctrines to their own spiritual experiences

- Small-group discussion of key issues through analytic, synthetic and evaluative questions

- Reflection on case studies in light of key theological issues

- Role plays and theological reflection

- Debates

- Movie clips and theological reflection

Learning Resources

Grudem, Wayne A. *Systematic Theology: An Introduction to Biblical Doctrine*. Grand Rapids: Zondervan, 1994.

McGrath, Alister E. *Historical Theology: An Introduction to the History of Christian Thought*. Oxford: Wiley-Blackwell, 1998.

Migliore, Daniel L. *Faith Seeking Understanding: An Introduction to Christian Theology*. Grand Rapids: Eerdmans, 1991.

Mutual Commitments

What I expect from you as an emerging leader in the service of Christ:

1. I expect you to be diligent in preparing thoroughly for each session.

2. I expect you to submit work on time, or, if this is not possible, to request an extension adequately in advance of the deadline.

3. I expect you to participate fully and constructively in all course activities and discussions.

4. I expect you to show respect towards other students, being sensitive to national, cultural, gender and other individual differences, and listening courteously when others speak in class.

5. I expect you to provide accurate and constructive feedback on the course content and methodology that will help me as I teach this course and when I teach this material again in the future.

My commitments to you are:

1. I will prepare carefully for each class session.

2. I will encourage reciprocity and cooperation among you as a class of emerging leaders.

3. I will emphasize time on task, making the best use of the available time to promote quality learning.

4. I will promote active learning, respecting diverse talents and learning styles.

5. I will provide adequate opportunity outside of the class session times for you to discuss the course material with me.

6. I will do my best to provide prompt feedback on your work.

Contact Information

- I will be available in my office on Tuesday and Thursday afternoons from 2–5 p.m. (1400–1700)
- Email: dkouri@abcdseminary.org

Appendix 9.2

Sample Syllabus 2
ST 201 Introduction to
Systematic Theology

Spring 2007
Instructor: David Kouri
4 credit hours

Weeks 1–3: The Doctrine of God
Required Readings: …

Weeks 4–5: Theological Anthropology
Required Readings: …

Weeks 6–8: Christology
Required Readings: …

Weeks 9–10: Salvation History
Required Readings: …

Week 11: Pneumatology
Required Readings: …

Week 12: Divine Revelation
Required Readings: …

Weeks 13–14: Ecclesiology
Required Readings: …

Week 15: Eschatology
Required Readings: …

Course Requirements

1. Regular attendance, reading and class participation. 10%

2. Short class assignments as required. 20%

3. Mid-term examination. 25%

4. A 3,000–5,000-word research paper to be agreed upon with the instructor. 20%

5. Final examination. 25%

Methodology

Classes revolve around professorial lecture, with periodic breaks to field student questions.

Appendix 9.3

Verbs to Consider When Writing Aims

(Adapted and expanded from Martin 2006)

Cognitive

Knowledge	Comprehension	Application	Analysis	Synthesis	Evaluation
Count	Associate	Add	Analyse	Categorize	Appraise
Define	Choose	Apply	Arrange	Combine	Assess
Describe	Comprehend	Calculate	Break down	Compile	Compare
Discover	Compute	Change	Classify	Compose	Conclude
Draw	Convert	Classify	Combine	Contrast	Contrast
Enumerate	Defend	Complete	Compare	Create	Control
Identify	Define	Compute	Delineate	Design	Criticize
Know	Discern	Demonstrate	Design	Devise	Critique
Label	Discuss	Discover	Detect	Drive	Determine
List	Distinguish	Divide	Develop	Explain	Discriminate
Match	Estimate	Examine	Diagram	Generate	Evaluate
Memorize	Explain	Graph	Differentiate	Group	Grade
Name	Extend	Illustrate	Discriminate	Integrate	Interpret
Outline	Extrapolate	Interpolate	Distinguish	Modify	Judge
Point	Generalize	Manipulate	Examine	Order	Justify
Quote	Give examples	Modify	Infer	Organize	Measure
Read	Identify	Operate	Outline	Plan	Rank
Recall	Infer	Prepare	Point out	Prescribe	Rate
Recite	Paraphrase	Produce	Reflect	Propose	Select
Recognize	Predict	Show	Relate	Rearrange	Support
Record	Rewrite	Solve	Select	Reconstruct	Test
Repeat	State	Subtract	Separate	Related	
Reproduce	Summarize	Translate	Subdivide	Reorganize	
Select	Understand	Use	Utilize	Revise	
State				Rewrite	
Trace				Specify	
Write				Summarize	
				Transform	

Affective

Accept	Carry out	Marvel
Admire	Commit to	Obey
Appreciate	Continue	Practise
Approve	Decide	Prefer
Assume	Desire	Reject
Attain	Determine to	Rejoice
Be convinced	Enjoy	Show tolerance of
Be sensitive to	Enthuse	Support
Be willing to	Identify with	Sympathize with
Become interested in	Judge	Thank
Believe	Love	Value

Behavioural

Admit	Give	Prune
Apply	Go	Raise
Ask	Grade	Record
Assemble	Grid	Refill
Assist	Guide	Regulate
Attach	Harvest	Renovate
Avoid	Help	Repair
Balance	Highlight	Replace
Build	Implement	Reproduce
Bundle	Inspect	Retrieve
Buy	Instruct	Route
Calibrate	Interview	Save
Care for	Invite	Schedule
Clean	Lead	Search
Code	Lift	Secure
Collate	Line	Select
Collect	Listen	Send
Communicate	Locate	Separate
Compliment	Log	Serve
Conduct	Make	Share
Confess	Manage	Sharpen

Conserve	Measure	Show
Construct	Meet with	Simplify
Control	Mix	Simulate
Count	Obey	Sing
Create	Operate	Sketch
Demonstrate	Organize	Sort
Design	Package	Talk with
Diagram	Perform	Teach
Dictate	Plan out	Telephone
Direct	Plant	Terminate
Dismantle	Portion	Thank
Do	Position	Transfer
Draw	Practise	Treat
Duplicate	Praise	Trim
Edit	Pray	Troubleshoot
Eliminate	Prepare	Use
Encourage	Present	Visit
Execute	Press	Walk
Experience	Process	Wash
Experiment	Produce	Watch
Find	Programme	Write
Fix	Propagate	
Gather	Provide	

10

Lesson Planning for Multidimensional Learning

There is a general assumption that teaching should result in learning and that learning is the consequence of teaching. The problem with this assumption is that the student tends to be blamed for failure to learn. The thought is rarely entertained that teachers might not be teaching what they think they are teaching. (Smith 1986, 80)

One of the great tragedies of much theological education is the teacher-orientation of the lessons: the teacher does virtually all the thinking, most of the talking, and is often the only member of the class who learns much from the lesson. A variety of factors contribute to teacher-centred education, such as the perceived safety for both teachers and learners (Palmer 1998, 50–60), the tendency for teachers to teach as they have learned, and the sense teachers have that their role is to pass on the wisdom gained through years of academic research and writing.

Unfortunately, very few people actually learn much this way. The more passive the learning, the less content is learned, and the probability of applying the lesson in a meaningful way is next to nil. If our goal as theological educators is not simply the transmission of information but facilitating Christian maturation among those we are teaching, a fundamental perspectival change needs to occur. Lessons need to become learner-centred and learning-focused.

Teaching is a highly personal act, and quality teaching emerges out of the integrity of the teacher as a person (Cranton 2006, 112–15; Palmer 1998, 1–33). Consequently, excellence in learning facilitation will differ from teacher to teacher and from classroom to classroom. In this chapter a series of steps in lesson design will be presented; these steps are not a "law" but approaches that have been widely demonstrated to enhance learning. The goal is to provide you with new "tools" in your teaching "toolbox" as you seek to promote transformational theological education.

Step 1: The Purpose. Why Are You Teaching This Material?

The starting point for any lesson is to ask the simple question, "Why am I teaching this material anyway?" In chapter 8 on deep learning we saw that long-term embrace of material is directly related to the extent to which students find significance in what is being taught. For this reason it is important to start by considering questions such as:

- Why should the students care about this lesson enough to engage with me in significant learning?

- How might this lesson help emerging leaders in their preparation for future ministry?

If you cannot answer these questions, it is guaranteed that your students will not be able to either. Granted, there are times when the purpose of a lesson is to lay a foundation for what follows. However, if habitually you are unable to give meaningful responses to questions such as these, your students will tend to view your teaching as irrelevant and will lack motivation to engage with the content. A good starting point is to imagine a group of potential students who are under no obligation to attend your lesson. How might you seek to convince them that this lesson is crucial for their growth in life and Christian service?

It is valuable also to keep in mind the vision and mission of your school. When teachers throughout the educational programme are able to connect their lessons with the vision and mission of the school, this can become a unifying and integrating focal point in even the most fragmented curriculum. While it may not always be possible to connect your lesson purpose to the vision and mission statement of your programme, the more you are able to relate your teaching to the goal of strategic leadership formation, the more your teaching will be purposeful and transformative. If you are never able to connect your lesson purpose with the vision and mission statement, there is something fundamentally problematic, and it is likely that your teaching is primarily informational rather than transformational.

Step 2: Learning Objectives

Once you have a clear understanding of why you wish to teach a lesson, the next step is to clarify your learning objectives. In what ways do you want your students to be different cognitively, affectively and behaviourally as a result of this lesson?

Many educationalists advocate the expression of lesson objectives in terms of "behavioural objectives", specific and tangible actions that will be accomplished by the end of the lesson and can be measured. Such objectives are generally expressed in terms such as: "By the end of the lesson the student will be able to …" Behavioural objectives should demonstrate the following characteristics (Benson 1993, 168):

- *Clear enough to be understood.* This might seem self-evident, but all too often we aim at a different level from our students. As was discussed in chapter

8 on deep learning, students cannot learn what they do not understand. Making sense of material is one of the foundations of deep learning.

- *Specific enough to be achieved.* We are often tempted to say too much. As has been mentioned several times in this book, "less is more". Most people can only absorb one new item of truth at a time; a good aim will consist of only one specific objective.

- *Personal, geared to the individual.* An aim that does not relate directly to the students' life situations will not be owned and therefore is unlikely to be achieved. This is where our sensitivity to the students' life situations becomes significant. A good aim will relate to the contexts of the students.

- *Practical.* A "what am I going to do?" aim will see far better results than a "what am I going to think?" aim – although the latter aims do have their place.

The strength of behavioural objectives is that they hold teachers accountable to a learning focus. The task of education cannot be seen to be complete unless the students give tangible evidence that they have learned. However, care must be taken not to see behavioural objectives as a comprehensive measure of learning. Too great an emphasis on behavioural objectives can trivialize learning. Also, there is a tendency among those who emphasize the use of behavioural objectives to neglect the affective domain of learning due to measurement difficulties, despite the crucial role affect plays in holistic transformation.

Step 3: What Is/Are the Most Significant Point/Points in Your Lesson?

In chapter 8 on deep learning you were introduced to the value of "chunking" material around central ideas, and the use of appropriate redundancy (rehearsal) of those central ideas. A central main point helps to unify your lesson and gives the student a basis for connecting the various ideas. The main point seeks to answer the question, "If the students forget everything else in the class but they remember one thing through which they will have the essence of the class as a whole, what should that one central truth be?"

The heart of any lesson is the main point, and it is here that far too many teachers fail. They may study hard. They may present the content in an interesting way. The students may thoroughly enjoy the lesson. But an hour after the lesson, the students are unable to say what the lesson was about. The main point was not made clear.

A good "main point" has five chief characteristics. It is:

- *The main point of the lesson* – not some peripheral issue.

- *Short and easily remembered.* The main point should be brief enough to remain clearly in the mind of the teacher, so that he or she can repeat it frequently throughout the lesson. A good "rule of thumb" is to aim for ten words or fewer.

- *Stated in the form of a declarative sentence.* The title or topic heading is *not* the main point. The main point should be a statement of truth which can remain with the students.

- *Positive in tone.* Human beings resist rebuke – even where it is called for. There is an old saying, "When you insist, they resist"; hence quality main points are expressed in a positive or neutral form that invites student retention. Words like "should", "must" or "ought" will generally build a psychological barrier which causes the hearers to quickly forget the point.

- *Focused on one idea.* If we try to teach ten points in a lesson, our students will generally remember none.

Irrespective of how engaging and significant the material, students' minds rarely remain on task throughout a lesson. For this reason, it is best as a general rule to aim for no more than one main point for every hour of teaching. This central idea is then reintroduced and repeated frequently and in different ways throughout the lesson. In this way, while the student may forget many of the details, the central concept remains intact and is more likely to enter long-term memory.

Consider the following examples:

- Healthy churches are characterized by balance.

- The work of Jesus continues in the life of the church through the Holy Spirit.

- Working in teams brings power to Christian ministry.

- Healthy churches accept whoever God accepts.

- The work of evangelism and church growth needs openness and cooperation.

- Christian leadership is self-sacrificial but free of human manipulation.

- The source of power in Christian ministry is the cross.

- Effective leadership is a shared pilgrimage of spiritual influence.

- Effective leadership emerges through intentional selection and formative training.

- Postmodernity challenges the assumptions of truth and objectivity.

In each case, the main point satisfies each of the five criteria given above: it is the main point of the lesson, short and easily remembered, stated in the form of a declarative sentence, positive in tone and focused on one idea.

It is noteworthy that most of the proverbs and sayings that we remember so well ("Too many cooks spoil the broth", "A stitch in time saves nine", "Two wrongs don't make a right", "When the going gets tough, the tough get going", etc.) also satisfy these five criteria. The shape of these proverbs simplifies their retention.

Step 4: Approach the Lesson Psychologically Rather Than Logically

Learning is a dialogue between content and methodology. Student engagement with the content prepared by an instructor emerges through the use of effective methodology, and consequently, quality education gives equal weight in preparation to both content and methodology. Most teachers in higher education devote the greater bulk of their attention to the content they wish to present, without realizing that the delivery of content does not guarantee learning. While it is generally necessary for instructors to focus on content at the first presentation of material, outstanding teachers review and improve their methodology each time they teach a course or lesson.

The focus on content leads many instructors to design lessons as they would write research papers, through a logical step-by-step presentation. While this is often advantageous in written work, it is generally less than effective in the oral world of the classroom. Effective learning facilitation comes through a *psychological* rather than a logical approach to lesson planning.

A classic approach to psychological lesson ordering is that suggested over forty years ago by Lawrence Richards (1970): *hook, book, look, took*. While originally designed for church education, the principles are equally relevant for transformational theological education. Indeed, comparable approaches have been advocated for secular higher education (e.g., Sousa 2006, 275–76; Vella 2008, 32–47).

Richards suggests that teaching effective lessons involves a process that embraces four phases, which can be summarized as follows:

- The *hook* segment helps students focus on the lesson topic in an interesting and pertinent manner.

- In the *book* section, the main subject is investigated and explained.

- Next, the general implications of the subject for the contemporary context are broadly explored in the *look* segment.

- Finally, the lesson theme is privately addressed in the *took* section. The creative teacher does not simply present a creative lesson, but also leads the students to plan ways in which they might put elements of the lesson into practice.

The process of hook, book, look and took can be represented diagrammatically, as shown in figure 10.1. In the remainder of this chapter we will reflect on each of these phases, discussing the rationale behind their significance and the processes by which they might be implemented.

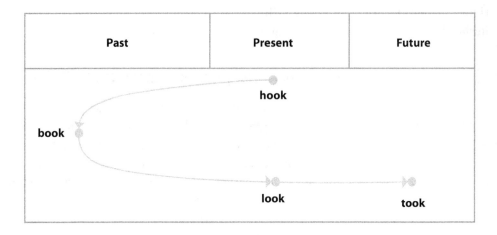

Figure 10.1 The movement of hook, book, look and took (adapted from Richards and Bredfeldt 1998, 160)

Hook: "beginning with a bang"

As you began reading this chapter, how did you feel? Where would you have placed yourself on each of the following parameters?

The opening few minutes of any class session is a very unstable time. As a committed teacher, you enter the class prepared and enthusiastic. You know your material and you believe it is valuable. You are ready to teach. But this does not mean that your students are ready to learn. In most cases, they are not thinking about your lesson. They have their own interests and concerns. Some are happy, some are sad. Some have grave preoccupying anxieties – the sickness of a loved one, an argument at home, financial difficulties. In reality, very few students arrive at the class fully prepared to learn. Their minds are dominated by the affective domain – feelings and attitudes that generally are not well focused on learning. The "hook" seeks to address the feelings and attitudes of our learners and turn their attention from that which is occupying their minds to a new phase of potential growth through the lesson at hand.

There are three basic qualities of a good hook:

- *It gets attention.* The best way to get attention is to involve your learners physically or verbally. The moment learners are doing something, they are hooked into the class. The moment learners have expressed their opinions in response to a controversial question or issue, they are hooked into the class. Involvement is the key to getting attention.

- *It sets a goal* – it gives the learners an answer to the foundational question, "Why should I listen to this?" From the students' perspective this is a fair question: "If I am to pay attention, this lesson needs to be about something important to me. Why should I pay attention to an irrelevant recounting of dusty data?" When your students have no reason to pay attention – that is, they see no reason that is important to them – you will find it hard to hold them. But if you set a goal *they* want to reach, they will come with you.

- *It leads naturally into the lesson* by being directly related to the main point. An attractive start is counterproductive if it does not connect directly with the material that follows.

A good way to begin is with techniques that offer currency (a recent news article), reality (case studies, interesting physical objects linked to the lesson), drama (role play, film clip), or vividness (pictures, slide show), and then to relate the essence of the lesson's main point to the students' own lives. These and other creative methodologies will be examined in the next few chapters.

Many teachers find that one effective opening is a strongly worded statement (Brookfield 2006, 127–28) that provokes and challenges, producing strong emotional responses in students. This is then followed by small-group discussion or debate in which students wrestle with the reasoning and circumstances that might elicit such a statement. By being forced to take seriously opinions with which they strongly disagree, students are drawn into the discussion at an emotional level.

Edwards (1988, 55–56) comments that "a group's readiness to learn is frequently determined within the first few minutes of a class session. During that time a 'psychological set' is established that often persists through the entire period. Happily, that set may be positive as well as negative". Some common pitfalls Edwards warns against include:

- Consuming too much time with "administrivia" (taking roll, making announcements).

- Offering "dead time" with no expected activity (gathering materials, waiting for others to arrive).

- Stifling interest with a hackneyed introduction ("Please open your Bibles to …").

In chapter 8 on deep learning we discussed the primacy–recency effect. What you do in your first activity, your first idea, even your first sentence, may provide the most significant learning that students retain. Effective teachers engage in careful planning of exactly how they will open the class and engage the students. Whatever method is used, the principle is the same – the need to engage students actively from the beginning of the lesson.

Consider, for example, the following openings to classes:

1. "Well, I think we should get started now. I'd like to begin by reading to you Philippians 2:1–11."

2. "I think everyone is here now. Let's call the roll before we get into the lesson."

3. The teacher writes on the board, "The Sermon on the Mount: Unreachable Ideal or Reachable Instructions for Christian Living?" The class is divided into two and the teacher conducts a debate on this topic.

4. The teacher opens the class by reading a short extract from the week's newspaper which talks about the rising local divorce rates, and then asks the students to say how they feel in response.

5. The teacher opens by reading a case study, and the class is divided into groups of three or four to discuss it.

Option 1 assumes that students are ready from the beginning of the class, and does little to attract interest and attention. Option 2 begins with administrivia, and wastes the key opening prime time of the class. In contrast, options 3 to 5 all engage and direct the class. While the three last "hooks" are all strong openings, even these have associated challenges: both the debate and the discussion on the newspaper extract will probably be dominated by a handful of voices; the case study will more likely engage all students, but can be time consuming and may not be suitable for shorter class sessions. Good "hooks" need creativity and wisdom.

Book/look: "text and context"

While Richards makes a distinction between the "book" and "look" phases, in practice the ideal is for the central part of the lesson to be a dialogue between text ("book") and context ("look"), in which the main subject is investigated, explained, reflected upon and analysed.

Lecture is by no means the only method for delivering the book/look phase; in fact, other methods are generally more effective. Some of the more significant of these methods will be discussed in subsequent chapters of this book. Whatever method is used, the purpose remains constant: through meaningful and intentional instructional strategies, a deepening understanding takes place of the main point of the lesson and its significance for developing effective men and women for ministry.

A learning orientation will not be satisfied with the mere delivery of the book/look phase. Rather, a focus on learning will seek student engagement through which the learners demonstrate both their understanding of the texts and their ability to connect the texts to their contexts. It is in this phase that the genuine "artistic" ability of the teacher shines out. As Willingham (2009, 161–62) describes it,

> Teaching is like being a guide on a journey. A teacher tries to guide the thoughts of the student down a particular pathway, or perhaps to explore a broader swath of new terrain. It may be novel country even for the teacher, and their journeys occur side by side. Always the teacher encourages the student to continue, not to lose heart when he encounters obstacles, to use the experience of previous journeys to smooth the way, and to appreciate the beauty and awe that the scenery might afford. As an author must convince the reader not to drop the book, so too must the teacher persuade the student not to discontinue the journey. Teaching is an act of persuasion.

In general, a good lesson will:

- Relate each issue to the central main point(s) of the lesson.

- Move rhythmically between the theoretical and the practical.

- Lead students from factual knowledge to deepening understanding, to living application.

- Incorporate affective (feeling) questions.

- Keep students involved and engaged throughout, through the use of varied methodology.

Took: "towards transformation and not merely information"

In 1976 the first gathering of the Ecumenical Association of Third World Theologians took place in Dar es Salaam, Tanzania. They concluded their meetings with the following statement:

> The theologies from Europe and North America are dominant today in our churches and represent one form of cultural domination. They must be understood to have arisen out of situations related to those countries, and therefore must not be uncritically adopted without our raising the question

of their relevance in the context of our countries. Indeed, we must, in order to be faithful to the gospel and to our peoples, reflect on the realities of our own situations and interpret the word of God in relation to these realities. *We reject as irrelevant an academic type of theology that is divorced from action. We are prepared for a radical break in epistemology which makes commitment the first act of theology and engages in critical reflection on the praxis of the reality of the Third World.* (Torres and Fabella 1978, 269; italics mine)

A missional-ecclesial understanding of theological education implies a need to embrace the Great Commission mandate to teach for obedience. For many theological educators this is a new concept, and yet the evidence of genuine transformative learning is informed heart action – the ability to act upon the learning that has taken place and allow cognitive growth to impact affect and behaviour. For our education to be not merely informational but transformational, it is imperative that our teaching not only connects text with context, but also leads to active response. While not every subject matter lends itself readily to application in action, if praxis response never takes place, the education our programme is offering cannot claim to be formative and missional.

An old Arab saying is that "a fifty-mile journey begins with one step", and effective application seeks not so much a large general change as specific actions that represent steps on the path towards Christian maturation. One common shape is the development of "SMART" responses – Specific, Measurable, Attainable, Relevant, Tangible – which demonstrate the following characteristics:

- *Specific* applications give names, places, details.
- *Measurable* applications give numbers and time, such that after a fixed period we can measure whether or not the message has or has not been applied meaningfully.
- *Attainable* applications can be accomplished.
- *Relevant* applications are directly related to the message.
- *Tangible* applications are visible acts. In other words, it would (at least theoretically) be possible to observe the person doing the application.

By way of example, imagine that you have just given a class a Bible study on Matthew 5:13–16 and have asked the students to write down how they are going to apply the message to their lives. The following are their responses:

- "I want to be light and salt in the world."

- "I want to be a Christian example to those around me."

- "I want to bear witness to my faith."

- "I want to visit my friend Ahmad during the coming week and tell him about Jesus."

- "I want to help George and Dikran to reconcile their differences, and so I plan to telephone each of them before next Sunday."

Each of these responses is an acceptable application of the passage. However, the last two are more likely to lead to action than the others because they are specific, measurable, attainable, relevant and tangible.

When it comes to planning an actual lesson, most students need to be guided through the process towards applying the message in a specific, measurable, attainable, relevant and tangible way. Although not to be seen as the "law of the Medes and the Persians", one possible means by which students might be led into meaningful action is the following four-step process:

1. As the lesson draws near to its conclusion, ask students the following behavioural questions: "Name two or three ways in which the main point is not practised. What are some of the main barriers to the practice of the main point?" The reason for teaching is that there is some aspect of the main point that is not being lived; if the students are already living the main point, there is no point in giving the lesson. A question such as this provides the students with the opportunity for general reflection on the possible life implications of the main point from a negative standpoint, enabling open expression of the students' doubts and fears.

For example:

- Give two or three of the main factors that make it difficult for churches to be fully open and accepting. You may wish to consider issues of age, race, and socioeconomic background.

- Give two or three of the main factors that create barriers to genuine teamwork in your own local church and other churches you know.

- Why is it difficult for us to embrace cross-shaped life and ministry? Give two or three of the factors that cause us to fear the patterns of cross-centred life we discussed in the lesson.

2. Having looked at why it is difficult to practise the main point, it is then important to look at positive possibilities. And so a second behavioural question should follow, along the lines of: "State two or three specific and practical ways in which you have seen the

main point practised in your own life or in the life of someone you know." Practical living-out of truth is most effectively facilitated when people have specific examples or models to follow. This sort of question provides such a model.

For example:

- Have you ever seen a church that was able to create an environment of genuine and open acceptance to all? Name two or three of the main factors that enabled the church to do this.

- Have you ever seen a church in which quality teamwork was widely practised and where this teamwork brought power and effectiveness to the church's ministry? Name two or three of the main factors that enabled the church to develop this sort of team ministry.

- Have you ever seen a Christian leader who demonstrated something of the power of cross-centred ministry? Describe how this worked out in practice. Give two or three factors that helped this person to embrace this approach to ministry.

It is often valuable for these questions to be discussed in small groups of three to five students.

3. Through the previous two questions the students have shared together in general terms both the barriers to living out the main point and the possibilities for changing their current behaviour. This next question challenges them to personal reflection and response: "Write down one specific area of your life in which you wish you could live out the main point more effectively. Considering how you or others have seen the main point lived out in the past, give an example of how you think it could be lived out in the future."

For example:

- In light of the material that we covered in the lesson and our discussion of actual churches from our region, give at least one specific and tangible action you personally could take during the coming two weeks to promote in your own local church an environment of genuine and open acceptance to all.

- In light of our discussion today, give at least one specific and tangible action you personally could take during the coming month to promote team ministry in your own local church.

- Considering the principles discussed in class today, give at least one specific and tangible step that you could take during the coming week towards living out a life of cross-centred ministry.

Because of the personal nature of the question it is often best to have the students complete their responses privately on paper in a "personal response form", perhaps with the personal covenant shown below.

4. The students have now articulated *specific*, *relevant* and *tangible* ways in which they could apply the message. To make the application *measurable* and *attainable*, it is often helpful to have them complete the study by filling out a covenant form, along the lines of either "During the next week, at least once I will act upon the main point by doing …" or "With God's help and strength I covenant that for the next week I will not …." This response is private between the students and God, but it is possible for the teacher to ask the following week whether any of the students were able to apply the message in a practical way. Where there is a good level of trust among students, I have found it possible and helpful to have a student sign the covenant and then get a friend to countersign it. The witnessing of the covenant adds an additional level of seriousness and commitment to the process.

An alternative process which many instructors have found helpful is to conclude blocks of learning (perhaps once every three to four hours of learning) with a centring activity or daily journal. The following series of questions can be used to conclude virtually any sort of learning activity, giving students the opportunity to reflect on their cognitive learning, their affective engagement and their behavioural response to material covered in class:

- Briefly list the main points from today's session.

- For you personally, what was the most important thing you heard or read in today's session? Why was it important for you?

- Was there anything you found challenging in this week's class or readings? Why? Was there anything that made you uncomfortable or with which you disagreed? Why?

- Have you ever seen the principles discussed in today's session at work in your own life or in your church? Briefly describe what happened.

- In light of today's session, describe at least one specific, measurable and attainable action you could take during the next few days as a response to what was discussed.

- In light of today's session, describe at least one way in which your future life and ministry might be impacted by what was discussed.

Conclusion

Most instructors in theological education have spent years in research and writing, and have come to value system and logic in thought. A shift to psychological ordering in no ways seeks to denigrate the value of carefully structured ideas. However, an appreciation of the holistic nature of learning, and in particular the importance of building positive affect, will greatly strengthen our lesson planning. In addition, a shift to psychological ordering, with its conclusion in meaningful application, is better positioned than a traditional approach to lead to learning that is transformational and not merely informational.

Steps in Lesson Design

Consider a lesson that you intend to teach in the near future.

1. *Purpose statement.* Why do you intend to teach this lesson? To what extent does the material speak to the deep concerns of the learners? How might this lesson help to fulfil the vision and mission (purpose) of your programme or school? Write out a clear purpose statement for the lesson.

2. *Main point.* What is/are the main point(s) of the lesson? Using the sample main points given in the chapter as a model, formulate a simple statement that gives the essence of what you are seeking to communicate in your lesson. Check your statement(s) in light of the five characteristics of a quality main point: that it is (a) the main point of the lesson; (b) short and easily remembered – ten words or fewer; (c) stated in the form of a declarative sentence; (d) positive in tone; (e) focused on one idea. Keep in mind that quality teaching seeks to present only one main point for every forty-five to sixty minutes of teaching.

3. *Hook.* How might you begin the lesson "with a bang", ensuring that the primacy–recency effect will result in students retaining what is significant for the lesson as a whole? Suggest a way to engage your students actively from the beginning of the lesson. Keep in mind the three elements of an effective hook: it gets attention; it sets a goal; it leads naturally into the lesson.

4. *Book and look.* List in summary form the main issues represented in the content, briefly explaining how each issue relates to the main point. Give some initial suggestions for how you might be able to engage students in active learning and not simply deliver material through lecture. (In subsequent chapters you will be introduced to a variety of creative teaching methods which should help bring life to the book/look phase of the lesson.)

5. *Took.* Using the four-step process described in this chapter, or some other approach, develop an appropriate "took" phase for your lesson. Remember that a strong "took" will be specific, measurable, attainable, relevant and tangible.

6. *Time.* Allocate appropriate time periods to each phase of the lesson, ensuring that adequate time has been given to reflection and application at the close. While suggested times should never control our teaching, a failure to consider time will likely result in a focus on information delivery rather than genuine

transformational learning which facilitates thinking, attitude formation and action. As you consider the use of time, remember to change activities regularly so as to retain a maximum of twenty to thirty minutes for each learning episode, hence maximizing the prime-time learning for the class.

7. *Resources.* For each phase of the lesson make a list of all the resources you will need. If these resources include technology it is important that you arrive and test the technology at least ten minutes prior to the start of the lesson.

Exercises

1. Consider the last class you taught. What went well and why? What went poorly and why? What learning took place, and how do you know that the learning took place?

2. Palmer (1998, 1–33) sees the starting point of quality teaching not in the content or methodology, but in the person of the teacher. To what extent do you agree with Palmer? Why? How would you describe yourself as a teacher? How are your personality and character seen in your classroom teaching? In what ways is your personality an asset to your teaching? In what ways is it a liability?

11

Traditional Versus Non-Traditional Instructional Methods

The gift of teaching is not the gift of talking! (Duane Elmer)

Ultimately, the success or failure of our education rests on what happens in the classroom. Implementation of the finest holistic and integrated curriculum eventually comes down to the teacher–learner dynamic. Unfortunately, too few of our faculty have more than an elementary understanding of the way people learn, and they consequently revert to the approach by which they themselves have learned – lecture and assignment. There are better ways.

In this chapter you will be introduced to a variety of instructional strategies that can be employed in the process of encouraging and facilitating learning. Traditional methods (such as lecture and classroom discussion) will be assessed in light of educational research, and suggestions will be given for strengthening traditional approaches, making them more learning-sensitive. You will also be introduced to a variety of non-traditional strategies, such as forums, debates, interviews, and the use of images and literature. The following two chapters will engage in a more detailed discussion of question design for deep learning and the particularly powerful technique of case study, which is readily converted into a simulation or role play.

Throughout this whole process it is important to keep in mind that whatever methods are used, they are simply servants of the learning process, and no single technique is the "silver bullet" that will solve all educational challenges. In this regard Fink's (2003, 138) words are particularly pertinent:

> There is a fundamental difference between an instructional strategy and a teaching technique. Instructional strategy is by far the more important. Teachers still need to be effective and proficient with whatever techniques they use. But it is the particular way those techniques and learning activities

are combined and sequenced that determines whether a course creates synergy among its component parts. It is the strategy that creates the energy necessary for significant learning, not the techniques themselves. Hence, for teachers who want a truly powerful course, my admonition is: Don't think technique; think strategy.

Educational research over the past thirty to forty years has established as fact that business as usual – preparing and delivering lectures to passive students who are then asked to regurgitate the information in tests and essays – is no longer an adequate approach for promoting learning. Perhaps it never was. Meyers and Jones (1993, 14–15) give the following uncomfortable findings:

- While teachers are lecturing, students are not attending to what is being said 40 per cent of the time.

- In the first ten minutes of a lecture, students absorb 70 per cent of what is said; in the last ten minutes, only 20 per cent. Most of the 70 per cent is lost within one hour of the lecture, and virtually none of what is said in the last ten minutes is retained.

- Students lose their initial interest, and attention levels continue to drop, as a lecture proceeds.

- Four months after taking an introductory psychology course, students knew only 8 per cent more on the topics covered than a control group who had never taken the course.

- Research has shown that learners retain in six weeks perhaps 5 per cent of what is learned through traditional teaching strategies (lecture, question and answer), and in two years the recall is inconsequential.

There are two keys to effective educational methodology – involvement and application. Involvement means that the learner is drawn into and engages with the material in such a way that he or she comes to "own" it for him- or herself. Application means that, once the learner has "owned" the content in principle, he or she is helped to apply that content in specific, tangible ways. Over sixty years ago Edgar Dale (1946) recognized the relationship between active involvement, memory retention and learning, and developed his now-famous "cone of experience" (fig. 11.1).

In the remainder of this chapter we will discuss a variety of instructional strategies in light of Dale's diagram, working from the more verbal to the more active forms of educational methodology. The powerful instructional strategy of case study will receive detailed attention in chapter 13.

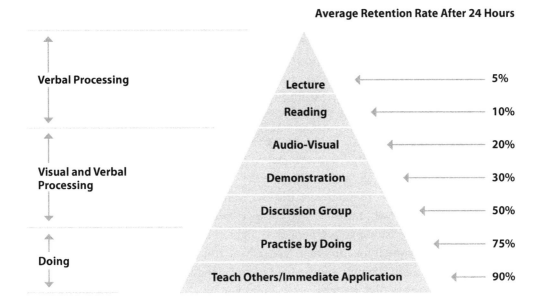

Figure 11.1 Edgar Dale's cone of experience

Lecture

> Lecturing is an unnatural act, an act for which providence did not design humans. It is perfectly all right now and then to speak while others remain silent, but to do so regularly, one hour at a time, for one person to drone on and on while others sit in silence, I do not believe that this is what the Creator designed humans to do. (Barth, 2001, 34–35)

Although faculty across the disciplines of higher education express the desire to promote higher-level and deep learning, about 80 per cent of college-level faculty continue to choose lecture as their primary instructional methodology, despite a long history of research (Fink 2003, 3) that suggests that lecture has limited effectiveness in helping students:

- Retain information after a course is over.
- Develop an ability to transfer knowledge to novel situations.
- Develop skill in thinking or problem solving.
- Achieve affective outcomes, such as motivation for additional learning or a change in attitude.

There are many myths which contribute to the continued popularity of lecture as a dominant instructional methodology. Elmer (1993, 142–43) suggests the following:

- *The myth of omniscience.* As teachers are those who have undergone higher studies and done extensive preparation for the class, they believe that they are the only ones who have anything important to say and that others will be served best by listening. As was discussed in chapter 5 on the hidden curriculum, in such situations the teacher equates education with schooling rather than with quality learning – problematic in any context of higher education but a grievous concern in theological education.

- *The myth of ignorance.* There is a frequent assumption that since it is the teacher who is trained, experienced and equipped, why should we waste time having students "share their ignorance"? While often the teacher does have greater expertise in the theoretical elements of the material, many students come to class with knowledge and experience from which both the teacher and the other students can benefit. In light of our goal of forming faithful men and women for missional leadership, which implies active living of the content, there is much to be gained from having students hear how their peers have applied the message in their own lives. This becomes particularly imperative in contexts where learners are in their thirties, forties or fifties. In such contexts, while the learners may have some level of ignorance of the theory, they are sometimes more expert at the practice than is the instructor.

- *The myth of change* assumes that telling people changes people. The "action–attitude principle" presented in chapter 4 on multidimensional learning suggests that the reverse is true – that actions change attitudes far more than attitudes change actions – pointing to the need for more active approaches to learning.

- *The myth of disinterest* refers to the reluctance of learners to interact. According to this myth, students are happier to sit passively and don't want to participate in active learning methods. Generally, this myth is held by those who either have never used active teaching methods or have not used them well. Those who have learned the skill of involving students recognize that students are eager to engage in learning that makes sense and has significance (see chapter 8 on deep learning).

While the lecture has fallen on hard times and there are significant grounds for challenging its use as a dominant instructional methodology, there remains a place for lecture in quality learning-centred instruction. However, effective instructors use lecture sparingly and are careful to ensure that its purpose is understood.

The typical lecture tends to present a systematic, concise summary of the knowledge to be covered that day, an approach Chang et al. (1983, 21) describe as "conclusion oriented", by which the beginning, middle and end are presented to the students as a finished package. McKeachie (1999, 75) suggests that this approach is misdirected: that the lecturer's task is not to be an "abstractor of encyclopedias, but to teach students to learn and think".

The greatest danger of lecture is the tendency of the instructor to focus on teaching rather than learning, and to present information in logical rather than psychological ordering. When lecture requires little in the way of response from the students, dependency and passivity are promoted. The student may keep notes, but little in the way of deep learning takes place.

Lecture is generally most effective as an introduction to the overall contours of a field, followed by whole-class or small-group discussion of the implications of the material. In this regard excellent instructors are aware that "less is more" – that is, less material taught well, with time for reflection, discussion and analysis, leads to greater long-term learning than the presentation of vast amounts of material with little opportunity for reflection and discussion (O'Brien, Millis and Cohen 2008, 12).

For quality learning to take place through lecture, instructors do well to remember some of the basic principles of memory retention and deep learning:

- In light of its questionable long-term value, only lecture if you have no other choice. Always consider alternative instructional strategies (Juengst 1998, 90–91).

- Clarify in your own mind why the material being presented might be of value and significance to students. Do not hesitate to communicate this value with enthusiasm and passion. Enthusiasm is contagious.

- Establish a clear main point that is repeated at regular appropriate points throughout the presentation. Other ideas are then connected to this one foundational concept. As a means towards better comprehension, provide students with clear outlines that help them follow the flow of thought and "scaffold" their learning.

- It is often worthwhile to provide the listeners with relevant reading materials (significant questions, case studies, extracts from texts, annotated bibliographies) prior to the presentation (Farrah 2004). This encourages a sense of anticipation in the learners and eases the connection between the known and the unknown on the path towards meaningful learning. Likewise, distributing an outline of the content at the beginning of the lecture can give an organizing framework, allowing the flow of the presentation to be followed.

- Be aware of the phenomenon of primacy–recency (see chapter 8 on deep learning), and consequently ensure that the first sentence and the first paragraph of the lecture are striking, relevant and worth remembering. Giving opportunity for student feedback and response after the first ten to fifteen minutes will allow minimum loss of retention in down times.

- Break your lecture into "chunks" of ten to fifteen minutes, with interludes of buzz groups, whole-class discussion, reflective silence, the showing of short video clips, or other means of creating space for a new learning episode to begin (Brookfield 2006, 105).

- Ensure that students can make sense of what is being presented. Define terms, clarify concepts and regularly ask for student feedback. Be sensitive to what students are actually hearing and learning.

- Model desired learning behaviours by introducing early in the lecture key questions that you are seeking to answer, deliberately introducing a variety of alternative perspectives that challenge students towards synthetic thinking, incorporating periods in which underlying assumptions are assessed, and concluding with a series of questions that have remained unanswered by the lecture (Brookfield 2006, 109–13).

- Know your material so well that you can produce a "relaxed familiarity" (Habermas 1995, 217) that reduces student fear of the material.

- A conversational tone of delivery with good eye contact and appropriate gestures is more likely to hold the students' attention than an academic and pedantic approach. Speak with authority balanced with humanity and warmth.

- Use vivid and lively examples and illustrations, and visual resources, but always ensure that these remain a servant and not a master to the learning process.

- Keep the lecture component as short as you can. Leave students hungry for more rather than bored and longing for you to end.

Whole-Class Discussion

In more traditional classrooms, learning-sensitive teachers break lecture material regularly with opportunity for class discussion of what has been presented. In light of such factors as the need for psychological ordering and the primacy–recency effect, class discussion can provide students with the opportunity to pause, think, respond and engage.

Sadly, in practice, *quality* classroom discussions are few and far between. The instructor's preparation is devoted primarily to the arrangement of the content. The focus is on teaching. Little attention is paid to how students might be led to engage with and reflect upon that content – a focus on learning. For whole-class discussion to be effective, instructors must devote time not only to the content but also to the questions that will be used to facilitate reflection. (The next chapter is devoted to question design for deep learning.)

Good questions are foundational to quality whole-class discussion. But equally significant is the need to be sensitive to classroom dynamics. In particular, effective class discussion takes into consideration the following:

- Quality facilitators develop means by which the voices are heard of both the confident and articulate class members, and the more silent members. In general, men are more likely to contribute than women, and white Westerners are more likely to contribute than Africans or Asians. One effective way to give voice to more silent students is to change the classroom geography from auditorium style to workshop format in groups of three to five students, with the more vocal members placed together in the same group, and more silent members together in other groups (see fig. 11.2). The reflective questions are then discussed in the small groups, and each group is given equal opportunity to share. For example, rather than giving an open forum to speak (in which case the more vocal students will dominate), each group is allowed to offer only one or two key responses. Such an approach also helps learners to develop and focus their ideas more clearly. Even when a change of classroom geography is not possible, something comparable can be achieved through a "discuss with neighbours" approach.

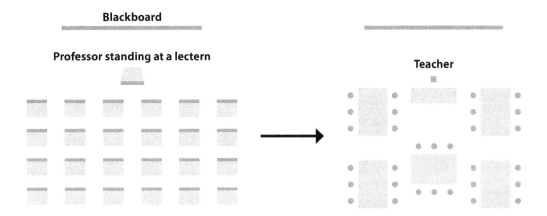

Figure 11.2 From auditorium-style to workshop classroom layout

- The traditional pattern of classroom interaction requires the instructor to speak at every turn. The secret of good discussion facilitation is to withdraw from the focus and play guide rather than controller. Quality instructors provide appropriate leadership of the discussion through balancing the open and honest expression of their own opinions with the need to keep their perspectives private. There are times when students are so off-track that they need help from the instructor in seeing major connections. However, when facilitators are too quick to offer the "right" answer, students rapidly become wary of expressing their opinions lest they be inconsistent with the "approved" or "acceptable" view.

- Quality non-verbal communication plays a very important role in fostering healthy class discussion. Moving away from the podium and creating an open space between teacher and students encourages more timid students to speak. Providing eye contact communicates value and relationship. It is also important to give time for students to reflect before speaking, and to demand an environment of acceptance and respect in which students will not chat to their neighbours while one of their peers is speaking (Weimer 2013a).

- The starting point of transformative learning is "cognitive dissonance", a disorienting dilemma that requires learners to undergo critical self-examination (Cranton 2006, 20). Instructors need to find a balance between challenging students towards significant learning and being sensitive to the anxiety that students experience when confronted with an idea that is different from their previously held paradigm.

- Quality discussion takes time. For example, if you have a class of twenty-four and you divide them into six groups of four students, for each student to share for two minutes in the small group, and then for each group to share for two minutes with the class as a whole, will take a total of twenty minutes. While many instructors will see this as lost time, from the learner's perspective the active involvement has greater potential for deep learning than twenty minutes of lecture. Effective balance between lecture and discussion will entail careful selection of the most important substance and the careful design of accompanying questions to ensure deep engagement.

- People process information differently. Some develop their ideas *by talking*, while others need to organize their ideas *before speaking*. Consequently, it is sometimes valuable to allow a brief period of silence before entering into class discussion, to provide opportunity for the latter group to prepare their initial ideas. One of the greatest errors committed by instructors is to respond to silence by answering their own questions. Students rapidly come to expect this, and what began as a thoughtful silence will end in student non-participation. If there is an extended silence it is possible that your question is not understood. Student engagement is more likely to be promoted through rephrasing the question or even asking a student to explain what he or she understands you to be asking.

- It is possible to develop critical skills in students by playing "devil's advocate", presenting opposing points of view and challenging the students to give reasons for their views, or by asking other students for a counter-example: "Who can think of a different point of view or an argument against that?" (Fisher 2008, 126).

- Quality instructors foster perplexity in students (Issler and Habermas 1994, 60). In general, what hinders students from asking questions is the hidden curriculum that it is not appropriate for students to show ignorance in class – as evidenced by some teachers' responses or by the groans of other students. In most classrooms, only questions about the subject at hand are permitted – even though changing the direction of the thought may raise an important implication of the issue. Inviting and affirming student questions opens the window to understanding the students' learning processes.

- When people recall significant learning experiences, they frequently describe discussion situations where the unexpected took place (Brookfield 2004). Effective instructors welcome these "learning moments". Often, these unexpected learning experiences emerge when a member of the class raises an issue that is not directly a part of the teacher's agenda but which connects with a substantial number of the class members. When teachers avoid or dismiss these unexpected questions, classroom discussion can easily devolve into a frigid and lifeless experience, disconnected from the context of the learners' lives and ministries.

Small-Group Discussion

After lecture and whole-class discussion, perhaps the most commonly used teaching methodology is to break the class into small discussion groups. The most important principle in effective small-group discussion is the quality of the questions which are asked, a topic which is the subject of the next chapter. Beyond the art of question design and the principles of whole-class discussion given above, there are a number of important principles which are specifically relevant to the enhancement of small-group discussion:

- Keep discussion groups small, even as small as two to four people. In smaller groups, every person has the opportunity to express an opinion and it is far more difficult to remain silent and uninvolved. In groups larger than five, certain people tend to monopolize the discussion and it is possible to remain an uninvolved observer. Remember that the two keys to effective methodology are involvement and application. Students are more likely to become involved in a smaller group than in a larger group.

- Group size should vary according to the learning objectives (Meyers and Jones 1993, 66). If the goal is a lot of interchange that moves into a larger class discussion, pairing students or creating groups of three ensures an animated dialogue. However, for problem-solving tasks, larger groups of four to six work best. In groups larger than six, passive students find it easier to remain silent and the groups lose their overall advantages.

- Recognize that discussion takes time. If you break the class into smaller groups, set a time limit and remind them about halfway through, to ensure that everyone has an opportunity to participate. This gives the group permission to ask anyone who is monopolizing the conversation to finish so that others may have a turn. As teacher/facilitator you should move around the groups, ensuring that they have understood the questions and are progressing through them at an appropriate pace. Your presence will communicate interest and concern, and greatly motivate the students to stay on task and engage with the material.

- Where the material you are seeking to cover is extensive, a helpful adaptation is to create a "jigsaw" approach to the discussion (Barkley, Cross and Major 2005, 156–62). Each small group addresses a series of discrete and specific questions, and at the time of reporting, their "piece in the puzzle" is presented as part of a greater whole. While "jigsaw" small-group work can be a very engaging and satisfying way to have students delve broadly into a topic, it needs substantial prior preparation. The piecing together of the puzzle also needs careful management, otherwise students may pay attention only to their own piece and hence lose the overall picture.

- How well small groups operate depends on the clarity of the objectives the participants have been given ("Why are we doing this exercise?"), the parameters of the activity ("What exactly are we to do?") and the guidelines agreed upon for interaction ("How should we behave?"). Small-group dynamics are greatly enhanced through the clear communication of objectives, parameters and guidelines (Meyers and Jones 1993, 69).

- Closure is important. A time of reporting is valuable, but it needs five to ten minutes following the small-group work, and the class structure needs to be planned accordingly. It is generally best not to take extensive responses from each group, as this can become boring and counterproductive. A very effective procedure is to ask each group to contribute its one most important insight, and once every group has had an opportunity, only then to solicit additional responses. Sharp and short reporting can give an almost electric dynamism to the feedback process. Reporting serves several purposes. At the cognitive level, it reinforces for each group the content they have developed. It also enables different groups to benefit from each other's insights. However, perhaps most importantly, at the affective level, a time of reporting communicates to the students that the instructor values their hard work and insights, and considers it important for the others to hear these insights. Students are therefore more likely to be motivated to participate actively in future small-group discussion work.

Brainstorming

Brainstorming can be an effective way of launching discussion. Students, usually in small groups, are presented with a problem and asked to come up with as many different solutions as possible. The emphasis here is on quantity, not quality. Quantity often breeds quality. It is easier to modify a creative idea than it is to develop an uncreative one. Participants withhold judgement until all suggestions have been offered, or until about two-thirds of the time allotted to the brainstorming session has been spent. After a short break, the group select the best contributions from those suggested (or perhaps combine several ideas), refine the responses and bring the group's conclusions to the class as a whole. Each brainstorming group presents its solution in a total-class discussion. If class action is indicated, the students may want to decide which idea they would like to further refine and act upon. Generally, an effective brainstorming exercise will not exceed five minutes in total.

Brainstorming can also be a valuable whole-class methodology introducing a new idea or a body of teaching. The teacher presents a foundational issue in the form of a major question and asks the students to suggest answers. These are listed on the board and (if appropriate) organized into categories. The teacher then presents already developed material on the issue. Generally, the students have incorporated much of the material in their brainstorming session and hence have engaged in a form of "discovery learning". The subsequent formal presentation serves to reinforce the content.

The key to quality brainstorming is the design of a question which is tangible and significant to the students and for which there is no simple solution. Consider the following examples:

- The churches in many parts of the world tend to follow a dictatorial leadership approach which is in dramatic contrast to the body-life pattern seen in the Scriptures. In small groups list (a) the major reasons for this widespread practice and (b) specific steps emerging leaders could take upon graduation from seminary to address this divergence between theology and practice.

- [As part of a study on 1–2 Corinthians.] List all the characteristics of the Corinthian church – both good and bad. Which of these characteristics do you think are also common in the church in your context today?

- Our local churches would like to build better communications with … (other churches, parachurch organizations, government bodies, NGOs). How can we go about doing this?

Debate

Occasionally, a lesson subject lends itself to debate. There are many ways to organize a debate, from a two-minute informal structure to a prepared formal debate. A relatively effective way to open a class session can be to present a debatable statement, divide the class in two and have one side affirm the statement and the other side negate. While this form of impromptu whole-class debate will inevitably be dominated by the more vocal class members, nonetheless it can be an effective means of drawing students into a significant topic or issue. An adaptation of the whole-class debate is small-group brainstorming of the proposal followed by representatives of each group speaking for or against the statement.

More formal debates generally involve two teams of three members who are given the proposal statement a week in advance and work together to prepare their cases. In classic debates it is the affirmative side's responsibility to prove that the resolution is correct; the negative side has to prove that it isn't. Of course, the negative side may also want to present an alternative proposal.

Debaters give their speeches in the following order:

1. First affirmative speech

2. First negative speech

3. Second affirmative speech

4. Second negative speech

5. Third negative speech

6. Third affirmative speech

Since the burden of proof lies with the affirmative team, this team has the advantage of presenting the first and last speeches. Debate winners are determined by the ability of debaters in presenting their positions. In a classroom debate it is often good to open the floor for comments and questions following the last rebuttal, under the direction of the debate moderator.

A very effective means of promoting perspective-taking skills is to use a "critical debate" approach (Barkley, Cross and Major 2005, 126–31), in which students take the side of the issue that is *contrary* to their actual beliefs. Through wrestling with alternative viewpoints, students are challenged to delve into the foundational assumptions and commitments associated with the topic and to recognize the possibility of a range of perspectives on complex issues.

The key to effective debates is the resolution statement. Good debatable resolutions are clear, fairly precise and (most importantly) evenly balanced between the positive and negative sides. Too many debates fail because only one side is defensible and/or the resolution is too vague for arguments to be developed. Consider the following examples:

- "Hinduism is misguided human striving more than it is fundamentally evil."

- "Paul was wrong in refusing to take Mark with him on the second missionary journey."

- "The civil legislation in the Mosaic law is irrelevant for the church today."

Debates hold great potential for developing the critical thinking capacities of students and highlighting the complexity of sensitive issues.

Forum or Panel Discussion

In forums or panels, two or three experts are asked to prepare brief presentations, which are then followed by questions and answers from the floor. Forums are particularly valuable when:

- The subject is difficult and the students would not be able to participate in a meaningful discussion without a significant amount of background.

- People with special training or experience have insights that would not ordinarily be available to the students. Depending on the topic, it may not always be necessary for those participating in a forum discussion to be Christians.

The procedure for developing forum discussion is as follows:

- Panellists are chosen in advance and given not only the topic but also the particular elements of the topic to which they are being asked to bring their expertise. It is important that each panellist is personally convinced of the position which he or she is expected to take on the forum. The clearer the guidelines given to panellists, the more likely that the forum will be a success.

- The panellists are seated in front of the audience, next to a moderator.

- The moderator introduces the topic and the panellists.

- Each forum member should prepare a three- to ten-minute speech and be given uninterrupted time in which to present it.

- Questions from the audience and discussion among the panellists follow. The moderator needs to guide the discussion skilfully, to ensure fairness and to avoid clashes. In general, it is preferable that audience questions be submitted in written rather than oral form. Requiring written submission forces clarity and precision in the questions and reduces the risk of verbal attack from members of the audience. A notorious pattern in forum discussions is for certain audience members to feel the right and need to "be another expert" and present a verbose lecture, rather than seeing the question phase as simply an opportunity for further engagement with the visiting speakers. Written submission can remove the risk of this eventuality.

- The moderator thanks each of the participants and closes the meeting.

Consider the following examples:

- Panellists for a forum on women in ministry: a woman in full-time ministry (preferably ordained); a priest or pastor who is opposed to the ordination of women; a Christian sociologist or senior woman from the business world.

- Panellists for a forum on globalization: a businessperson; a computer scientist; a theologian with a strong background in what the Bible has to say about the key issues.

- Panellists for a forum on "What is 'church?'": a leader from a more traditionally structured denomination; a church-planter engaged in a creative ministry context; a missiologist or a theologian with particular expertise in ecclesiology.

You will probably want to make your forum topics more specific than the ones provided here. Slant them so the speakers deal not simply with their own pet interests but with the questions the students are asking.

Short Forum or Floating Panel

In point of fact, it is exceedingly difficult to arrange professional forums for a classroom context. The sort of high-quality speakers that enrich a forum are generally busy people, and it is problematic if not impossible to find a time that is mutually suitable for the class and all potential panellists.

However, the process of forum can be adapted at a much simpler level in the flow of a regular classroom. Sometimes you have a topic to which almost everyone in the room would have something to contribute –for example, marriage, love, work, getting along with people. With topics such as these, it is possible to stimulate thought and discussion through a student "floating" panel. Three or four people whose names are chosen at random (from a hat, perhaps) become "experts" for several minutes. These "experts" are given a few minutes to think through the issue and then become the panellists for a short forum similar to that described above.

Interviews

Interviews can be a very useful tool for learning from someone who has unique insights to share with the group. There are a number of reasons why an interview may be more effective than a lecture given by the visiting expert. To begin with, the visitor is generally not aware of the needs and interests of the learners, and the instructor or student interviewer can be a bridge between the visitor and the learning needs of the class. Many high-quality professionals do not have good public speaking skills, and interviews can help a visiting expert better connect with students. The movement from moderator to visitor also reduces the likelihood of disinterest among the members of the class.

While one person may take charge of the entire interview, structuring and asking questions, whenever possible it is preferable for the entire class to take part. Have each student write a question for the guest to answer. As with the forum, it is preferable that student questions be submitted in written rather than oral form. Requiring written submission is more likely to result in clarity and precision, will reduce the risk of verbal attack on the speaker, and limits the prospect of one single student dominating the discussion through poorly constructed and/or long-winded questioning of the visitor. Written questions from the students will also press the speaker to talk in depth about the subject and deal with specifics rather than generalities.

Through wise use of interview, the moderator, being one who knows the group better than the visitor, can give direction to the visitor both in terms of content and style.

The following are some suggestions for the effective running of an in-class interview:

- Have a goal or focus as you prepare and put questions. Ask yourself, "What is the purpose of this interview? What do I want to achieve?" Visitors are less likely to ramble on and on if they know precisely what is expected of them and what sort of student learning is desired.

- Establish a good relationship with the visitor being interviewed. Find out what you can about the visitor's background before the interview. Remember that in most cases the visitor is feeling uncomfortable in an unfamiliar environment. The interview is more likely to be a success if the visitor feels relaxed in the context. It can often be beneficial to take a couple of minutes to introduce the students to the visitor.

- Before the interview, have a list of four to six foundational questions which can guide the initial phase. It is generally best to provide the foundational questions to visitors beforehand, ensuring that they understand the questions, and giving them the opportunity to prepare initial responses in advance. The best questions begin with the words "who", "when", "where", "what", "why" or "how", because they require a detailed answer. Avoid questions which call for a yes/no answer, as this makes for uninteresting listening.

- As the interview progresses, be ready with follow-up questions which probe in greater depth the topic under discussion. For instance, if a "difficulty" has been mentioned, find out the nature or causes of the difficulty. Always keep in mind the goal or focus of the interview, and do not hesitate to gently interrupt when the visitor has moved too far off the topic. However, do not comment on the flow of the visitor's ideas with comments such as "Aha", "I see", "Naturally" and "Of course". While you may believe that these are affirming, they tend to distract both the speaker and the listeners.

- Ask the sorts of questions that an average listener would ask. Do not be too technical or detailed. Above all, do not give in to the temptation to ask questions about *your* interests, or those which show off your knowledge.

- Having to do two things at the same time makes interviewing an art which demands much practice. You not only have to pay full attention to what the visitor is saying, but you also need to have the next question ready. So you must both listen and think while the visitor is speaking.

The Flipped Classroom

With growing accessibility to new technologies, a variety of creative educational approaches have emerged. One of the most fruitful concepts is that of the "flipped classroom", first popularized by Khan Academy founder Salman Khan. In the flipped classroom, what would traditionally have taken place in the classroom (lecture) is now done through streamed video outside the class, and class time becomes devoted to tasks that traditionally were required out of class, such as research, reflection and writing.

There are numerous advantages to the flipped classroom (Hill 2013; Kachka 2012):

- As the video lectures can be edited, polished and rerecorded, they are generally of much higher quality than those delivered in the classroom.

- Students can pause, replay and watch videotaped lectures repeatedly at their convenience.

- In the past, diligent faculty would devote many out-of-class hours to working individually with students to tutor them through complex material. In the flipped classroom, greater in-class time is available for this sort of mentoring process.

- There is more time available in the classroom to explore collectively the interface between theory and practice, and to engage in synthetic and evaluative reflection.

Simply switching the lecture to streamed video will not guarantee improved learning. Quality planning and preparation make or break a flipped classroom. In order to maximize the benefits of this approach, consider the following suggestions (Kachka 2012):

- Have the students submit in advance of the class session a list of questions that emerged from their viewing of the online video. This process both ensures that students have actually seen and engaged with the lecture material, and provides clear direction for the class session. Over time, experienced practitioners of the flipped classroom are able to gather a dossier of key questions related to specific lecture material.

- It is preferable for the instructor to understand the key issues being raised by the students and to provide appropriate scenarios that connect the theoretical material presented in the lecture with practical exercises. The instructor should at all costs avoid teaching what students already understand.

- While it is appropriate for some of the class time to be used to clarify elements of the lecture that were not fully understood, it is preferable for the bulk of the time to be devoted to challenging students to dialogue at analytic, synthetic and evaluative levels of thinking.

The Language of Images and Literature

Image is powerful. For educators living in the twenty-first century, technology has opened up the possibility of access to a wide variety of video clips, photographs, pictures and drawings. Through their evocative and suggestive power, images can be a valuable means of crystallizing a problem and dramatizing it before a group. In the same way, fine literature can elicit emotions and ideas that a simple discussion is unable to arouse. Images are a particularly effective way of connecting the affective and cognitive dimensions of learning.

There are many ways of using pictures and literature. The following are some possibilities:

- *Discussion of symbolism.* The group studies a picture or a poem in silence for two to three minutes. The members then share what they understood it to symbolize.

- *Comparing interpretations.* Two or three different paintings of the same story are compared. Class members are asked to explain which of the paintings they feel best captures the story, and why. A far deeper understanding of the story will inevitably result.

- *Discussion of a theme.* Various pictures are displayed, or one or two powerfully written but controversial texts are given out, which the group studies for two to three minutes. Each member is asked to select the picture or text which best expresses his or her own views on the theme, to share with the group the reasons for his or her choice, and to respond to the others' questions about the choice.

- *Discovering inner reactions.* Close-up photographs of people are displayed. The group studies the photographs for a period in silence, and then discusses the inner sentiments revealed in the face of each person portrayed. Perhaps further questions can be developed, such as "What could be some of the possible causes for the sorts of feelings portrayed in this photograph?"

Consider the examples shown in figures 11.3 and 11.4

This painting by Titian is one of the most famous portrayals of the day of Pentecost. In what ways is it an accurate portrayal? In what ways is it inaccurate? If you had the artistic skill, how would you portray Pentecost?

Figure 11.3 Comparing interpretations: a painting interpreting a story

12 years 11 months   **14 years 8 months**

Youth is a time of dramatic change. What are the most important changes that take place in youth –physically, mentally, socially, emotionally, spiritually?

Figure 11.4 Observing change: studying photographs

A few additional comments on the use of images and literature:

- If you have access to digital projectors (LCDs), it is worthwhile taking basic training in the use of PowerPoint and other helpful computer programmes. However, be careful to ensure that the images remain a servant of the learning process and do not consume an inordinate amount of time in preparation.

- Become familiar with online search engines. Google Images and YouTube are particularly well-known resources for images that can be used in class. However, effective use requires practice.

- For biblical instruction, specialized databases and websites are available. A particularly user-friendly site is Biblical Art (www.biblical-art.com), which provides links by topic and passage to artistic representations of most biblical narratives. Links include classical fine art, contemporary popular art and illustrations from picture Bibles. One of the great challenges in teaching biblical material is motivating students to undertake a close reading of the text. Providing an image and asking the students what is accurate and/or inaccurate leads to an almost immediate response of enthusiastic engagement with the biblical text. However, caution must be exercised: because of the power of image there is the possibility that the image remains more vividly in the memories of the students than does the text.

- Be aware of copyright laws. These vary from country to country and are not always consistent. In most parts of the world an image available online can be used on a PowerPoint slide, but you should be very careful to ensure "public domain" permission for anything that you print and distribute. In many countries, penalties are severe for infringement of copyright.

Conclusion

I have come to believe that a great teacher is a great artist and that there are as few as there are any other great artists. Teaching might even be the greatest of the arts since the medium is the human mind and spirit. (John Steinbeck)

Emerging generations of learners are growing up surrounded by multiple images and sounds. Effective teaching for the twenty-first century must move beyond a methodology which was originally developed in a world before the invention of the printing press, when books were scarce and the primary means of imparting knowledge was oral transferral. In this chapter you have been presented both with ways to enhance traditional instructional methods such as lecture and discussion, and with more creative techniques of instruction, such as brainstorming, debate, forum, interviews, and the use of image and literature.

These are only a sample of the creative educational methodologies available to the learning-focused instructor. You are urged to watch and learn from outstanding teachers, and to share ideas openly with other instructors in your programme of study. In the following chapters two particularly helpful approaches will be examined in greater depth: the design of questions for deep learning, and the engaging method of case study, and with it simulations and role plays.

The task of theological education cries out for teachers who are great artists. Creativity in education is always a risk, but inasmuch as we engage the creative spirit in ourselves and in our students, we reflect the character of our creative God and open the potential for holistic transformative learning.

Exercises

1. Make a list of the methods that were used in some of the most interesting and memorable learning experiences you have ever had. Suggest some key factors that helped make them so memorable.

2. Give at least one specific way in which you could incorporate one or more of the principles of effective lecture into a lesson you are planning to present in the near future.

3. Suggest at least one element of quality classroom discussion suggested in this chapter which you could incorporate into your teaching.

4. For specific lessons in a course you are likely to teach in the near future, try to develop each of the following: (a) a relevant brainstorming question; (b) a relevant forum topic, and possible participants in such a forum; (c) a debate topic that could equally be argued from the affirmative or the negative side; (d) a series of interview questions; (e) a dialogue between an image and the material you are seeking to present.

5. The foundations of good teaching are found in the integrity of the teacher. Give at least two suggestions for how you might develop more creative instructional methods while respecting your own integrity as a person.

12

Question Design for Deep Learning

[A professor] is a person who professes something, especially one who openly declares his or her sentiments, religious belief, subject, and so on. Therefore, an educator-professor is one who leads out toward truth, in a manner that encourages dialogue with the emerging inner authority of the student. (Parks 2000, 167)

Throughout this book you have been urged to view ministerial training as an integrative and holistic endeavour. In chapter 4 you were introduced to the cognitive, affective and behavioural domains of learning, and in other chapters you have been encouraged to incorporate a balance between these elements into every facet of the theological education programme. In practice, however, many instructors struggle to know how best to promote this sort of holistic integrative learning in the classroom. What follows is a major tool in your "toolbox" that can help your students in their pilgrimage of leadership formation – the formulation of quality questions.

Research over the past forty years has demonstrated that thinking, emotions and behaviours are inextricably linked (Goleman 1995, 18–25; LeDoux 2000), and any attempt to separate these different aspects of the human personality is inappropriate and dehumanizing (Damasio 2005). Consequently, it needs to be made clear from the outset that the boundaries between the cognitive, affective and behavioural domains are somewhat artificial, as are the supposed levels within these learning domains. Learning is a complex and multifaceted phenomenon in which each element affects the others. Nonetheless, using the frameworks presented in chapter 4 can be a helpful discipline and guide as we seek in the classroom to respect our students as whole persons.

Cognitive Questions

As discussed earlier, the pattern of most traditional classrooms has been to focus almost exclusively on the cognitive domain. A number of reasons can be posited for this emphasis. Some more cynical voices suggest the social ineptness of many academics, and the anti-social nature of the book research necessary for success in higher education (Drane 2008,

132). More measured assessments would focus on the ease of design and assessment of cognitive learning, compared with those for affective or behavioural learning. However, even within the cognitive domain, a desire for controlled design and assessment can lead instructors to focus on lower levels of thinking (knowledge and comprehension), with minimal attention given to the higher-order learning associated with analytic, synthetic, evaluative and creative reasoning. It therefore should not surprise us that the majority of classroom questions are directed at the basic knowledge level of learning (Cotton 2010; Fredericks 2010) and there is little attempt to stretch students' thinking.

Our fixation on lower-order cognitive learning fails to provide the sort of deep learning and integrative thinking skills necessary for meaningful ministry in a complex world. While the foundational basics of knowledge and comprehension have essential value, it is only when we reach the level of analysis, synthesis and evaluation that we can say that quality learning has taken place. The design of quality divergent questions at the analytic, synthetic and evaluative levels can play a significant role in stimulating this sort of higher-order thinking.

Before we begin our examination of question design, it is worth noting that the boundaries are somewhat artificial between the levels of analysis, synthesis and evaluation, just as they are between the cognitive, affective and behavioural domains. Keep in mind that our goal is not the development of discrete analytic, synthetic or evaluative questions, but rather the development of substantial divergent questions that challenge students to think. The process of examining the nature of analytical, synthetic and evaluative questions is simply a guide along that path.

You will undoubtedly also discover that careful question design takes time. It is very straightforward to deliver convergent knowledge and comprehension questions while you are teaching, but it is a rare teacher who can develop a good divergent question in the middle of a class session. Quality teachers devote as much time (or more) to preparing the lesson methodology as they do the lesson content, recognizing that good content with poor methodology will not lead to quality learning. Effective question design must be seen as a part of this lesson-preparation phase.

Although we often reserve analytical, synthetic and evaluative questions for research papers, I suggest that they can and should be part of the warp and woof of everything we teach. Complex divergent questions are not difficult to design, but they do need careful preparation. As a beginning, a simple way to develop more complex cognitive questions is given below.

Analysis questions

A key approach to developing analytical questions is to compare two ideas, passages, and so on, which have points of similarity. Consider, for example, Philippians 2:6–11. Some possible analytical questions are:

- In one or two sentences, explain the relationship between Christ's example in 2:6–11 and Paul's teaching on Christian unity in 2:1–4.

- In what ways are the stages in the descent of Christ recorded in 2:6–8 reflected in the stages of his glorification in 2:9–11?

- Compare Philippians 2:6–11 with Mark 10:42–45. Based on these passages, give at least two ways in which Christ's model of humility should be expressed in the lives of believers.

Consider also the following:

- Make a list of each of the characteristics of the ideal of church life recorded in Acts 2:42–47. Consider each of these characteristics in turn and give one or two ways in which your local church does or does not reflect this ideal.

- Give at least one point of commonality between "communication" and each of the following terms: (a) "common"; (b) "communion"; (c) "community".

- Draw up a chart which shows points of similarity and differences between the calls of Abram (Gen 12:1–9), Paul (Acts 9:1–18) and the disciples (Matt 28:16–20; Acts 1:8) with respect to (a) the action of God; (b) the content of the call; and (c) the reaction of those called.

- Give at least one point of similarity and two major differences between 1 Peter 2:9–12 and the Islamic concept of *umma*.

- Give at least four points of similarity between the factors that led to the Crusades and the factors that contributed to the sixteenth-century wars of religion.

- Give at least two points of similarity and at least two major differences between the Christian and Muslim understandings of God's sovereignty.

In each case, the comparative shape of the question requires the student to analyse the parts and come up with shared principles. These principles can then become the basis for application to the contemporary life context of the student.

Note in particular the different forms used to challenge students in reading and wrestling with biblical texts. The first question asked on the Philippians passage challenges the students to look at the literary context. The second asks students to investigate the internal structure of the text. In many classrooms the teacher answers these questions for the students, particularly where lecture predominates, and thereby the opportunity is lost to train students to read texts carefully for themselves. The third question on Philippians reflects a general form that moves beyond the text to discussion of broader biblical themes through appropriate comparison of comparable texts. However, even this kind of question will often result in students engaging in a closer reading of the text than they would do otherwise. A Bible with quality referencing materials can make designing such questions straightforward.

In the second cluster of questions, the first three questions can readily be answered by students without substantial prior knowledge, but the last three require significant preliminary knowledge and comprehension.

We often ask students to respond in research papers to profound analytical questions such as the last three examples without having trained and prepared them in class. My experience is that a very high level of analytic reflection takes place when, with complex analytic questions such as these, we take time to engage in initial discussion in small classroom groups (three to five students) and then ask the students to complete their reflections in writing outside the classroom. Students have already taken steps on the path, and are often enthusiastic about pursuing ideas in the library that they began to investigate orally with their colleagues in class.

Other types of analytical questions

The shapes I have suggested are not comprehensive and there are many other varieties of analytical questions. Cunningham (2005, 314) suggests the following:

- *Hypothetical questions*, used to encourage consideration of issues and consequences outside of what is expected or actual:
  (a) What if the resurrection were not true?
  (b) What if the giving of the Ten Commandments had not occurred?
  (c) What if there were no church buildings?
  (d) What if Jesus had turned up in the garden to stop Adam eating the fruit (after Eve had already tasted it)? (Heaton 2013)
  (e) What if Moses had joined his brother Aaron in making the golden calf?

- *Reversal questions*, investigating the implications of an event by considering what might have been the consequences if the details of the event were reversed or changed:
  (a) What if Adam had tasted the forbidden fruit and offered it to Eve? (What if we reverse … and …?)
  (b) What if Jesus had been taken to heaven before the crucifixion? (What if … had happened first?)
  (c) What if Peter had kept his eyes on Jesus instead of on the waves? (What if … did … instead of …?)

- *Web analysis questions*, considering the short and long-term web of consequences of a particular event. When asking web analysis questions, instructors should press students to think further: "And what else? … And what else?"
  (a) How extensive were the effects of King Josiah's decision to have the Law of God read?

(b) How many effects can you imagine from Stephen's stoning?

Quality questions take time to design. They need sufficient clarity and direction that students feel confident in responding. Numbers can make questions less threatening: "Give at least three aspects of …", "Name at least four points of similarity", "Describe at least one specific thing you could do". While there may be dozens of possible responses, the students are more likely to feel confident that they can achieve a handful of correct possibilities. As responses are elicited from the class as a whole, the broader variety of potential answers will emerge naturally.

Many instructors leave their questions too vague and general. Consider the following examples:

- "Compare Augustine's and Calvin's attitudes towards the church." The students are likely to ask themselves, "Where do I begin? What aspect of the church is being asked about? In what ways am I being asked to compare?" A better formulation would include numbers and greater precision; for example: "Give at least two points of similarity and two points of difference between Augustine's and Calvin's understandings of the relationship between church and state."

- "Explain the significance of Piaget's theory of cognitive development for Christian teaching." Again, the question is too large. Better is: "List at least three significant ways in which Piaget's theory of cognitive development might impact the teaching of young adolescents in a church youth group." Requesting "at least three" makes the question manageable without being limiting. "Christian teaching" has been clarified to "the teaching of young adolescents in a church youth group".

- "Research the attitudes of believers towards their local churches." It is not clear what this question is asking. The question needs substantial clarification and direction. For example: "From each of three different churches, ask at least one lay leader (youth-group leader, Sunday-school teacher, home-group leader, etc.) and one lay congregant to give you the two things they like best about their local church and the one thing they like least about their local church. Make a list of these features, and give at least two substantial observations as to the attitudes reflected in these responses." Note the length of the revised question, and its step-by-step nature. In general, the more vague the question, the more vague the responses.

Synthesis questions

The key approach in the development of synthetic questions is to compare two ideas, passages, and so on, which are different, contradictory, apparently unrelated or need reconciliation. A beneficial form is: "This writer or passage says …, but that writer or passage says …. Which of these is better/How can both these be true? Why?" Some possible synthetic questions for Philippians 2:6–11 are:

- We tend to hold up the life of the early church as an ideal. And yet, in Acts 6:1–4 (and elsewhere) the apostles seem to have considered "serving at tables" as below their dignity. Do you think that in their early example of Christian leadership the apostles had failed to understand Christ's example of humility? Give two or three key reasons for your answer.

- How do you reconcile the need for active, initiative-taking leadership, necessary for the church to move forward, with the model of humility in leadership given by Christ?

Consider also the following:

- "The blood of the martyrs is the seed of the church" was true for the early church, but not for the church in Japan, where the church was destroyed through persecution rather than built. How could this have been the case? Name two or three factors which might enable persecution to contribute positively to the life of the church. What factors may work the opposite?

- What are some of the strengths and weaknesses of Augustine's and Luther's respective understandings of the relationship between church and state? Building on the ideas of these two great theologians, develop your own theologically based understanding of the relationship between church and state.

In each of these cases, students are asked to weigh up the pros and cons of different perspectives in order to reach a personal synthetic position. In so doing, there is an expectation that students will understand and embrace a larger picture. A comparison between a good thing and another good thing makes for a particularly strong synthetic question: in wanting to affirm both, while not being able to do so, students are forced to think through the foundational issues at stake and formulate a personal position.

It can be highly beneficial to incorporate short readings into the design of synthetic questions (Weimer 2013b). For example:

- Assign a short reading in which an expert disagrees with the conventional wisdom. For example, you may have students read a short extract by a contemporary writer who advocates the chronological priority of Matthew (rather than Mark or "Q"), and have students defend or disagree with the expert's position.

- Share contrasting quotations and have students respond – agreeing, disagreeing or finding some place in the middle. For example, compare an extract from a person who advocates a "just war" approach with an extract from a person who presents a "pacifist" or "peacemaking" perspective. There are numerous publications that present multiple Christian views on such topics as war, the millennium, the meaning of Christian spirituality, divorce and remarriage, salvation and divine providence.

Evaluation questions

The key approach in developing evaluative questions is to ask some or all of the following questions: "Can we believe this? Is this acceptable? Is it realistic? In all seriousness, can it be applied today? If we did it, what problems and/or benefits might result?" Some possible evaluative questions for Philippians 2:6–11 might be:

- Is it realistic to ask someone to humble themselves to the extent described in Philippians 2? Won't other people take advantage of this? Explain.

- What are the main factors which prevent us from following Christ's example of humility? Don't you think these reasons are good and healthy? Isn't there a danger of becoming like a "doormat" which everyone walks on if we don't assert ourselves? Discuss.

- If everyone put others first, who would lead? Are there limits to humility? Give some reasons.

Consider also the following:

- Consider Hudson Taylor's understanding of contextualization. To what extent do you think he did it right? In taking his stand, he opposed his leadership and went his own way; wasn't this a wrong thing to do? Didn't the fact that the local Chinese regularly beat him up indicate that there were problems in his approach to contextualization? Discuss.

- Many people have a strong love for and identification with their home country. Yet, Paul (Phil 3:20) and Peter (1 Peter 1:17; 2:11) describe us as strangers and aliens in this world. Did Paul and Peter get it wrong in their understanding of our relationship to our countries? What does our status as strangers and aliens mean for us?

- Evangelistic events (evangelistic services, spiritual-revival meetings, evangelistic concerts, etc.) are very popular in evangelical churches. In what ways does the fact that communication is not a one-time event challenge the relevance and effectiveness of these events?

Sound education seeks to lead students from where they are to a more mature position. While many students may verbalize the desired change, genuine embrace of a new perspective is often hindered by doubts and questions. Evaluative questions seek to put student doubts into words so that the doubts or challenges can be dealt with honestly and barriers to genuine learning can be addressed. A skilful teacher will be sufficiently aware of student concerns to articulate relevant evaluative questions.

Other forms of divergent question

While the shape of analytic, synthetic and evaluative questions given above is a useful tool for the formulation of quality divergent questions, these models are not comprehensive. There are numerous other forms of divergent question which can equally contribute to quality classroom discussion. Shulman (2006) suggests the following:

- *Deductive* questions, in which specific conclusions are drawn from general principles:
  (a) Based on our discussion of the sovereignty of God, what are some of the implications for Middle Eastern Christians facing discrimination and persecution?
  (b) Given the incarnational foundation of contextualized mission, what might be the implications for the training of South Indian Christians looking to serve in Hindu North India?

- *Inductive* questions work in the opposite direction, drawing generalizations and principles from specific examples:
  (a) What are two or three possible broader implications of the patterns of institutionalization we have observed in the history of the Roman Catholic, Lutheran and Presbyterian Churches?
  (b) What are three or four of the most notable patterns and themes you have observed in our discussion of early mission practice in Africa?

- *Adductive* questions seek evidence for an argument or position:
  (a) What research evidence supports the notion of the hidden curriculum in seminary education?
  (b) What proof exists for the relationship between ideological hegemony and censorship?

- *Refutation* questions seek evidence against an argument or position:
  (a) What are some of the main biblical and theological arguments against Arian understandings of Christology?
  (b) What research evidence exists to question the classic understanding that "the blood of the martyrs is the seed of the church"?

- *Perspective-taking* questions challenge learners to move out of their own religious, racial, socio-economic or gender world and see an issue from another's viewpoint:

(a) In light of the Asian value of paradox (yin/yang), how might a Chinese Christian view the classic Calvinist–Arminian debate?

(b) Why might many Arab Christians feel particularly negatively towards dispensational theology?

- *Personality-in-context* questions, which are used to challenge students to a close reading of texts, and to connect text with context. In these questions a person from the past is brought into the present, and students are asked to suggest what might happen.

  (a) If Paul were to come to Beirut today, how do you think he would launch his ministry? On what basis do you make this assessment? How do the narratives of Acts and/or Paul's teaching in his letters shape your response?

  (b) If Augustine was the bishop of twenty-first-century Colombo (rather than fifth-century Hippo), in what one or two possible ways might he have taken a different approach to his City of God? Give reasons for your response.

  (c) If Dietrich Bonhoeffer were to meet with the leaders of the twenty-first-century Presbyterian Church of Egypt, what might be his two or three most important words of advice regarding the nature of the church in an environment of discrimination and persecution? Give reasons for your answer.

An excellent means of pushing students to wrestle deeply with class readings is to ask them to address a question to the author. These questions not only test whether students have actually completed the readings, but also move them to something of an evaluative posture with the readings, challenging the material and delving into the content at a deeper level:

- If Chris Wright were to visit our school, what question would you ask him about today's readings from *The Mission of God*?

- If you were asked to interview Augustine about his *Confessions*, what are the two or three most important questions that you feel would best help the other students in your class understand what Augustine was trying to accomplish in this text?

- If Paulo Freire were to visit your school, what question might you ask that would challenge the significance of his *Pedagogy of the Oppressed* for your own local context?

From closed to open questioning

One of the greatest challenges in question design is to provide what Palmer (1983, 69–75) has described as bounded but open space; that is, the questions must have sufficient substance and direction that meaningful responses can ensue, but they also need to be open enough for students to be able to investigate the issues at stake. In designing questions, it is important to be aware of and to avoid three particular categories of question that can kill discussion (adapted from Goodman 2011):

Yes/no questions

Questions that can be answered by a simple "Yes" or "No" kill discussion. As the teacher has a clear desired response, most people consider this kind of question a waste of time or degrading to their intelligence. If the teacher has a particular piece of information or a perspective that he or she wishes to deliver, let's hear it and move on to more substantial discussion! This is where careful preparation of questions beforehand is important. Vigilant teachers will restructure yes/no questions so that the questions move from convergent to divergent in form.

Leading questions

A leading question assumes the answer in the question. In other words, the teacher already has an answer in mind and tries to force the students to agree with that answer. Leading questions begin with phrases like, "Don't you think that …?" or "Isn't it true that …?" The following are leading questions:

- Don't you think that a personal encounter with Christ is necessary for a person to become a Christian?

- Isn't it true that all effective churches have a strong small-group ministry?

- Isn't it true that the greatest challenge confronting the church today is postmodern secularism?

The subconscious aim of many of these questions is the indoctrination of students into the perspective of the teacher through a level of emotional pressure. Leading questions are generally resented by students, as they give value only to the teacher's voice and leave little opportunity for disagreement and dialogue.

Limiting questions

Limiting questions seek a very definite answer. Rather than devoting their attention to the significant issues at stake, very often the learners expend their creative energies on trying to discover the specific answer buried in the folds of the teacher's brain. Examples of limiting questions are:

- In what three ways did the Samaritan woman seek to divert Jesus's attention from her past (John 4:1–30)?

- In Matthew 19, what was the reason Jesus gave why the Pharisees would have a difficult time getting to heaven?

The reason these questions are limiting is because they tell the learners to provide a specific answer. The first question asks for three items. Everyone sitting in the group tries to figure out which three the teacher wants. They may find four, but equally they may only find two or they may find five. The person who thinks of three items may be as correct as the person who thinks of two items; the only difference may be the way in which they categorize the information and answers. The second question limits because it asks for *the one* reason why the Pharisees would have difficulty getting to heaven.

Careful teachers will ask themselves, "Do I have a specific response in mind?" If so, there is no need to waste time with a question. Far better is to give the students the information and move with them on to higher orders of thinking. Where the problem with the question is simply a matter of design, it is possible to convert closed questions into open questions by incorporating one of the following at the beginning: "To what extent …"; "Give at least three ways in which …"; "Why do you think that …". Alternatively, closed questions can be made open by adding one of the following at the end: "Give reasons for your answer"; "Explain why you have responded in this way"; "Describe how and why others may give a different response from yours".

Affective Questions

While it takes time and preparation to design divergent cognitive questions like those given above, they are largely familiar and relatively non-threatening. The pervasive influence of Enlightenment rationalism on education – even on theological education – makes us comfortable with questions that address the mind, but less comfortable with questions that probe the deeper heart emotions, attitudes, values and motivations. However, recent research has demonstrated not only that cognition and emotions are entwined (Caine and Caine 1990), but also that the thinking parts of the brain are not effectively engaged unless positive affect is in place (Sousa 2006, 84). In short, we ignore the affective dimension of learning at our peril.

There is also a theological imperative. As mentioned in chapter 4, the heart plays a central role throughout the Bible in the process of knowing, as seen in the great commandment to "Love the Lord your God with all your heart" (Matt 22:37) and in the attitudinal characteristics of the mature spiritual Christian – love, joy, peace, patience, kindness, goodness, faithfulness, gentleness and self-control (Gal 5:22–23).

In chapter 4 we observed that the heart of affective learning is the quality of the teacher–student relationship (Brookfield 1986, 62–64; Cranton 2006, 112–15). However, affective components of learning can also be addressed through carefully designed questions. Consider the following template examples:

- "What was the most important/exciting thing you read/heard in this week's readings/lectures? Explain why you found it so important." As we have seen in chapter 8 on deep learning, what students value is generally what they will remember and apply. I have found it extremely helpful to ask this question routinely at the end of a class or as a part of weekly journaling – sometimes orally, sometimes in written form. Through such a question we can gain a glimpse of what the students' greatest Teacher is doing in their lives.

- "In what ways did the lecture/reading impact your relationship with God? With others?" Part of our goal in theological education should be a growing relationship with God. Simply asking the question communicates to students our desire for the material they are studying to enhance that relationship. Asking the question also holds us as instructors accountable to the fact that our education should be genuinely "theo-logos" (a word from or about God).

- "Was there anything you found challenging? Was there anything that made you uncomfortable? Why? To what extent do you feel you can trust the source of this information? Why?" Asking questions such as these enables us to work alongside our students as they struggle to understand, apply and grow.

- "How did you feel about a particular statement/idea/theory …? Why?" Ted Ward (2001, 123) reminds us that "real people have real feelings, not just disembodied information systems called brains". Learning about new perspectives and developing new skills in thinking and acting are activities that prompt strong feelings, and asking students about their feelings is a valid learning exercise that enables us to understand their attitudes and possible openness to change. Many students have difficulty articulating their feelings, and it is often helpful to give a list of possible feelings of various sorts – both positive and negative – which can be a springboard from which students can discuss their own affective responses.

- "Describe how … might change your attitude towards …" A question like this challenges students to see learning as more than the acquisition of knowledge and provides a bridge into possible response in action.

- "What attitudes or feelings do you see in this passage? Have you ever struggled with/enjoyed/seen in your own life similar attitudes or feelings? How does the affective dimension of the text relate to your own affective experiences?" We can easily forget that all texts are written by human beings who write within particular affective states, irrespective of the apparent "objectivity" sought by the writer. Wrestling with these attitudes and emotions can lead us into a deeper understanding of the text, the writer and ourselves. In theological education, this can be a particularly significant (although often neglected) element of studying biblical texts.

Affective questions such as these transform the learning context from unidirectional impartation of instructor expertise to one in which the students and instructor join together in a mutual pilgrimage of discovering what God is doing in life.

Behavioural Questions

Too often in our desire for students to master the challenging corpus of theological knowledge, we forget that Jesus's Great Commission was not to make disciples by "teaching them … everything" (a cognitively oriented message), but rather by "teaching them to *obey* everything" (an obedience-oriented message). In my own years of theological study and teaching I have frequently felt sympathy with the little girl who, returning home from Sunday school, told her parents how disappointed she was with the class: "We were taught to go into all the world and make disciples of all nations … but we just sat."

Obedience can only genuinely be worked out in practice, and behavioural learning is at its strongest when we engage students in the doing of the faith through some form of active discipleship or apprenticeship. However, even in the classroom, behavioural learning can be encouraged through the questions we ask. Consider the following template questions that touch elements of the behavioural domain, and the sample questions that follow:

- Have you seen … at work in your life/church/community? Explain.

- What are some of the things you wondered about while this was happening?

- What would you have done? Why do you think this is the best choice?

- How would you put … into practice in your own context?

- Imagine how your family/church/community would be different if … had not happened.

- Imagine how your family/church/community would be different if all of us in this class/in your church/in your community … [practised the main point].

- Name one specific thing you could do at least once during the coming week/month in response to …

Sample behavioural questions

- Have you ever been the recipient of dictatorial treatment from a Christian leader? (Please do *not* specify names.) Describe your feelings. What positive reasons can you give for why that particular leader might have functioned dictatorially? How might the leader have related to you more creatively and redemptively? What insights might Marshall's *Understanding Leadership* (1991, 42–73) give on this experience?

- Imagine how the church in your region might be different if every leader embraced team leadership both at the local-church and regional-cooperation level. List two or three of the benefits that might emerge.

- What is the difference between transmission and communication? Give an example from your experience of ministry in which transmission has taken place, but not necessarily communication.

- A central element of effective ministry is the development of patience and perseverance. Describe a situation when you have found it difficult to be patient and persevering. If a similar situation arose again, describe at least one way that you might work out patience and perseverance more effectively.

- Give one or two erroneous concepts common in the Crusades that you also see at work in the Middle Eastern evangelical churches today. Give at least one lesson from the errors of the Crusades that you believe your own local church needs to learn. Describe at least one thing you could do this week to help your church become stronger in this area.

- Imagine how the world would be different if the Crusades had never happened. How might the Western church be stronger or weaker? How might witness to Muslims be different?

- "If God's revelation is thoroughly affective, we who seek to communicate that message should make use of thoroughly affective styles of communication." Describe at least one practical way in which this truth might impact (a) evangelism; (b) teaching in the local church; (c) preaching.

By asking students to relate their own experiences to the substance of course content, we encourage an ongoing dialogue between theory and practice. Experiential questions do not need to be restricted to skill-based courses. In the teaching of history there is a place for comparing the events of the past with the experience of the present, and a call to act in the future. The teaching of theology should move from theology to doxology, then to a life lived in response to worship of the Almighty. The end point of sound exegesis is not simply gleaning eternal principles from the text, but connecting these principles with the lives of the students; such it was with the teaching of Jesus and Paul, and we do well to follow their model.

One of the most frequently lost "learning moment" possibilities in seminary education is the way we close our lessons. Very often, we have spent an hour or more building our session around a central main point – Jesus's teaching on love, the divisiveness of the wars of religion, Paul's call to live in the Spirit, the model of servant leadership, the need to listen before we speak. Sadly, our students rarely act upon these principles because they haven't had the opportunity to wrestle with and reflect on the why and how of the main point. If we are serious about seeing students "walk the talk", a process along the lines of the four steps suggested under the "took" section in chapter 10 both communicates the imperative of application and guides the students into a means of carrying it out. Appropriate behavioural questions can play an important part in this process.

Even more effective is where time is taken in subsequent lessons to ask students whether they have followed through with their commitments. My experience is that, when I ask, I generally get only about a 10–20 per cent response rate, but even this has a huge impact: for the student who has applied it, the message of the class has entered into experience; for the other students, they now have a peer model to follow, not merely the exhortations of the teacher.

Conclusion

In most theological schools, we try to do far too much. As we have noted several times in this book, educational research is increasingly discovering that "less is more": in the long term, when less quantity is presented, but in greater depth, students remember, value and apply more than when they are asked to listen, read and digest vast quantities of material. Asking quality questions that challenge deeper cognitive reflection, connect with student emotions, attitudes and motivations, and guide them to application in practice – all this takes time. But the level of holistic deep learning that can take place is far more likely to lead to the sort of life transformation that all responsible theological educators long to see in emerging Christian leaders.

Exercises

1. Consider a lesson that you are likely to teach in the near future, and drawing on the principles and patterns presented in this chapter:

- Write an appropriate cognitive question that requires analysis.
- Write an appropriate cognitive question that requires synthesis.
- Write an appropriate cognitive question that requires evaluation.
- Suggest two or three quality affective questions.
- Formulate two or three behavioural questions that help students connect the content with their own personal contexts.

2. Drawing on the suggestions for behavioural questions given in this chapter, and the suggested four-step process for the "took" component of the lesson, presented in chapter 10, write down a series of behavioural questions that might be used to challenge students towards practical application of the material presented in the class.

13

Case Studies in Theological Education

God so loved stories that he created man. (Rabbi Nachman)

We must realize that ultimately meaning in our lives is found not in an understanding of our human structures, but in our human stories. (Paul Hiebert 2008, 31)

In chapter 11 you were introduced to Edgar Dale's "cone of experience". According to Dale, the teaching methods which provide the greatest potential for active learning are direct, purposeful, personal experiences. While good in theory, in practice, direct personal experiences cannot generally be planned in advance – particularly in formal classroom contexts. We can, however, do the next best thing, which is to *simulate* reality through games, role plays and case studies. The power of teaching methods which simulate reality is that they embrace the two keys to effective methodology, requiring the students to become involved and to apply their knowledge in practical situations. In so doing, the students are engaged in active learning.

Of all these forms of active learning, case studies are perhaps the easiest to design and use. Moreover, as role plays are largely dramatized case studies, developing skills in writing case studies can facilitate the creation of role plays, and, from them, simulation games and extended dramas. In this chapter you will be guided through the formation and design of case studies.

Jesus used stories as the foundation of his teaching. While we recognize that this was natural in a largely oral society, it was also a product of Jesus's practice of seeing his "learners" as whole people. For Jesus, making a connection between text and context was an imperative, and stories were an ideal methodology for driving his learners to do this. While Paul did not use story as much as Jesus did, nonetheless we see in his letters a profound commitment to embodied faith that is consistent with a storytelling approach to theological education.

The teaching method of Jesus and Paul is rooted in key theological convictions – our creation in God's image as whole people, the great reconciliatory message of the Scriptures in which relationship is central, and the wonder of Christ's incarnation and his invitation to his people to make the message of redemption relevant to each age and each context in which they find themselves. Using stories is one of the most effective and appropriate means for making relevant the eternal message of God's mission in the world.

Corcoran (2007) suggests that since human experience is narrative or story-like in nature, teaching only doctrine and theology will not provide growth in faith and life in the way that narrative can accomplish. If we take Scripture as our benchmark, story is a better methodology than theology and doctrine for communicating the way God relates to believers. For too long we have restricted our understanding of texts worthy of study to the works of academics. In the process of developing an integrative missional approach to theological education, it is imperative that we embrace contextual realities as "cultural texts" (Vanhoozer 2007) in dialogue with traditional texts. Case studies can be a significant element in this process of reflective practice.

The Power of Case Studies

Read carefully the following case studies and the accompanying questions:

Lucy

Lucy is a believer who can be relied upon to do her duty. She is a faithful wife and mother. She keeps her house neat and beautiful, cooks wholesome and delicious meals, and does much with her children: helping them with their homework, reading to them, taking them to the park, and so on.

Lucy is active at her church in both attendance and service. She visits and prays for the sick in her neighbourhood, and she shares the gospel with them when she can. She reads her Bible and prays daily for a long list of people. People think well of Lucy and are grateful to her.

But Lucy is not really happy. She has a suspicion that God is not happy with her either. There is no big problem in her life – just things like dullness in prayer, irritability with the children for childish behaviour, and annoyance with people at church who are not faithful in attendance, leave others to do all the work, or dress or behave inappropriately. Lucy wouldn't dream of creating a fuss about these things, but there's a resentment inside, and people, although they respect her, sometimes feel that she's unhappy with them, that they're never quite good enough.

· What do you think are some of the main factors that influence Lucy's life decisions?

· Do you believe that Lucy is "living by grace"? Give reasons for your answer.

Pastor Paul

Paul is the pastor of a church in a politically unstable country. Shortly after he took over the leadership of the church, civil war broke out and a number of militias emerged in the country, each claiming to be purely defensive of the rights of one particular group in the country. Among them, there have arisen three fairly powerful "Christian" militias, substantially funded by Western powers that are concerned about the influence of "terrorist states" such as Iran and North Korea, who have been funding Islamic and Communist militias in the country. The leaders of the Christian militias have been actively recruiting among the young men of the Christian community, including members of Paul's church.

· What are some of the main factors that might impact Paul's responses to this situation?

· What theological considerations impact a response to this situation? You may like to consider some of the material we have discussed in class about salvation history, the kingdom of God, the church as a missionary community, redemptive love, and truth and justice.

· In light of both theological and pastoral considerations, how do you think Paul should respond:

(a) If some of the young men decide to join one of the Christian militias?

(b) If one of the Islamic or Communist militias enters the district of Paul's church and begins threatening church members and/or the church property?

(c) If the Christian militias begin fighting with one another, and young people in the church have aligned themselves with rival Christian militias?

Sarah and Lydia

About a year ago, Lydia began teaching children in Sunday school. This happened because Sarah, the active and gifted teacher who had taken the class previously, could no longer be depended upon: without any notice, she would simply not show up. Lydia had begun teaching to fill the gap. Sarah does still come from time to time, as the whim takes her – about once every six weeks – without letting anyone know that she is coming. On these "visits", Sarah expects Lydia to drop what she had planned and follow the programme that Sarah has in mind. Even though Lydia knows that Sarah is a far more gifted teacher than she is, nonetheless Lydia has worked hard to improve her teaching skills, and her lessons are always far better planned and organized than the lessons Sarah gives – which are often presented without any preparation whatsoever. As if this isn't enough, Sarah is married to one of the elders of the church, and he is always telling everyone what a great job Sarah is doing heading up the Sunday school. At every church event, Sarah is thanked publicly and profusely by the pastor and elders for "all her work with the Sunday school children", while Lydia's name is never even mentioned.

· What might be some of Lydia's feelings in this context?

· If you were a friend of both Lydia and Sarah, describe two or three constructive actions you could take to enable the significant contributions of both to be a benefit to the children in the Sunday school.

· If you were the pastor of this church, how might you address the situation in a positive and redemptive way, particularly with respect to Sarah's husband, who is a valued and committed elder in the church?

Which of these three cases engaged you the most? Why do you think this case particularly interested you? What feelings did the story elicit within you? Why? In general, the extent to which a case study engages your attention and feelings is directly related to the level of connection it has with your own life experience. A case study is more likely to aid in transformational growth if it deals with a topic or experience that has in the past elicited strong emotions and/or required challenging decision-making.

Case studies are powerful and effective as an educational methodology:

- The most effective learning moves from the known to the unknown, whereby the learner is introduced to new concepts and skills from the starting point of prior experience. Case studies give points of connection through which students can better remember and understand the details of the new content. In this way (returning to Bloom's taxonomy), the knowledge and understanding components of cognition are enhanced.

- Quality case studies challenge the students to think about contextual issues through the lenses of principles that are found in texts. This comparative work generally entails analytic, synthetic and/or evaluative thinking.

- When the situation described in the case study is close to the life experience of the learners, it thoroughly engages them, and frequently elicits a strong affective response.

- Case studies help build problem-solving skills, particularly those that are valuable when applied but are likely to be used infrequently. Opportunity is thereby given for practice that might not otherwise be available in essential skills for life and ministry.

- Realistic case studies help bring reality to theoretical material, and hence encourage reflective practice and deliberate action (Merseth 1991).

- Specifically in the realm of theological education, case studies are ideal for integrative seminars or integrative papers in which students are trained in bringing a variety of biblical, theological, historical and pastoral perspectives to bear on a practical situation.

- Case studies can promote team-building. When a team gets together to solve a case, different opinions, methods and perspectives need to be heard. The development of effective responses to the case will emerge to the extent that the group works cooperatively towards the shared goal. The hidden curriculum of the group work that generally accompanies the case-study approach promotes the sort of team cooperation that is an essential element of effective Christian ministry.

- Most importantly, case studies help learners to evaluate themselves, but from a safe distance, thereby isolating key issues from personalities.

Characterization, Setting and Plot

Case studies are stories, and as with other stories, the more closely they reflect the experience of the reader, the more gripping they will be, the more emotions they will elicit, and the more likely they are to result in some sort of active response. Consequently, the key to an effective case study is for it to reflect a real-life situation known to the students.

For many teachers new to the case-study approach, there is a tendency to present dramatic or extreme stories. However, these are generally not very effective, as the stories do not connect with the students' life experiences and the students are consequently unable to relate to the narrative. Powerful stories are ordinary and routine, the sorts of events that occur repeatedly in life. It is more likely that elements of these "routine" stories will be common to the experience of the students, and consequently the students will enter more intimately into the narrative and wrestle more passionately and realistically with the issues that are at stake.

As with any story, case studies involve three important features – characterization, setting and plot.

Characterization

The first important feature is *characterization*. The success of a story depends in large part upon its ability to develop interesting, real people with whom the readers can identify. Stated simply, characters can be one-, two- or three-dimensional. One-dimensional characters are largely decorative. They enter the stage of action only briefly and play little direct role in the overall plot. They are, however, crucial in that they provide mood and realism – particularly in longer stories.

Consider, for example, the well-known story of David and Bathsheba in 2 Samuel 11–12, in which there are numerous one-dimensional characters, including "the king's men" (11:1), "the … Israelite army" (11:1), "someone" (11:3), "messengers" (11:4), "servants" (11:9, 13), "the men of the city" (11:17), "some of the men" (11:17), "the messenger" (11:19), and so on. In each case, we know virtually nothing about the characters, but without them the story would not "live". The one-dimensional characters give depth and breadth to a story.

In the sample case study about Lucy, some of the one-dimensional characters are her children and "people" at church and in her neighbourhood. In the story of Paul, one-dimensional characters include "the church", "militias" and "the young men". In the story of Lydia, we see the children of the Sunday school, "one of the elders" and the pastor. In each case, we know little if anything about these characters, but the story could not function without their existence.

Two-dimensional characters have more substance, but are generally (but not always) painted with one predominant personality characteristic. Two-dimensional characters interact with the key characters and give greater substance to the story, but their role is supportive rather than central. Again, from the story of David and Bathsheba, we see a variety of two-dimensional characters, such as Uriah, Bathsheba, Joab and possibly Nathan (although it could be argued that Nathan is three-dimensional). In each case, we learn a number of key characteristics about the personality, but overall the picture has a dominant feature: good, bad, strong, weak. It is difficult for us as readers to relate to the personality in depth. The only notable two-dimensional personality in the three sample case studies is Sarah. Although we know that Sarah is gifted, the portrayal remains largely negative. We don't "feel" with Sarah as we would tend to "feel" with Lydia.

The most important characters in any story are three-dimensional. These are the central characters in the story, those around whom the plot moves. Effective stories give sufficient information about these characters for them to seem real to the readers. The goal is that the readers will personally identify with them, or at least associate them with people with whom they are intimately acquainted. It is through this process of identification that the storyteller seeks to engage the readers, communicate the message of the story and elicit a response. In effective stories, the three-dimensional characters will show a variety of characteristics, moods and actions, all of which contribute to the sense of reality. In the David and Bathsheba story, the key three-dimensional character is David.

While the David and Bathsheba story clearly plays a significant role in the overall explanation of the Davidic line, at a more local level the storyteller clearly wants the reader to identify with both David's sin and his subsequent repentance. As with David, so with the reader: secret sin is endemic and destructive, but through repentance we can experience God's forgiveness.

In the three stories given earlier, Lucy, Paul and Lydia are all three-dimensional characters. They have a variety of personal characteristics, and the respective conflicts revolve around them. The extent to which a reader engages with the story is directly related to the extent to which he or she identifies with the three-dimensional character in the story.

Setting

The second important feature of good stories is *setting*. The setting of the story can be geographical, temporal, social or historical. Although the reader generally pays little attention to the setting, it is this that provides the basic context within which plot and characters develop. The setting serves many functions: generating atmosphere, determining conflict, revealing traits in the characters who must deal with problems or threats caused by the setting, and evoking associations with the current situation of the readers.

The David and Bathsheba story is set in a period of war with the Ammonites (a central feature of the story), with a rhythmic movement between the palace and the war front. With respect to the three stories given earlier in this chapter, the historic setting is the present. The geographic settings of the stories of Lucy and Lydia could be almost anywhere, although the elements of the stories are particularly strong in honour–shame societies. The setting in the story of Paul is more specific and implies a multi-religious and conflictual context such as Lebanon, Nigeria or Sudan. The extent to which the stories grip the readers is directly impacted by the extent to which the setting is close to their own life settings.

The key to giving realism in story characterization and setting is the provision of a moderate amount of seemingly unnecessary detail.

For example, in the story of Lydia and Sarah, the following details seem irrelevant to the actual story:

- Why name them Lydia and Sarah? Why not Katie and Janice? Or why not Tim and Chris?

- Lydia began teaching about a year ago. Why not six months? Why not three months?

- Sarah comes about once every six weeks. Why not once a month? Why not every two weeks?

- Sarah is married to an elder. Why not make her the daughter of an elder? Why not the pastor's wife? Why have any relationship to the leadership at all?

In each case, the reason for the choice is actually quite arbitrary, and other choices would have been just as acceptable. What was important was the provision of some detail, because the detail creates an image in the reader's mind of a real person – very often a person with whom the reader is familiar, sometimes even themselves. The clearer and more familiar the image created, the more likely the story is to connect with the readers and impact their learning.

While detail is essential in providing stories with realism, it is important (particularly with case studies) that readers should not be buried under an avalanche of information. Length must be tailored to the time available, and the complexity of cases must be matched to the level of learning students have attained. Cases for beginning students should make the most important facts and issues obvious. As students grow in their sophistication in terms of what they know and how they handle case-study exercises, they can advance to materials that are more complex. Details must add to the realism but not distract from the main issues being discussed. Notice, for example, that in the story of Lucy, we gave no specifics about her husband and children, nor was her church context described in any detail. Information was intentionally excluded that may have distracted the readers onto tangential issues – such as the topics of her marriage relationship, her children's school difficulties or conflict in the church.

Plot

The final important feature of good stories is *plot*. Plot refers to the sequence of events, generally following a cause–effect order, which build to a *climax* and involve the reader in the narrative world of the story, and which are finally *resolved* and brought to a conclusion. The basic element of plot is *conflict*. Although the conflict may be interpersonal, it is more importantly intrapersonal – a struggle within the key three-dimensional characters which emerges out of choices presented to them. In longer stories, there will be a series of decisive choice-making moments which build in interest and suspense towards a climactic choice, roughly following the pattern represented in figure 13.1.

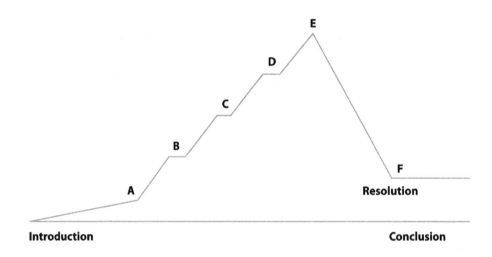

Figure 13.1 The sequence of events in the plot of a story

For example, in the David and Bathsheba story, the following choices are seen:

- Should David lead his people to war or stay behind (11:1)?
- Should David call for Bathsheba or not (11:2–4)?
- Should Bathsheba come in response to David's call (11:4)?
- What should David do when he hears of Bathsheba's pregnancy (11:5)?
- Should Uriah sleep with his wife (11:8–9)?
- What should David do when Uriah refuses to sleep with his wife (11:10–11)?
- Should Joab obey David's command (11:14–15)?

All these are stages towards the major intrapersonal conflict found in 12:1–12, where Nathan confronts David with his sin, and David needs to make the choice: to repent, to deny, or even to have Nathan put to death. Fortunately, David chooses repentance, and so the story reaches a satisfying resolution (12:13–25).

When the intrapersonal conflict reflects a situation of choice experienced by the reader, the reader is immediately drawn to identify with the story and speculate on his or her own possible choices in the situation. The eliciting of such responses from the reader is what gives power to well-written case studies.

If we return to the story of Lydia and Sarah, we see a series of choices that create intrapersonal conflict within Lydia:

- Should Lydia have responded to the unreliability of Sarah by beginning to teach Sunday school?

- Should Lydia have remained silent about Sarah's continuing to come to the Sunday school?

- On these "visits", should Lydia have allowed Sarah to take over?

- To whom might Lydia have spoken about Sarah's behaviour?

Your own connection with this story will be related to the extent to which you have yourself experienced a similar intrapersonal conflict because of comparable sorts of choices to those faced by Lydia.

It is at the point of crisis and resolution that case studies differ from regular stories. In most classic stories, the writer provides the reader with the resolution. In a case study, the reader must provide the resolution. Indeed, the interest and involvement that good case studies elicit is largely due to the different ways in which resolution might be achieved, based on the wide variety of experiences and perspectives people bring to these stories.

In the case of the story of Lydia and Sarah, the story ends with Lydia in a position of significant choice. Should she quit teaching? If so, how might this impact the children? How might this impact her relationship with other members of the church? Should Lydia speak to someone? If so, who?

Case studies with obvious outcomes are generally not particularly valuable, as the students have little motivation to wrestle with the tension between the ideal and reality. Case studies with multiple possible outcomes are far more powerful, as they require students to delve deeply into the issues that are at stake.

Writing a Case Study

Now it is your chance to design a case study. I should warn you that the first time you write a case study, it will require a lot of work and imagination. You may well forget key details or provide distracting information. Learning to write effective case studies takes practice. However, it is worth the effort, for case studies are among the most powerful tools in the effective teacher's methodological kit, engaging students in active learning, and promoting quality theological reflection on practice.

First, to gain practice in the process of writing a case study, complete the following brief exercise:

For each of the following situations, name a book of the Old Testament which addresses a similar situation. In each case, describe the central issue that provides the connection between context and text. Note that in most of these cases there is more than one possible answer; you are invited to suggest a variety of alternatives.

1. The Iranian government has ordered the closure of the Persian-speaking churches and threatened the leadership of these churches with imprisonment and even death.

2. A man approaching fifty begins to wonder if his life has any meaning at all. Everything has become a rut and it all seems so empty.

3. Members of a congregation in South Sudan, all of whom were forced to leave Khartoum after the separation of North and South Sudan, ask their pastor how God could allow his people to suffer at the hands of the Sudanese government. Why doesn't God do something?

4. The leader of the church's young-adults group has been doing a series on grace, and the young people have begun revolting against the church's legalism, the girls wearing skimpy clothing to church and some of the guys taking up smoking. Since the gospel is about grace, everyone should be able to do as he or she likes.

5. A major tragedy has occurred in your community: a school bus went over a precipice. Several of the children were killed and others were badly injured.

It is probable that you did not encounter too much difficulty in establishing links between these contemporary situations and various biblical texts. Now see if you can reverse direction: for the following Old Testament stories or passages, suggest a comparable situation that you personally have experienced.

1. David and Bathsheba
2. Jonah
3. The tower of Babel
4. The defeat at Ai
5. Psalm 137: "By the rivers of Babylon …"

In order to connect the text with your own personal context, you will need first to describe what the central issue is in the text. For some of these texts, there are a variety of issues at stake and/or levels within the issue. For example, while the story of David and Bathsheba is ostensibly about sexual immorality, at a deeper level it speaks to the natural human tendency to seek to cover up sin, and to the fact that a sin leads to sin which leads to sin.

In suggesting contemporary examples, you should try to give "routine" situations that you have seen and which are common in your own church, school or local community, preferably situations in which you personally have been involved. As we move towards case-study design, the end result will be more effective if the situation from which the story is drawn is "ordinary".

The next step will be to develop a fully fledged case study based on one of the "routine" situations that you have suggested in the previous exercise. Effective case studies need forethought and planning. I have found that one of the best ways to develop the case is by applying the following five steps:

1. *Think of the key controversial issue* that you are seeking to address in your lesson as a whole.

2. *Consider a real situation* you have encountered related to this issue or dilemma. Transformational learning begins with what has been variously termed "cognitive dissonance" (Festinger 1957; Gawronski and Strack 2012), "disorientation" (Mezirow 1991; Cranton 2006) and "intrapersonal conflict" (Loder 1982), whereby a dilemma catalyses the development of new perspectives. Well-designed case studies are able to discover and present the essential dilemmas embedded within key issues. The key is to present information so that a "right" answer is not obvious. It is generally preferably (if possible) to use two or three situations, and amalgamate features from each of these. For example, when I wrote the Lydia scenario, I had three different women in mind from three different countries. By amalgamating their three stories, you cannot be accused of "directing" the story towards any one individual.

3. *Change all names and places*, and perhaps all the incidents. If you have a particular class for which you are preparing the case study, try *not* to include names of members of your class, or specific locations from which the students come, as these details will likely distract the students from the issues at stake.

4. *Give sufficient seemingly "irrelevant" details* to make the situation seem real, but not so many that the issue gets "swamped" in the details. In particular, it is generally best to give the characters names and, where appropriate, personal details such as age, marital status, number and ages of children, and so on. The readers will be more likely to engage with the story if the story seems "real", and the details are a key to creating a sense of reality.

5. *Provide appropriate discussion questions.* The more complex the case, the more complex the questions should be. In some classes, a well-written case can become the hub around which a whole lesson can turn. Possible questions that could be used or adapted include the following:

- What are the main factors that contributed to the crisis described in this story?
- What do you consider are the main issues in this case study?
- If you were a friend of …, how would you advise/help/relate to him/her?
- If you were the pastor of …, how would you advise/help/relate to him/her?
- Which items in this case stand out as significant issues?
- Which of these issues are you familiar with from your own experience?
- Which of these issues have you had some success in resolving?
- Which of these issues arouse apprehension, and why?

The number of questions used will depend on the time available. For example, I often use a case study as a "hook" into the lesson, in which case I do not want to devote more than ten to fifteen minutes to it. Where this is the case, I will generally only give three or four questions, have groups discuss the questions, and then give each group the opportunity to share only one or two key responses in total. In other situations, the case study follows theoretical material and becomes a means of connecting the theory to practice; a more extended series of discussion questions is then appropriate. In longer case studies, it is worthwhile to bring in some debrief questions, such as:

- What new insights did you gain from this case study and its discussion?
- What questions do you still have?
- What new ideas do you want to try out?

Case studies are at the heart of problem-based learning (PBL), discussed in chapter 6. PBL reverses the traditional pattern of theory to practice: students are confronted with a real-life problem, they are challenged to bring different elements of theory to bear on the problem, and finally they suggest solutions. This process has been widely used in the study of medicine and law, but rarely in theological education, even though the nature of Christian ministry demands the sort of integrative learning that PBL promotes.

Conclusion

Around the world, people love stories. In oral societies in particular, stories are a key cultural strategy in the communication of truth. Even in Western contexts, the power of story for effective learning has been seen in the growing use of PBL as an educational strategy.

Too easily we become so preoccupied with our specific course material that we forget the complex realities that confront our graduates in ministry. Educators who are serious about preparing leaders for real-life contexts will help students to connect text with context in their teaching. Case studies are one of the most effective means by which this can be accomplished.

Exercises

1. Based on your own experience and the material given in this chapter, make a list of significant advantages to using case studies in theological education. Give one or two cautionary observations about using case studies.

2. Using the suggested five steps for case-study design above, write a case study based on one of the Old Testament texts presented earlier in the chapter.

3. Consider a lesson that you are likely to teach in the near future. What is a key issue that you wish to address in the lesson? Working through the stages of development described in this chapter, write a case study that highlights this key issue.

4. In light of what has been presented in this chapter and the description of problem-based learning (PBL) given in chapter 6, what do you believe is the most significant strength of PBL? Why? What are some of the main barriers to using PBL in your own educational context? Suggest at least one specific step that you could take to help overcome these barriers and promote a greater level of context-to-text learning in your programme of study.

5. Using as a starting point the ABTS Integrative Project sample given in appendix 6.1, design a comparable or more developed integrative project for your own educational programme, using an adapted form of PBL for promoting skills in theological reflection on practice.

14

Teaching, Learning Styles and Cultural Context

Over the past forty years, a growing body of research has increasingly affirmed the extent to which people learn in fundamentally different ways. A variety of models and taxonomies have been suggested to describe these diverse learning patterns and preferences. While none of these fully capture the complex nature of learning, a discussion of major theories of learning difference can sensitize serious teachers to the need for greater variety in instructional strategy in response to diverse learning needs. In this chapter you will be introduced to a number of influential models of learning styles, Gardner's concept of "multiple intelligences", and material that has emerged from intercultural and gender studies on learning.

Kolb's Model of Learning Styles[1]

One of the most influential models addressing learning and teaching style differences is David Kolb's (1983) learning style theory. Kolb's model is based on research suggesting that individuals have a tendency to both perceive and process information differently, as follows:

- *Concrete and abstract perceivers.* Concrete perceivers absorb information through direct experience, by doing, acting, sensing and feeling. Abstract perceivers, however, take in information through analysis, observation and thinking.

- *Active and reflective processors.* Active processors make sense of an experience by immediately using the new information. Reflective processors make sense of an experience by reflecting on and thinking about it.

Kolb's learning theory can be visualized as two perpendicular axes demonstrating a continuum between active experimentation and reflective observation, and between concrete experience and abstract conceptualization (fig. 14.1). An individual whose

---

1. This section is adapted from Williamson and Watson (2006).

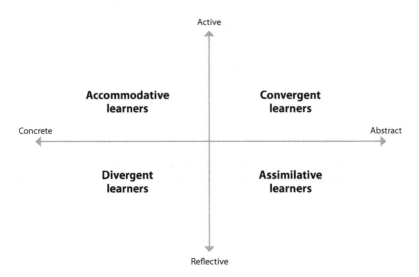

Figure 14.1 Kolb's learning styles

learning style is located close to the intersection of the axes will have a more balanced approach to learning and will be more adaptive in learning situations. On the other hand, an individual whose style is located away from the intersection will be more dominated by one style in learning:

- *Divergent* learners prefer concrete experience and reflective observation during learning experiences. Divergers tend to rely on feelings, imagination and intuition. They are open-minded and typically engage in thoughtful understanding. However, weaknesses are found in areas of decision-making, thinking skills, use of theories and systematic thought processes. Researchers have determined that Divergers will excel in learning situations that include individualized learning, open-ended assignments and sensitivity to feelings. Learning strategies should include evaluating current information, creating examples, using illustrations and evaluating implications. Divergers tend to struggle in learning situations that emphasize theoretical background or theoretical models.

- *Assimilative* learners prefer abstract conceptualization and reflective observation. Assimilators depend upon sound logic, accuracy, inductive reasoning and the ability to assimilate a wide range of ideas. They have the ability to create multiple perspectives in learning, to use a systematic approach, to organize information and to analyse abstract concepts. Weaknesses within this learning style include the tendency to be less focused on people or feelings, to minimize personal involvement and to exert little influence on others. Assimilators are not usually action-oriented, artistic or decisive. Researchers have determined that Assimilators will excel in learning situations that include organized information, conceptual models, testing of theories and analysis of data. Learning strategies should include validating sources, forecasting predictions and evaluating implications. Assimilators are challenged in learning experiences involving simulation or applying real-world situations.

- *Convergent* learners prefer abstract conceptualization and active experimentation. They are strong in the areas of problem-solving and decision-making. Convergers tend to be unemotional, focused and pragmatic. They have the ability to apply ideas practically, to use a systematic and analytical approach, to influence others and to get things done. Weaknesses can include having narrow interests and being relatively unemotional, close-minded and unimaginative. Convergers tend to focus less on people or feelings and more on concrete tasks. Researchers posit that Convergers will excel in learning opportunities that include creating new ways of thinking and experimenting with new ideas. They enjoy goal-setting and decision-making. Learning strategies should include goal-setting, repetition of important information, outlining information and outcome-predicting.

- *Accommodative* learners prefer concrete experience and active experimentation. Accommodators' strengths are being action- and results-oriented, seeking new experiences and being willing to take risks. Accommodators have the ability to carry out plans, to adapt to new situations, to influence and lead others, and to achieve results. They are often intuitive, artistic and people-oriented. Weaknesses can include relying on other people for information, lacking confidence in personal analytic ability, disregarding theory and being perceived as controlling. Researchers have found that Accommodators will excel in learning that includes the opportunity to set objectives, seek opportunities and influence others. They enjoy using concrete examples to apply information and prefer active participation instead of individual or group reflection.

While Kolb's model is an over-simplification of what is in fact a complex network of learning (M. Smith 2001; Tennant 1997), the evidence for diverse learning styles is substantial. Nonetheless, traditional schooling continues to favour abstract perceiving and reflective processing, particularly in higher education. If we are to affirm and benefit from the various gifts that people bring to the learning context, we need to provide space for intuition, feeling, sensing and imagination, alongside the traditional skills of analysis, reason and sequential problem-solving. Teachers need to design their instruction methods to connect with all four learning styles, using various combinations of experience, reflection, conceptualization and experimentation through broadening the sorts of experiential elements that take place in the classroom, incorporating sound, music, visuals, movement, experience and talking. They also need to employ a variety of assessment techniques – beyond the traditional essay and examination approach – appreciating the development of "whole brain" capacity and respecting each of the different learning styles.

Other Approaches to Learning Styles

While Kolb's model is helpful, it falls short of a thoroughgoing explanation of the different ways in which people learn, and a number of other approaches have been suggested.

Neil Fleming (2012), for example, divides learners according to their sensory preferences – visual, aural, reading/writing or kinaesthetic/tactile. In Fleming's model, the preferred learning method of visual learners is through image. Consequently, visual learners benefit from graphic displays such as charts, diagrams, illustrations, hand-outs and videos (Cherry 2012). Aural learners prefer listening, and tend to be among the minority who can benefit from lectures, although they value discussion and verbal interaction. Reading/writing learners prefer to absorb information through text. Kinaesthetic/tactile learners need experience – moving, touching, doing – and consequently appreciate laboratory activities, field trips, role playing, and other forms of active learning.

A completely different learning styles inventory has been developed by Felder and Silverman (1988). In this model, learning styles are a balance between four pairs of extremes: Active/Reflective, Sensing/Intuitive, Visual/Verbal and Sequential/Global, with learners being rated along each of these continua (see fig. 14.2).

Learning is a complex and multifaceted phenomenon, and no single model is able to capture the ways in which people appropriate and process information. Each of these models makes a contribution to our overall understanding of learning and should sensitize us to the need for diverse instructional strategies to meet the diverse needs of learners.

Multiple Intelligences

A totally different approach to understanding diversity in learning has been the model of "multiple intelligences" (MI). In the 1970s, Howard Gardner, a professor of education at Harvard University, started questioning the traditional approach taken by IQ tests. Gardner worked with talented children and adults whose gifts and abilities were not necessarily reflected in the traditional notions of intelligence. His observations and reflections culminated in his highly influential text *Frames of Mind* (1983), in which he outlined seven different types of intelligence. Ten years later (Gardner 1993), he added an eighth type. According to Gardner, all humans have all eight of these intelligences, but to a lesser or greater extent, and consequently we each have a different intelligence profile. An understanding and acknowledgement of different profiles can better guide educators in nurturing the various latent abilities in learners. Gardner's eight intelligences are as follows:

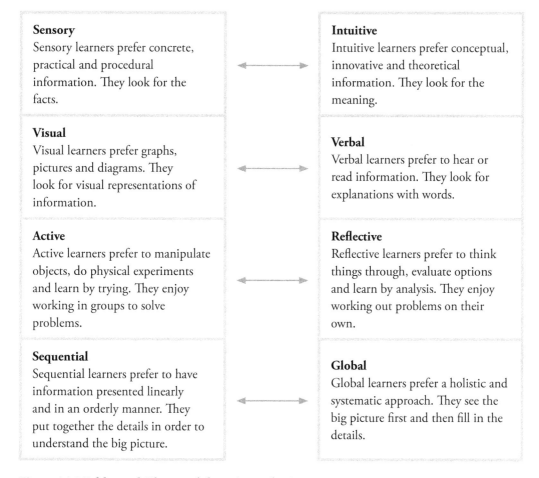

Figure 14.2 Felder and Silverman's learning styles inventory

- *Linguistic intelligence* – the ability to use spoken and written language effectively to express yourself. Lawyers, writers and speakers tend to have high linguistic intelligence.

- *Logical–mathematical intelligence* – the ability to analyse problems logically, work effectively with mathematical operations and use deductive reasoning. People working in the scientific and mathematical communities tend to be high in this type of intelligence.

- *Musical intelligence* – the ability to perform, compose and appreciate musical patterns, including changes in pitch, tone and rhythm. Successful musicians, composers and people involved in music production have high levels of musical intelligence.

- *Bodily–kinaesthetic intelligence* – the ability to use the body for expression. Professional dancers and athletes are good examples of those who have high levels of this kind of intelligence.

- *Spatial intelligence* – the ability to recognize, use and interpret images and patterns and to reproduce objects in three dimensions. Successful architects, sculptors and designers are likely to have high spatial intelligence.

- *Interpersonal intelligence* – the ability to understand people's intentions, motivations and desires. Professions like therapy, teaching and sales attract individuals with high interpersonal intelligence.

- *Intrapersonal intelligence* – the ability to understand yourself, and to interpret and appreciate your own feelings and motivations. Therapists, actors, caregivers and writers are all people who can bring high levels of personal awareness to their work.

- *Naturalist intelligence* – the ability to recognize and appreciate our relationship with the natural world. Astronomers, biologists and zoologists are examples of professions with a high level of naturalist intelligence.

While the idea of multiple intelligences seems intuitively attractive, a key criticism is that no valid measurement tool is available. This has made MI difficult to prove. It is therefore accused of being overly ambiguous and subjective. However, Gardner's model has substantially contributed to a broader appreciation of diverse ability, and when used cautiously can help us better respond to diverse abilities in our learners.

Culture and Learning

An overwhelming body of research has established what cultural anthropologists have intuited for decades: people from different cultures think in fundamentally different ways. While the differences are not absolute, and there is wide diversity and individual variation, there are strong, statistically significant differences between the ways in which information is processed by people from different cultural backgrounds, and this has a profound impact on the ways in which learning takes place from culture to culture.

One of the most influential and extensive series of studies in this field has been that conducted by Richard Nisbett (2001, 2003) with colleagues at the University of Michigan, who focused on differences in thinking and learning patterns between East Asians and European Americans. Nisbett's team suggested four areas in which Westerners and Easterners process information differently:

- *Attention and control.* In general, East Asians tend to focus on the overall field, seeing wholes and observing co-variations. Westerners tend to focus on specifics, isolating and analysing the elements as the necessary step towards generalization.

- *Relationships and similarities vs. rules and categories.* East Asian students are more likely to group words and ideas on the basis of some kind of relationship, while European-American students are more likely to group words and ideas on the basis of a shared category. These different results are consistent with the communal nature of East Asian society as against the analytical–individualistic character of most Western societies.

- *Experiential knowledge vs. formal logic.* When engaging in deductive reasoning, East Asian students tend to prefer beginning with experiential knowledge based on intuitive understandings emerging from direct perception, reflecting a general understanding of truth and reality as relational and changeable. In contrast, Western students tend to rely on logic and abstract principles, reflecting a general understanding of truth and reality as consistent and logical.

- *Dialectics vs. the law of non-contradiction.* East Asians and European-Americans have differing levels of commitment to avoiding apparent contradiction in deductive reasoning. For example, in Western logic, rules such as the following have played a central role:
  - The law of identity: A = A. A thing is identical to itself.
  - The law of non-contradiction: A ≠ not-A. No statement can be both true and false.
  - The law of the excluded middle: any statement is either true or false.

  In contrast, East Asian logic is based on Chinese dialecticism, which embraces principles such as the following:

  - The principle of change: reality is a process that is not static, but rather is dynamic and changeable. A thing need not be identical to itself at all because of the fluid nature of reality.
  - The principle of contradiction: partly because change is constant, contradiction is constant. Old and new, good and bad, exist in the same object or event, and indeed depend on one another for their existence.
  - The principle of relationship or holism: because of constant change and contradiction, nothing either in human life or in nature is isolated and independent, but instead everything is related. It follows that attempting to isolate elements of some larger whole can only be misleading.

In summary, Nisbett's team suggested that Western students tend towards information-processing that is linear, specific, analytic, theoretical and individualistic-competitive, while East Asian students prefer to think through patterns that are circular, interconnected, holistic, experiential and communal. While the focus of Nisbett was on

East Asia, similar intercultural research from elsewhere in the world suggests that the linear–analytical thinking of Greek philosophy and the Enlightenment, which has so shaped Western educational systems, is globally atypical. While the specifics differ, the general pattern of information-processing throughout most of the non-Western world tends towards holism and networked thinking, in contrast to the tight specificity so typical in Western academia (see, for example, Bauman and Skitka 2006; Merriam, Caffarella and Baumgartner 2007, 238–39; Schwartz 1992; Triandis 1989).

Gender and Learning

The recent report of the "Global Survey on Theological Education" (Esterline et al. 2013) reported that the number of women students engaged in theological education is growing in every denomination and in every region. Yet the shape and focus of the education that takes place in most programmes of ministerial training remains biased towards typical male ways of appropriating and processing information.

The dominance of approaches that favour male learners should not surprise us. Our traditional model of theological education was developed in the West and in its earliest generations was a virtual "closed shop", for male students only. Still today, the most admired academic institutions in the world are in the West and are dominated by white male faculty and administration. These institutions have enormous influence on the shape of international accreditation, which in turn globally dominates the curricular decisions of higher education. The approach is rarely questioned. In part, this is because most white Western males cannot understand how people could learn otherwise; more than once I have been asked by male colleagues in the West, "Doesn't everyone learn this way?"

Research into gender differences in learning suggests statistically different ways in which men and women prefer to learn. While there are always exceptions, and these are tendencies rather than absolutes, it has been found that the typical male brain tends to be attuned to specificity in tasks, and prefers to compartmentalize and simplify tasks as much as possible: it is hardwired for understanding and building systems around specific content (Baron-Cohen 2003). In contrast, there is a tendency for the typical woman's brain to be geared to see multiple implications and the big picture when completing tasks (Goleman 2006, 139; Gurian and Henley 2001, 41–42). Consequently, there is a tendency among men to enjoy abstract arguments, philosophical problems, and moral debates about abstract principles, and to do big-picture theoretical philosophy or theology divorced from day-to-day life. In general, women have difficulty understanding the value or meaning of theory without specific, concrete examples, and tend to do best in learning opportunities which involve hands-on, practical experiences from which the theoretical material can be deduced (Philbin et al. 1995; Williamson and Watson 2006, 348). Stated simply, men tend to prefer to go from theory to practice, while women tend to prefer to go from practice to theory.

Women also have greater interconnectivity between the verbal, reasoning and emotional parts of the brain, and consequently tend to prefer learning in community by talking through the issues and ideas being presented (Belenky and Stanton 2000, 82; Stonehouse 1993, 117). In contrast, males tend to prefer processing ideas and issues without having to exercise the language parts of their brains; or, if they use speech in learning, it tends to be through debate and argument over very specific points.

These differences have been challenged by some, particularly by feminist writers concerned that a sharply dichotomous understanding will reinforce gender stereotypes. Nonetheless, a sensitization to gender difference can empower serious educators to provide appropriate learning contexts for all. I have observed that when women are given opportunity and time to process their thinking in gender-specific groups, they often bring a breadth of interconnectivity that groups of male students miss. On the other hand, the male groups are sometimes better able to simplify processes into a "step one, step two, ..." approach that greatly facilitates understanding.

Conclusion

This chapter has introduced you to various attempts to explain the diverse ways in which people learn. While there is substantial debate about the specifics, and no model adequately addresses every element of learning, nonetheless serious educators will recognize the need for diverse learning contexts and approaches to assessment so that the teaching–learning dynamic can become more inclusive.

Exercises

1. What do you see as the two or three major strengths and weaknesses of the theories and models presented in this chapter? For you personally, what is the most significant lesson that might contribute to your own development as an instructor?

2. Which of the various models presented in this chapter most resonated with you? Why do you think that was the case for this particular approach? How would you best describe your own approach to learning?

3. Consider your normal instructional patterns. Which kinds of learners are most likely to benefit from your instructional methodologies? Why? Which kinds of learners are most likely to feel excluded by your instructional patterns? Suggest at least one specific instructional methodology that might better include these sorts of learners.

4. In what ways do you see the normal learning patterns of your local context as more reflective of the West? Of East Asia? On what bases do you make these assessments? What other unique features of learning do you see in your local context? Give at least one specific implication of your observations for the practice of theological education in your context.

5. Given that the wider education system in most countries has largely been shaped by Western education, initially in the colonial era and reinforced through globalization and accreditation, to what extent do you see Western patterns of education to be a problem for theological education? Why do you make this assessment?

6. To what extent does the material on gender difference presented in this chapter reflect your own personal experience? Give two or three examples to illustrate your point. Suggest at least one specific action you might take during the next few months to better empower both male and female voices in your classes.

15

The Grading and Assessment of Students

In theological education, the easier something is to assess, the less important that something is likely to be.
(Graham Cheesman)

One of the most pervasive and unquestioned elements of education is the grading and assessment of students. However, the allocation of a number or letter to a student's work is a relatively recent phenomenon in the history of education, dating back only some two centuries (Pierson 1983, 310; Stray 2005, 94–95). Nonetheless, it is today perceived as so standard that few instructors in higher education are aware of the philosophical and practical problems inherent in our grading practices. In this chapter we will investigate the purpose of assessment, the drawbacks associated with grades, and some possible ways forward that respect the missional-ecclesial vision for theological education.

What Is the Purpose of Assessment?

The starting point of any discussion on grades and assessment is to determine the purpose of the assessment process. The simplest answer is that the goal of assessment is *learning* – both as a means by which students can evaluate the extent to which they have attained the desired learning, and as a way through which teachers can assess the extent to which they have enabled the desired learning to take place.

Suskie (2009, 4–5) describes the ideal of assessment as a continual four-phase cycle in which:

- The teacher establishes clear and measurable learning outcomes.
- Students are provided with adequate and appropriate learning opportunities by which it is possible for them to achieve these outcomes.
- The teacher systematically gathers, analyses and interprets evidence to determine the extent to which student learning matches the desired outcomes.

- The teacher uses this information to help students to adjust and improve their learning towards the desired outcomes.

This process can be represented diagrammatically as shown in figure 15.1.

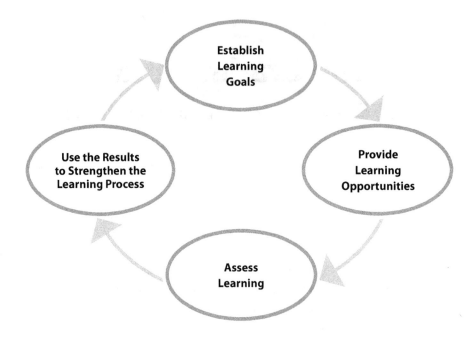

Figure 15.1 The four-step cycle of assessment (adapted from Suskie 2009, 4)

Fink (2003, 83–84) contrasts what he calls "audit-ive" assessment with educative assessment processes. Audit-ive assessment looks backwards by focusing on the "auditing" of student learning at the conclusion of the course. Educative assessment looks forwards, through first establishing learning goals – preferably goals which are shared with the learners – and then working with the learners towards those goals through the use of multiple, diverse and frequent feedback processes.

A distinction is often drawn between "formative" and "summative" assessment. Formative assessment refers to phases of assessment that take place during the course, by which the teacher is able to see the extent to which students are walking the desired path, and, if necessary, redirect or "reform" their learning processes towards the desired outcomes. Summative assessment takes place at the end of the course and seeks to evaluate the sum total of learning that has taken place. Although a common practice, the inclusion of formative assessment in the final grade allocation is questionable: if a grade is to be allocated, it should be for the final level of learning and should not include mistakes and wrong turns that were taken earlier along the path.

The Problems with Grades in Theological Education

While some form of assessment process is an essential element in promoting learning, the allocation of grades is a more dubious exercise. Genuine learning entails engagement in the cognitive, affective and behavioural domains, and in each of these domains the goal should be student attainment of increasingly high levels of learning. The allocation of a letter or number is generally only meaningful at the lowest levels of cognitive learning; the assessment of more significant learning is best done dialogically, through comments and reflection.

Wlodkowski and Ginsberg (1995, 275) observe that the giving of grades is "a context-dependent judgment, which is assigned and registered as a unidimensional symbol for a multidimensional conglomerate of teacher information, attitude, bias and error". When we subjectively apply a single letter or number to the complex process of multidimensional learning, we both promote the illusion of an objectivity that rarely exists and provide little of meaning that might help promote student learning. Because students subconsciously are aware of the highly subjective nature of grades, such grades tend to be received more at the emotional than at the informational level: the grade is seen primarily as a measure of the extent to which the instructor values the student as a person. The emotional response is justified: numerous research studies over the past forty years (Dennis 2007; Kahneman 2011, 83; Landy and Sigall 1974) have documented the power of the "halo effect", in which teachers were found to give higher-than-deserved grades to students they considered attractive or likeable, and the opposite to students they liked less.

The subjectivity of grades is also evident through a number of common scoring errors, particularly in the assessment of written work (Suskie 2009, 44):

- The instructor assesses work better than others would ("leniency" errors), or uses only the high, medium or low end of the rating scale ("generosity", "central tendency" or "severity" errors).

- The instructor lets extraneous features of the student (physical attractiveness, dress, loquaciousness, gender, race, age, etc.) influence the grade that is given, either positively ("halo effect bias", mentioned above) or negatively ("contamination effect bias").

- Instructors give higher grades to students with similar interests and personalities to their own ("similar-to-me effect bias").

- Instructors give higher grades to students who have presented better-quality work in the past, irrespective of the quality of the current piece of work, and vice versa ("prior impression effect bias").

- Particularly where a diversity of grades is expected by the administration, instructors may assess based on comparisons between students rather than according to established standards ("contrast effect bias"). For example, an instructor might give a rating of "unacceptable" to the worst paper received, even though the paper meets the minimally acceptable standards stated in the syllabus.

- Particularly when a large number of papers need to be assessed, it is common for the bases for grade allocation to drift during the marking process ("rater drift"): as instructors tire while assessing student work, some become irritable and progressively harsh in their grades, while others skim work more quickly and score more leniently.

Grades are built on the assumption that some students should succeed and some should not. Cannell (2006, 314) relates her attempt at promoting a course and its assessment in such a way that students would be trained to develop self-educational and self-assessment strategies, essential tools for lifelong learning. Because of the nature of the course, it was appropriate that most students achieved the learning outcomes at a very high level and consequently were deserving of an A. The dean of her seminary asked her to stop this practice as it was interfering with the school's awards system! I recognize that grade inflation is a growing challenge in higher education, but the frequent concerns expressed about grade inflation are voiced only because grades exist in the first place. A shift towards assessment processes that de-emphasize grades is less likely to encounter the same issues.

Grades assess product more than they assess learning. By way of example, I once taught at a small school that offered a Master of Christian Education degree. I had one student who took eight courses with me, and by the eighth course the incremental learning that took place was minimal. However, she knew the material so well that I had no choice but to give her an A for the course. In that same eighth class was another student for whom this course was her first in the field of Christian education. She began with no background knowledge and learned an enormous amount, but her final work was not of the calibre of the student who had greater expertise; consequently, the final product of the second student received a B+. The first student, despite learning little, was rewarded more substantially than the student who had demonstrated notable growth and learning. If the basis of assessment was upon the quantity of learning that took place, I would have given the first student a C and the second an A – but in the current grade structure, this would be seen as unjust. If the purpose of education is learning, the focus of grades on product rather than learning must be seen as problematic.

One of the main arguments offered in favour of grades is their perceived motivational efficacy. Without grades (so the argument goes), students would not make the effort to learn; students make effort in order to get the desired grade that comes through satisfying the learning requirements. While there may be an element of truth to this, grades are likely to be a very temporary form of motivation. As we observed in chapter 8, the basis for deep learning is the extent to which a student gives value to the learning; if the only value is the attainment of a grade, as soon as that grade is achieved there is little reason for the student to retain the learning, and it is improbable that the desired learning outcomes will last substantially past the end of the course. Where the grades are perceived to be the goal, students will do whatever they need to do to attain the grade – even cheat.

Wlodkowski and Ginsberg suggest that grades are more coercive than educative: "Many more students would object to and confront poor teaching, irrelevant content, sexual harassment, unfair evaluation, and prejudiced comments and practices if it were not for the intimidation of teachers lowering their grades" (Wlodkowski and Ginsberg 1995, 276).

The problem with the motivational argument is that it assumes (albeit unconsciously) that the extrinsic motivational nature of grades will evolve naturally into long-term intrinsic motivation: if we coerce the students into learning, they will naturally come to value the learning. Extensive research over four decades (Deci, Koestner and Ryan 2001) has demonstrated that the opposite is the case: external rewards such as grades, when used to motivate or coerce people, substantially undermine curiosity, interest, self-motivation and persistence. Stated simply, the more we depend upon extrinsic motivators, the more we undermine intrinsic motivation. In the world of education in particular, it has been found that a focus on rewards or punishments substantially undermines students' desire to learn for the sake of learning (Dobrow, Smith and Posner 2011; May 2003).

Kohn (1999, 76–92) has suggested a number of key factors that contribute to the destructive nature of extrinsic motivators such as grades:

- Anything presented as a prerequisite for something else – that is, as a means towards some other end – comes to be seen as less desirable. "Do this and you'll get that" automatically devalues the "this". Promising a reward for an activity is tantamount to declaring that the activity is not worth doing for its own sake.

- Rewards are usually experienced as controlling, and we tend to recoil from situations in which our autonomy has been diminished.

- The more we want what has been dangled in front of us, the more we are likely to dislike whatever we have to do to get it.

The process of grading is a particular challenge in collectivist societies. Especially in small schools (the norm in theological education), a grade is perceived by those from collectivist societies as a measure of the extent to which an instructor likes the student. In these societies, the relational component of teaching is particularly influential, and it is natural for instructors to want to give an A to every student as an element in strengthening the teacher–student relationship. Most collectivist societies also place a high value on personal and communal honour. Receiving an A is honouring; receiving a B falls short of honour; receiving a C is a great dishonour; and receiving an F is shameful in the extreme. In such contexts, it is virtually impossible to promote any sort of objectivity in the giving and receiving of grades, except in cases where the grade is based on the repetition of facts.

I sometimes wonder whether this reality may contribute to the ubiquitous emphasis on rote learning in collectivist societies.

The above concerns with grades apply generally in higher education. However, the particular missional purpose of theological education raises further questions.

While any notion of grades is totally absent from the Scriptures, we see an evaluation process evident in the story of the Pharisee and the tax collector (Luke 18:9–14): the Pharisee lists the various ways in which he deserves an "A", and is condemned; while the tax collector recognizes his shortcomings, and is honoured. The implication for theological education seems to be that evaluation should be based on the extent to which students are teachable: irrespective of where they are in their current pilgrimage, if they are willing to recognize their shortcomings and respond to formational guidance, they are affirmed. It is those who believe they already "know it all" who are subject to judgement. Grades rarely assess teachability; their focus is on product. I have too often encountered students who come to the school already with strong background knowledge and whose primary goal is the "piece of paper" they receive at graduation. They learn little; they grow little; and yet, because of our focus on product, they often receive high grades – even academic honours. I have also encountered students who come with much weaker background who are like "sponges", absorbing every opportunity to learn, and yet, because of their weaker background, are unable to achieve top grades. While our grading systems honour the former, I suspect Christ would honour the latter!

In line with practice common in North America, for some years ABTS kept a record of the Grade Point Average (GPA) of students, and those who achieved high GPAs were given various levels of honours at graduation. The problem we observed, however, was that many of the students who achieved high GPAs did so because they were more comfortable with books than with people, and in some cases they were constantly in conflict with other students. We were honouring students with good academic skills but poor social skills, while students less academically able who were leaders in peacemaking and relational ministry at the school and in the church received no recognition – even though they inevitably succeeded better post-graduation. This pattern is not unique to theological education: similar issues arise in many of the people professions – education, social work, medicine, and even law and engineering. Good grades do not make good teachers, good social workers or good doctors. In the people professions, social and emotional competence has been found to have a greater role in professional excellence than raw academic ability (Goleman 2006, 88).

Fortunately at ABTS, we no longer honour students based solely on academic evaluation. The high honour of student graduation speaker, for example, is now based on holistic evaluation by both students and faculty, rather than simply academic performance. However, our experience at ABTS highlights a number of more general questions and issues related to grades in theological education:

- What is rewarded is valued. Grades are a form of perceived reward, and in general, we only issue grades for academic achievements. While the academic learning of our students is important, it is only one of several areas that are crucial to the formation of missional leaders. It is difficult enough to give meaningful grades in the cognitive domain; it can be even more challenging to evaluate growth in the behavioural domain, and it is nigh on impossible to know what is happening in the affective domain. It is therefore not surprising that most of our grade assessments occur in the cognitive domain. However, by giving "value" through grades only to the cognitive domain, through the hidden curriculum we essentially devalue what is needed in the affective and behavioural realms of learning.

- Grades promote conformity. Cano-Garcia and Hughes (2000) found that those students who achieve the highest grades academically are actually those who prefer to work individually and who show a willingness to conform to existing rules and procedures. As the purpose of grades is to satisfy the desires of the instructor, an emphasis on grades frequently discourages the sort of creativity that is so needed for effective missional leadership in the twenty-first century.

- The more a school emphasizes grades, the less likely the school is to promote group-learning tasks. Where grades are emphasized, students will oppose group work, concerned that less competent or committed students will bring their grades down. Teachers will avoid group work as it is notoriously difficult to be "fair" to all students in a group. In short, grades promote individual competition and squelch cooperative learning. In light of the missional-ecclesial vision for theological education, the hidden lessons embedded in this approach are disastrous: through this highly individual and competitive emphasis, students are very effectively trained to see ministry as an individual and competitive activity, rather than as team servanthood in the image of our Triune God.

Some Possible Ways Forward

Despite the resounding and repeated critiques brought by educationalists, the giving of grades is still pervasive in education – in every country of the world and in every field of study. Moreover, many of the key gatekeepers – accrediting agencies, admission committees for advanced studies, employers, denominational leaders, even school boards – believe that "good grades" are synonymous with competency and knowledge of the field (Cannell 2006, 312), even though this assertion is highly questionable. While a small but growing number of schools have turned their backs on grades, moving to assessment based solely on learning reports, I suspect that few of our theological colleges are ready for this level of dramatic change. Consequently, in the remainder of this chapter I suggest some possible ways to function within the world of grades while minimizing their negative impact and maximizing the focus of assessment on learning.

The first step towards decreasing the negative effects of grades is to minimize the number of possible grades. In fields such as theological education, the allocation of a number grade is extremely arbitrary in all but knowledge-based subjects such as languages. There is generally a high level of inconsistency among teachers, and consequently, students often sense a level of injustice in the system. The giving of a letter with pluses or minuses is barely an improvement. A simple system of A, B, C is far more likely to result in the giving of meaningful grades.

The use of rubrics rather than grades is one of the most straightforward ways to shift the focus of assessment towards learning. The term "rubric" refers to a set of standards. In education, the standards should be related directly to the desired learning outcomes that are given prior to the students' beginning a learning task or tasks. There are two possible ways of approaching educational rubric: narrative or specific elements. Appendix 15.1 gives a typical narrative rubric that describes the general meaning of A, B and C for written work in a course of study. Appendix 15.2 provides a rubric for assessing oral work through the evaluation of specific elements. Appendix 15.3 provides a detailed rubric for the integrative project given in appendix 6.1, in which the assessor would simply check relevant boxes, concluding with some substantive summary comments. You will note that the second and third rubrics avoid terms such as "excellent", "good", "fair" and "poor", instead using "extensive", "medium" or "slight" treatment (appendix 15.3) or different terminology for each parameter (appendix 15.2). Outstanding students know where to emphasize and where to de-emphasize, and a scattering of results should be expected in the rubric assessment of a good paper. Where the more evaluative terms of "excellent", "good", and so on, are used, there is a tendency for an instructor to get an overall feel for the paper and grade the elements based on the general assessment, rather than deal with each element according to its own merit. Detailed rubrics provide far more information to students than a simple letter or number, and are more likely to promote learning.

In most schools, the only grade that is actually required is that given at the end of the course. In such circumstances, it is best not to place grades on papers, but rather to provide students with extensive substantive comments and some sort of rubric such as that given in appendix 15.2. My experience is that the moment you write a grade on the paper, the student's eyes will go to the grade and ignore most of your comments. When you place no grade, the student actually reads the comments, and hence there is greater potential for learning. This is confirmed in research that found that the destructive impact of grades was not substantially reduced by the addition of comments; positive outcomes were observed only when comments were given without a grade placed on the students' work (Kohn 1999, 202). Of course, some students are so used to defining themselves according to their grades that it may be important (at least initially) for the instructor to make time to talk with students about what their grades might be if given (Kohn 1999, 209). Even better would be to ask the students how they would assess themselves based on the comments and the rubric. If their self-assessment is inaccurate, the opportunity is then provided for discussing their learning processes in greater detail.

Removing identifying information from student work (Suskie 2009, 45) and/or having more than one faculty member correct work can help reduce the level of subjectivity in grading. In many schools, faculty members are already overworked, and because few instructors get any pleasure from evaluating student work, sometimes getting a single assessment from teachers can be a challenge! In these contexts, a second marking of a representative sample – say, 20 per cent of the papers – can at least promote some level of consistency and fairness.

Part of the goal of assessment is to train students in the process of self-monitoring. It can therefore be beneficial to have students develop learning contracts in which the students themselves define which tasks will be accomplished and when they will submit their work. The instructor informs them beforehand which grade would be applied depending on the approach taken to the course. This approach places a large amount of the responsibility on the student and the process is clear from the beginning.

Among the most important characteristics of outstanding leaders is their ability to self-evaluate and develop new strategies based on their own self-assessment. Consequently, a valuable approach can be to incorporate student self-assessment into the process: the students (perhaps using a rubric as the starting point) provide a description of the strengths and weaknesses of their work and then the grade is developed in dialogue. Having a level of peer assessment can reinforce this process. In more relational societies, this approach of self- and peer-assessment would need to be very carefully designed and explained in order to succeed; students are prone to give responses they think will please the instructor and their peers, and miss the opportunity for growing in self-evaluative skills.

Throughout this book we have focused on multidimensional learning – cognitive, affective, behavioural. This holistic approach somehow needs to impact our assessment and evaluation processes – but it is not always straightforward. Who is able to determine the level of growth a student is experiencing in the fruit of the Spirit? How do we assess a person's spirituality? Patterns of inner-life growth are subtle and often only discernible over a period of time. However, to ignore the affective and behavioural dimensions is to deny something of our missional-ecclesial purpose. Consequently, a part of our assessment process should include periodic reviews of students' holistic progress.

At ABTS we have listed some of the key elements we seek in students as they move towards graduation:

- A teachable spirit – not just in academic courses, but also in personal and ministerial formation. Of particular concern is a teachable sprit even where ABTS is not providing boundaries and direction.

- Reducing levels of ABTS-initiated "maintenance". While some students may need substantial "maintenance" at the beginning of their time with us, possibly with formal warnings and disciplinary actions, if this continues into the second and third years we should question their long-term effectiveness as leaders.

- An increasingly positive influence on other students. In particular, we should be able to see second- and third-year students having a positive influence on first-year students. Our belief is that a growing relationship with God should be reflected in a growing positive influence on other students.

- Self-initiated disciplines of growth, in which students recognize areas of weakness and take positive steps to address these weaknesses.

In order to assess student growth in these areas, we have faculty meetings in which we share any major concerns we have with students. For those students about whom the faculty members express notable concerns, the dean of students and the academic dean together develop a set of documented expectations for the remainder of the year. About six weeks before the end of the academic year, those students whose documented expectations have not been adequately met are subject to appropriate discipline or are advised to conclude their programmes of study.

While there are shortcomings in this approach, it does move beyond the mere assessment of academic learning to broader holistic concerns. As you consider the approach to assessment at your school, you should investigate context-relevant holistic approaches that can ensure that your school is nurturing emerging leaders who have growing competence in all areas of their person.

Conclusion

The purpose of assessment is learning. Quality assessment seeks means for minimizing the negative impact of grades and maximizing the focus on substantive comments and descriptive rubrics. Particularly in theological education, we need to do all we can to honour teachability and holistic growth, and be cautious of an overemphasis on pure academic ability. How we grade and assess communicates powerfully through the hidden curriculum our actual educational values. In this as in all that we do, our focus should be on the developing of whole people who are effective in helping the church fulfil its missional task.

Exercises

1. Why do you give grades at your school? What shape does your grading system take? In what ways do you find grades helpful or unhelpful?

2. In what ways might giving grades produce negative spiritual consequences which are particularly problematic at theological seminaries? Our long-term vision is to develop men and women who are agents of empowerment in the church for God's mission in our region. In light of this vision, to what extent do you believe that grades are helpful and/or unhelpful? Why?

3. What are some of the main barriers to changing the grade system? Can you suggest some ways of overcoming these barriers?

4. How do you decide how to give a grade in your classes? What do you assess and how do you make these assessments?

5. Consider a learning task that you are likely to give students in a forthcoming course. Try to design an assessment rubric along the lines of those given in appendices 15.1, 15.2 and 15.3.

6. Using the approach taken at ABTS as a starting point, try to develop (a) a series of descriptive statements for holistic growth of your students; (b) a process for assessing and following up with students which promotes not only academic competence, but also affective and behavioural growth.

Appendix 15.1

ABTS Bachelor of Theology (BTh) Grade Descriptors

In general, bachelor-level students should be able to:

- Show an increased vision and purpose in regard to their calling to ministry and have a clearer understanding of how they might implement their vision.

- Use a variety of newly developed skills and experiences within a range of ministry settings.

- Demonstrate growth in the values and practice of authentic and effective worship; missional ministry; Christlike leadership; kingdom-mindedness and empowerment; reflective discernment and practice; incarnational ministry; personal and spiritual development.

- Demonstrate knowledge and understanding in the field of study that builds on their general education and is supported by both advanced textbooks, and current knowledge and practice within the field of study.

- Apply their knowledge and understanding within a professional approach to their work or vocation, including the ability to develop and sustain arguments, solve problems, and transfer skills and understanding from different contexts into their current context.

- Gather and interpret relevant data that will inform their judgements that include reflection on relevant theological, social and ethical issues.

- Communicate information, ideas, problems and solutions to both specialist [such as within the context of training events] and non-specialist [such as a church congregation] audiences.

- Use their acquired learning skills to continue to undertake further study with a high degree of autonomy and at a higher level.

Grade	Description
A	Overall, the student has demonstrated an excellent level of work, reflecting a broad and deep understanding of the subject. There is clear evidence of the ability to analyse a variety of perspectives reasonably and logically. The student has used available resources (texts, journal articles, etc.) appropriately, with a high standard of referencing and footnotes. A strong attempt to integrate other appropriate disciplines. A good awareness of practical implications with a solid degree of personal, social and theological reflection. The student has shown excellent progress in attaining the course learning outcomes.
B	The student has demonstrated a good level in all his or her work, which reflects a sound general awareness of the issues involved in the subject matter. All the student's work is presented with accuracy and clarity. The student has made a good attempt at relating theory to practice, with some effective theological, social and personal reflection. Use of available resources (texts, journal articles, etc.) is sound. Generally, the student's work is clear and well presented, but there is still room for improvement. Overall, the student has shown good progress in attaining the course learning outcomes.
C	The student has made a satisfactory attempt to engage with the subject matter, but there are still significant gaps in his or her knowledge and understanding. The student has tended to be descriptive, with only a limited attempt at critical analysis and personal, theological or social reflection. Use of resources or footnoting is inconsistent or inappropriate. Overall, the student has shown satisfactory progress towards attaining the course learning outcomes, but there is still room for improvement.
I (Incomplete)	The student's work is unsatisfactory or incomplete, or the student's attendance has been too erratic to merit the granting of a passing grade. The student shows poor engagement with the material. Written work is poorly presented and lacking clarity. Compensatory work is required to attain a passing grade.

Appendix 15.2

Rubric for the Assessment of Oral Presentation

Student's name: _____

Course/Project: _____

Content

1. Clear purpose/answer to main question
– from clearly stated and understood (6) to not stated at all (1)

6	5	4	3	2	1

2. Broad and deep understanding of subject
– well done throughout presentation (6) to rarely (1)

6	5	4	3	2	1

3. Covers the issues at stake
– from fully (6) to never (1)

6	5	4	3	2	1

4. Lesson development from stated purpose
– from clear and logical (6) to vague and illogical (1)

6	5	4	3	2	1

5. Connection with practice
– from very meaningful and helpful (6) to vague and unhelpful (1)

6	5	4	3	2	1

6. Conclusion
– developed logically and delivered clearly (6) to a vague, unconnected conclusion (1)

6	5	4	3	2	1

7. Demonstrates progress in learning outcomes
– from exemplary (6) to mostly missing (1)

6	5	4	3	2	1

Method

8. Creative/engaging methodology
– from varied and interesting (6) to boring lecture throughout (1)

6	5	4	3	2	1

9. Appropriateness of methodology for audience
– from appropriate (6) to inappropriate (1)

6	5	4	3	2	1

10. Faithfulness to time restraints
– from right on schedule (6) to grossly over or under time (1)

6	5	4	3	2	1

11. Verbal skills
– from coherent fluid delivery (6) to incoherent and distracting (1)

6	5	4	3	2	1

12. Overall impression of the lesson
– from exemplary (6) to needing improvement (1)

6	5	4	3	2	1

13. _____ **(assignment specific criteria)** _____

– from always (6) to never (1)

6	5	4	3	2	1

Exemplary (A)   -   Proficient (B)   -   Developing (C)   -   Needs Improvement (I)

Overall Evaluation: _____

Comments:

Appendix 15.3

Rubric for the Assessment of Integrative Project (Appendix 6.1)

Component	Extensive Treatment	Medium Treatment	Slight Treatment	Not Evident
Focus Group				
Description				
How many leaders? What are their chief characteristics?				
How do leaders relate to one another?				
How does decision-making take place?				
How are new leaders incorporated into leadership?				
Other pertinent information about the focus group				
Group in Lebanon				
Reports on observations				
Reports on interviews				
Analysis of the leadership patterns at work in the Lebanon group				
Comparison of the strengths and weaknesses of the Lebanon group against the patterns evident in the focus group				
Biblical-Theological Lens				
Careful exegesis of specific texts:				
(a) Literary context				
(b) Historical-cultural context				
(c) The literary genre and its significance				
(d) Cross-references				
(e) Use of multiple translations				
Broader biblical-theological themes				

Component	Extensive Treatment	Medium Treatment	Slight Treatment	Not Evident
Engagement with material from Leadership Insights course				
Connections with the case study				
Appropriate referencing				
Historical-Theological Lens				
Comparable situations in history and relevance to the case study				
Quality of inferences from the historical situations				
Understanding of the significance of the historical context				
Theological works				
Relationship between theological reflections and historical context				
Connections with the case study				
Appropriate referencing				
Social-Contextual Lens				
Impact of culture on the situation				
Psychological dynamics				
Social dynamics				
Power relations				
Hidden curriculum				
Processes of institutionalization				
Other elements from the social sciences				
Appropriate referencing				
Personal-Ministerial Lens				
How do you see your own role in being a transformative agent in this situation?				
Reference to elements from the Personal Journeys course				
In light of the material given in the Personal Journeys in Leadership course, what should you be and do as a leader in this context?				
Appropriate referencing				

Component	Extensive Treatment	Medium Treatment	Slight Treatment	Not Evident
Integration				
How do these lenses come together? What shared principles do you see here?				
How can you nurture multiple lenses for looking at situations such as this?				
Recommendations				
How might the focus group better become the face of Christ to their communities?				
How might genuine impact on the world be nurtured?				
Grounded in Scripture and sound theology				
Specific, attainable and measurable				
Holistic – looking at the members of the group as whole people				
Comprehensive, dealing with multiple aspects of the situation				
Personal, explaining how you personally will think, relate and act differently in order to facilitate appropriate change				
Appropriate referencing				
Process Elements				
Participation in 3-hour workshop				
300–500-word progress report (18 November)				
20–30 minute presentation of the findings of the project				
Participation of each member of the group				
Project on time and formatted appropriately				
Details of the contributions of each member of the group				
Balance in Life				

Comments:

16

Excellence in Teaching

A teacher affects eternity: He (sic) can never tell where his influence stops. (Henry Adams)

Excellence is to do a common thing in an uncommon way. (Booker T. Washington)

The purpose of the second half of this book has been to enhance skills in the art of teaching, providing tools for intentionality and engagement. Bob Ferris (2006) has asserted that "the Faculty are the curriculum", and this final chapter is a word of encouragement and challenge as you strive towards excellence in teaching.

What makes a good teacher? To start on your road to increased self-discovery, try this reflective exercise. Take a piece of paper and draw three columns labelled respectively "Teachers", "Teaching Qualities" and "Response".

- In the first column: list the names of the three teachers who had the greatest impact on your life positively *and* the three teachers who had the greatest impact on your life negatively. Listing the bad ones often reveals as much as listing the good ones.

- In the second column: record the personal characteristics that caused their influence to be remembered or significant, positive or negative.

- In the third column: write down your personal response to their presence in your life, including in learning as well as in behaviour.

Take a moment to reflect on your lists. The goal, of course, is to emulate the good behaviours and eliminate the bad from your teaching. No matter how gifted – for some teachers have natural teaching gifts – all teachers can profit from a review of their skills.

- On the basis of what you observed in the chart, what do you see to be some of the chief characteristics of an effective teacher?

- Which of these characteristics do you see in yourself and in your own teaching? Which of these characteristics do you long to develop further?

Despite some level of ambiguity, research indicates that there are several general characteristics which have been found commonly to characterize excellent teachers.

While few teachers exhibit all of these characteristics, the more of these characteristics that are evident in a teacher, the more likely that teacher will excel in his or her teaching.

A Hospitable Relationship with Students

It has now been well established that the quality of relationship which exists between instructor and students is one of the foremost characteristics of excellence in teaching. In a wide variety of formal studies (see, for example, Cervantes 2007; Cranton 2006, 112–15; Harvie 2004; Murdock and Miller 2003; Pianta 1999; Taylor 2000; Teven 2007; Webb and Blond 1995), it has been found that while such qualities as a passionate love for the subject, knowledge of the material and creative teaching styles are common among exceptional teachers, even more so are warmth, genuine concern for the students' learning, and a sense of care and affection for those they teach.

One of the unfortunate realities of education is that it is a "fearful enterprise" (Palmer 1998, 36). Both teachers and students enter the classroom with a wide variety of concerns, and these are often resolved by creating an emotional distance that limits the quality of learning. The classroom is imbued with power relationships between teacher and students (Vella 2002, 11), and the inappropriate exercise of power can serve to exacerbate the fear and uncertainty that are endemic in education.

The only way in which educational fear and hostility can be transformed into trust is through relationship – a form of in-class hospitality in which teachers acknowledge (at least privately) their own fears and the fears of their students, and seek to reduce the natural hostility that exists through their own openness towards and welcome of the ideas, challenges and most of all the personalities of their students (P. Shaw 2011). As teachers actively encourage the more reticent of their students to speak, and deliberately withhold their authoritative speech in order to leave room for others, a hospitable environment is created in which true education can take place (Thompson 1995, 131). It is only in a context of openness and welcome that such activities as exposing and correcting ignorance in ourselves as well as in our students, experimenting with ideas, and mutual criticism of thought and action can take place with freedom and honesty (Palmer 1983, 74).

The provision of hospitable space is a theological act through which we are able to reflect the character of God – a God who from the beginning created bounded and ordered space in which the voice of all is encouraged. The act of separating light from darkness (Gen 1:4–5) and the waters above from the waters below (1:6–7) reflected God's divine value of both order and space. With the creation of Adam, God saw the need for a bounded and ordered space in the garden, a space within which the first task given was for Adam to use his voice in naming the animals (2:19–20), a task for which he needed a partner so that together they could complete the steward-ruler task God had given them (2:20–22). When we create ordered and bounded space in which others might express their voices, we fulfil our identity as created in the image of God.

An important element of this hospitable relationship is trustworthiness, through which students sense that the teacher can be trusted to seek the best for them (Fink 2003, 249). Trust must be earned. Trust emerges out of behaviours such as following through with promises, having rational and understandable bases for assessment, and treating all students with equity. Providing immediate and helpful feedback, avoiding embarrassing students, and demanding mutual respect in the classroom are all important for winning trust. Another significant element of trust-building is what Rodgers and Raider-Roth (2006) describe as being "present" to students, valuing the students sufficiently to listen attentively to them in word, gesture and action.

Integrity and genuineness will naturally communicate commitment and enthusiasm. It is always a temptation (especially for younger teachers) to hide behind the image and role of "expert" and "teacher", and for all of us there is the temptation to seek to be liked by our students more than to see the students genuinely challenged to be effective leaders. It can help our fragile egos to perform the role of expert scholar rather than older brother or sister guiding emerging leaders in their pilgrimage. Only through our transparency and honesty, however, will students trust us and learn to trust themselves.

One practical step towards reducing fear and building relationship is to de-emphasize grades, instead emphasizing approaches to assessment that focus on helping the students learn and grow rather than simply strive to do what needs to be done to get a grade (Kohn 1999, 206–10). Fear-reducing hospitable education will also respond to differences in learning style (Gardner 1983; Kolb 1983; LeFever 1995; McCarthy 1996), showing care and understanding of student learning needs and promoting cooperative learning in the classroom (Siew 2006). Most importantly, as all genuine hospitality means a certain willingness to "bear with" the guests, so hospitable education will be characterized by patience, as teachers and students together seek in faith to grope towards understanding the purposes and ways of God (Newman 2003). As Daniel Willingham (2009, 50) puts it, successful teachers are nice people.

Another facet of hospitable education is the empowerment of students. Effective teachers recognize that an essential element of motivation is a sense of control and self-determination. Students are more likely to be committed to learning when they discern that their unique potential is being recognized and used. This sort of empowerment requires teachers to hold essentially positive assumptions about students, trusting them to respond to their expectations and delegation of responsibility (Knowles, Holton and Swanson 2005, 256). A good teacher rejoices, not when the students reproduce what is taught, but when they are able to catch the teacher's enthusiasm for the subject and go on to develop ideas which the teacher has never thought about (Smail 2005, 176). The glory of the teacher is to sit at the feet of the student and learn from him or her (Fernando 2002, 170).

An essential prerequisite for relational education is that the teacher has a sound self-esteem. Low self-esteem leads to agendas. When my self-esteem as a teacher is at stake, I will seek to find my worth from my status in relationship with the students.

Teachers with low self-esteem either distance themselves from their students, acting the role of the teacher with authority, or they will do all they can to ingratiate themselves with students, often through compromising standards, giving less work and inflating grades. Teachers with high self-esteem feel at ease sharing something of their genuine self (within appropriate boundaries), and are comfortable with the shortcomings of others, graciously correcting error in others and honestly acknowledging error in self (Bosniak 1998). When teachers do not need to find their self-worth in the students, they communicate a joy for learning that is contagious.

For Christian educators, the source of self-esteem in teaching, as in all of life, must emerge not from their relationship with students or administrators, but in their identity as loved by God. In this regard, the model of Jesus is striking: throughout his earthly life we see the source of his lordship in his relationship with the Father, not in the extent of his power and influence over his followers. It is perhaps at Jesus's baptism that this is seen most clearly. As Jesus comes to John, he has not yet even begun his public ministry. He has no followers. He has as yet made no public manifestation of his authority over the powers. Few if any have an inkling of his identity. And yet it is precisely in this context that the voice from heaven declares, "This is my Son, whom I love; with him I am well pleased" (Matt 3:17). Jesus does not need us in order to be Lord, and it is because his status does not rest on us that he can serve us (P. Shaw 2006b). The starting point of confident and effective theological education is the quality of the instructor's own personal relationship with God.

Competence

Quality teachers have a deep understanding of the subject matter. They have a broad understanding of the field, and can critically reference significant work of others. Without a firm grasp of the subject matter, teachers are unable to think on their feet and adapt to their class. Most importantly, they will not be able to focus on the big ideas. A teacher to whom the subject matter is a fog will probably focus on highly specific facts or else make broad generalizations that are not meaningful to the students.

Brookfield (2006, 59–63) notes that expertise and experience are both qualities highly valued by students. It is important for instructors to demonstrate the necessary skills and knowledge that they want the students to emulate. Students need to have confidence that their teachers know what they are talking about. In people-professions such as education, medicine, law or Christian ministry, quality instructors not only know the theory of their discipline but also have extensive field experience, and are able to model deeply reflective practice. Students value instructors with extensive experience in the field they are teaching and in the activity of teaching itself. It rapidly becomes obvious to students when a teacher not only knows the subject from beginning to end, but also has a long history of hearing and dealing with challenging questions and issues related to the material.

Wlodkowski (1999, 28–29) suggests six questions that a competent instructor should be able to answer affirmatively and with confidence:

- Do I myself understand what I am going to teach? Can I easily put it into my own words, or am I dependent on the words of others?

- Am I able to illustrate what I am trying to teach through multiple examples and means?

- Can I personally demonstrate the skill that I am wanting the learners to acquire? If I want my students to be good exegetes of Scripture, they need a model. If I want my students to move to learner-oriented instructional methods in the church, they need to experience this in my seminary classrooms.

- Do I know the limits and consequences of what I am teaching? Competent instructors have sufficient familiarity with the material that they are not only confident in communicating it, but also able to evaluate what they are communicating.

- Do I know how to bridge what I am teaching to the world of the learners? Can I connect text with context?

- Do I know what I do not know? Competent instructors understand their own personal limitations and are comfortable communicating these limitations to students.

Most seminary instructors come with a high level of qualification in their fields, and knowledge of the subject matter, while necessary, can become all-consuming, to the neglect of other features of quality teaching. While good instructors seek continually to update their knowledge in the field, they will also recognize that such knowledge in and of itself does not make for good teaching. Equally important are the ability to explain complex material lucidly and to answer student questions with respect and clarity (Fink 2003, 249).

Years of teaching do not equate with years of experience. Too often, after a few years of instruction, teachers stagnate, and twenty years in the classroom can too easily become one year of experience twenty times over, rather than twenty years of experience. Quality teachers are always seeking to develop and grow.

A challenge for smaller schools can be that courses are built into the curriculum for which there is no qualified instructor. In such circumstances, it may be preferable to change the curricular requirements rather than inflict upon the students an instructor with an inadequate knowledge of the field. The curriculum must always remain a servant to integrative and missional learning, and not a master that controls our decision-making.

Clarity of Communication

Effective educators teach in such a way that their students understand the subject matter. Here again is a truth which needs some qualification: good teaching is far more than just clear explanation, and sometimes, when teachers explain things too well, the students may become passive learners. Yet without sufficient clarity of communication, the teacher contributes very little.

Teachers must communicate clearly in both subject matter and procedure. Clarity in subject matter refers to having clear central concepts (main points), staying on the subject, being repetitive enough to allow for retention, following a sequence and providing clear explanations. Procedural clarity refers to making explicit the goals of the lesson and how the students are expected to achieve these goals.

There are six major attributes of clear teaching:

- It has an introduction that provides students with a framework on which to attach the material to be covered in a class.

- It shows how the parts relate to the whole, by such means as verbal cues at transition points, or the periodic summarization of what has been covered.

- It limits the amount of material covered. Novice teachers typically try to cover far too much content. In general, quality learning presents less content, providing more opportunity for reflection so that deep learning is promoted.

- It focuses on what is meaningful. Students tend to retain material that they find meaningful far more than presentations of material they judge to be irrelevant.

- It varies the level of discourse. Discourse refers to the level of abstraction in the content being presented – from simple facts and explanation to critical analysis and synthesis, to evaluative judgements and abstract possibilities, to concrete realities and practical application. Moving back and forth across the levels of discourse helps to deepen understanding, connect learning with life and creatively explore new possibilities with students.

- It is more concerned about what the students are learning than about what is being delivered. Quality teachers are sensitive to the learning state of the students, and adapt the instructional approach accordingly.

Without clarity, effective teaching is impossible; with it, the foundation is laid for productive instruction. Perhaps the best way to ensure clear teaching is to keep in view a picture of the major contrasts between clear and unclear teaching, as shown in table 16.1.

Marks of Clear Teaching	*Marks of Unclear Teaching*
The lesson objective is clear from the beginning of the session	Students are unsure what is the point of the lesson
Students are able to follow the flow and logic of the material	Students are confused and unsure where the lesson is going
Transitions from one major theme to the next are clearly signalled	Students are unsure when the instructor has moved from one theme to the next
Fluency in presentation	Scattered logic and unclear expression in the presentation
Careful monitoring of student learning	Unawareness or misreading of student cues
Use of demonstrations, examples and illustrations	Vagueness and generality in expression
Language and vocabulary are clear; professional jargon is explained or avoided altogether	Excessive use of professional jargon and complex vocabulary
Appropriate redundancy: key ideas and themes are repeated to ensure retention	An attempt to cover too much, too fast
Appropriate organization	Lack of organization

Table 16.1 Clear and unclear teaching

Creativity

Students need to be hooked into learning intellectually, psychologically and, where appropriate, physically, and an effective teacher has a repertoire of methods upon which he or she can draw. Effective teachers are able to choose from this repertoire the methods which are appropriate for a particular learning task and group, which will engage the students most effectively and which best facilitate the learning process.

Creative teachers also stimulate and reward creativity, recognizing that creativity is an increasingly necessary asset for thriving in a world of accelerating change. Through the example of their own creativity, such teachers provide an environment that encourages and rewards students' own expressions of creativity. Creative classrooms legitimize experimentation, treating failure as an opportunity to learn rather than an act to be punished (Knowles, Holton and Swanson 2005, 259).

Enthusiasm

Enthusiasm and passion are significant elements in quality classroom instruction. This should not surprise us; almost everyone would prefer an animated, colourful and dramatic presentation to one that is lifeless and dull. Jim Wilhoit (1991, 149–151) makes the following observations:

Enthusiastic teachers are more effective because they hold their students' attention, and students tend to project the positive feelings they have for charismatic teachers onto the material. What all the great teachers appear to have in common is love of their subject, an obvious satisfaction in arousing this love in their students, and an ability to convince them that what they are being taught is deadly serious. Student activation is related to learning, and enthusiasm serves to activate students.... Enthusiasm is clearly more than a natural trait. In fact, teachers can be trained to be more enthusiastic. It is worth noting that our term enthusiasm comes from a Greek word meaning "inspired by a god", which suggests that an enthusiastic teacher is one who is inspired by another force. For most teachers that force is a love for the subject, for teaching itself, or for the students. In a very real sense, however, the enthusiasm of the Christian teacher should come from God the Holy Spirit. To be inspired by God (enthusiasm) is particularly important for Christian educators because a vital part of their responsibility to their students is to serve as models of the Christian life.

Dynamic teachers communicate an excitement about the subject that is contagious. When students observe a teacher who is passionate about his or her subject, it is natural for them to have their curiosity provoked as to what exactly has enthused the teacher. High energy, responsiveness to the mood of the classroom and an element of unpredictability are general attractive elements to teaching (Fink 2003, 249). Effective teaching is to some extent truth through personality, and the transparent commitment of a teacher enables students to see both the person of the teacher and the significance of the subject being taught. The best teachers teach from the heart, not from the book. Dynamic teachers are able to communicate a view of learning as a wonderful experience of new vistas of life and meaning, rather than as an unending series of largely meaningless tasks (Fried 2005, 171).

Brookfield (2006, 64) makes an important distinction between conviction and charismatic passion. It is not enough to make fervid, exaggerated declarations as to the transformative power of a skill or idea. Rather, genuine conviction emerges when a teacher communicates to students the crucial importance of the material by exploring every facet of the topic and every route to learning.

A Well-Ordered Class

Effective teachers are able to keep students focused on the tasks of learning. Students can have fun in many appropriate ways, and some socializing is appropriate, but the job of learning must be engaged in with the best possible effort, energy and concentration. For this to take place, quality instructors evidence careful preparation and systematic presentation, with a good balance between content and process. The main concepts are clearly articulated, and significant new learning is evident in each lesson.

Students also tend to value a sense of purposefulness of and productivity in the class time. Consequently, effective teachers make clear where the class is going and guide students along the path to the goal, and teach their students how to get started quickly and maintain focus when working on assignments (Brophy 1999).

Simple, measurable elements can be significant. Students are shown respect when instructors arrive on time and finish on time, and when they read, comment upon and return student work within a reasonable time frame. Quality instructors make their expectations clear and provide a variety of opportunities for students to demonstrate their learning.

Appropriate Use of Praise and Criticism

Teachers need to criticize poor performance while affirming the student as a person. A moderate amount of appropriate praise is effective and helpful, and encourages the student to persevere. However, excessive unearned praise will promote distrust between student and teacher. One of the greatest challenges of quality teaching is getting the right balance between being supportive of students as they struggle to learn, and offering loving critique that challenges them to go further (Brookfield 2006, 274–75).

The source of transformative learning is the sort of disequilibrium that emerges out of having one's comfort zone shaken. This will never emerge from a purely congenial and easy-going classroom. On the other hand, when students feel they are continually being critiqued and put down, they will perceive the classroom to be hostile and develop negative emotional reactions that may lead to discouragement or passive resistance. Balance can best emerge by ensuring that students feel personally affirmed while challenging and critiquing their work. This can be a particularly sensitive process in honour–shame societies, where the distinction between person and product is not fully understood. In my own context of the Middle East, I have frequently encountered students feeling personally affronted when given a B in a paper, let alone a failing grade: the assessment is perceived to be personal rather than relating to their work. Students in these contexts need to be walked through the process of assessment and guided into an understanding that a balance between praise and critique better serves them in their growth as emerging leaders.

Many instructors have found a "sandwich" approach helpful. Assessment begins with an acknowledgement of any effort the student has made, together with details of positive qualities evident in the student contribution. Then comes critique – preferably as brief, specific and challenging as possible. Finally, a word of encouragement can provide students with incentive to learn from their mistakes.

High Expectations

Effective teachers expect good things to happen, and then they make them happen. If teachers do not expect much learning to take place, it generally will not. However, these expectations should not be so unrealistically high that students are unable to meet them. The goal should be to develop and communicate expectations that are as positive as they can be while still remaining realistic. Such expectations should represent genuine beliefs about what can be achieved; they can therefore be taken seriously as goals towards which to work with the students (Brophy 1999, 31).

A key element in promoting passion and commitment to learning is finding the balance between teacher expectations and student concerns and ability. Csikszentmihalyi (1997) has observed that when there is a harmony between what we feel (our emotions), what we desire (our goals or intentions) and what we think (our cognitive mental operations), and there are challenges that match our skills, there is potential for "flow". When people experience "flow", they become totally absorbed in what they are doing: all their personal and psychic energy is in tune and flows in one direction. When teachers present students with appropriate challenges and expectations which stretch their skills in areas of felt concern and need, there is a high potential for promoting deeply significant learning experiences.

Effective teachers not only have high expectations for their students, but also are aware of and avoid the "sustaining expectation effect" (Arends 2007, 46). This refers to the tendency of teachers to expect students' previous behaviour to be retained and continued over time. Students who have produced high-quality work in the past are expected to maintain a high level, and so even when they produce a mediocre piece of work, they are given a generous assessment. Likewise, when students who are chronically late or habitually produce shoddy work decide to change their study patterns, most teachers will continue to expect and assess based on the prior poor behaviour. Quality teachers are not distracted by prior experience, but continue to hold high expectations and judge the responses to those expectations fairly.

A Capacity for Self-Evaluation and Continuous Growth

A great deal of data indicates that teachers tend to improve during their first five years in the field, but thereafter stagnate and depend on prior experience (Willingham 2009, 149). Generally, a teacher with twenty years of experience shows little more instructional competence than a teacher with five years of experience. It seems that teachers work hard on their competencies in their early years of class instruction and then rest on their laurels.

Effective teachers, however, are learners. They pursue continuous self-study and analysis so that skills can continually be enhanced over time. They are open and able to receive the constructive criticism of others, and can evaluate such criticism honestly and fairly. Quality instructors continue to develop as teachers through involvement in teacher-education seminars and/or reading texts in education.

Conclusion

No teacher is characterized by each of the qualities of excellence described in this chapter. However, the more we progress in each of these areas and allow them to shape our lives as teachers, the better placed we will be to facilitate purposeful and integrated learning. Taking simple steps on that path can make life-transforming differences in our students and in us.

Exercises

1. How does your school recruit its teachers? To what extent do the elements of excellence mentioned in this chapter feature in the recruitment process? How might you assess whether a potential faculty member has a teachable attitude, spiritual depth and quality instructional skills? What other characteristics would you see as important for your programme of study?

2. Write down each of the characteristics of excellence in teaching, and for each characteristic give yourself a grade out of 10 – from 0 ("I am very weak in this area") to 10 ("I am outstanding in this area"). For which of the characteristics did you give yourself the lowest grade? Name one specific way in which you could enhance your skills in this area.

Epilogue

Steps on the Path

The journey of fifty miles begins with one step. (Arab proverb)

In this book I have provided so many ideas and suggestions that you may feel overwhelmed, unsure of where to begin. If so, you are not alone! Personally, I am constantly conscious of how far my own teaching and educational leadership falls short of the ideal. But this is to be expected: as a fallen and redeemed people, we live between the "already" and the "not yet": we have tasted the first fruits of God's power and grace, and now await its consummation. Hence, we need daily to draw on the power of the Holy Spirit as we strive towards the ideal.

I do not expect any reader to apply every suggestion given in this book; I do not apply everything myself. But my hope is that you will have discovered some specific areas where you can grow both individually as a teacher and together as a faculty.

To conclude, therefore, I would ask that you pause and consider each of the following questions:

- For you personally, what three or four ideas, statements, principles, and so on, that you have read in this book have had the greatest impact on the way you understand your life and ministry as a theological educator? What do you remember most distinctly? Why do you think that these have been significant for you?

- From all the material covered in this book, write down at least three specific and practical ways in which you might be able in the next few months to apply the principles and practices presented. Share these suggestions with a friend, and have your friend sign your list as evidence of your commitment to take new steps forward as a teacher and as a model of Christian leadership.

It is not in perfection but in faithful response and steady movement forward that we honour Christ and better promote the mission of God. Our holy calling to train and develop leaders who can help the church confront its contextual challenges is critical and demanding, and yet can bring great joy and satisfaction. I pray that the material in this book will have helped you take some new steps along the path towards excellence in theological education.

Works Cited

Abrami, P., L. Levanthal and R. Perry. 1982. "Educational Seduction." *Review of Educational Research* 52: 446–64.

Anderson, L., and D. Krathwohl, eds. 2001. *A Taxonomy for Learning, Teaching and Assessing: A Revision of Bloom's Taxonomy of Educational Objectives*. New York: Longman.

Arends, R. 2007. *Learning to Teach*, 7th ed. Boston: McGraw-Hill.

Argyris, C., and D. Schön. 1974. *Theory in Practice: Increasing Professional Effectiveness*. San Francisco: Jossey-Bass.

Atkinson, R., and R. Shiffrin. 1968. "Human Memory: A Proposed System and Its Control Processes." In *The Psychology of Learning and Motivation (Vol. 2)*, edited by K. W. Spence and J. T. Spence, 89–195. New York: Academic Press.

Avolio, B., K. Mhatre, S. Norman and P. Lester. 2009. "The Moderating Effect of Gender on Leadership Intervention Impact: An Exploratory Review." *Journal of Leadership & Organizational Studies* 15 (4): 325–41.

Baddeley, A. 2000. "Short-Term and Working Memory." In *The Oxford Handbook of Memory*, edited by E. Tulving and F. Craik, 77–92. New York: Oxford University Press.

———. 2003. "Working Memory: Looking Back and Looking Forward." *Nature Reviews Neuroscience* 4 (10): 829–39.

Bailey, J. 2001. "Technology and Change in Education." Online at http://bbh.usd451.k12.ks.us/staff/faculty/chgtech/change.html. Accessed 11 May 2003.

Banks, R. 1999. *Reenvisioning Theological Education: Exploring a Missional Alternative to Current Models*. Grand Rapids, MI: Eerdmans.

——— and B. Ledbetter. 2004. *Reviewing Leadership: A Christian Evaluation of Current Approaches*. Grand Rapids, MI: Baker.

Barkley, E., K. Cross and C. Major. 2005. *Collaborative Learning Techniques: A Handbook for College Faculty*. San Francisco: Jossey-Bass.

Barna Group. 2004. "Born Again Christians Just As Likely To Divorce As Are Non-Christians." Posted 8 September 2004 at http://www.barna.org/barna-update/article/5-barna-update/194-born-again-christians-just-as-likely-to-divorce-as-are-non-christians. Accessed 20 February 2012.

Baron-Cohen, S. 2003. *The Essential Difference: Men, Women and the Extreme Male Brain*. New York: Basic.

Barrows, H. 1996. "Problem-Based Learning in Medicine and Beyond: A Brief Overview." In *Bringing Problem-Based Learning to Higher Education: Theory and Practice. New Directions for Teaching and Learning Series, No. 68*, edited by L. Wilkerson and W. Gijselaers, 3–11. San Francisco: Jossey-Bass.

Barth, R. 2001. *Learning By Heart*. San Francisco: Jossey-Bass.

Bauman, C., and L. Skitka. 2006. "Ethnic Group Differences in Lay Philosophies of Behaviour in the United States." *Journal of Cross-Cultural Psychology* 37 (4): 438–45.

Belenky, M., and A. Stanton. 2000. "Inequality, Development and Connected Knowing." In *Learning As Transformation: Critical Perspectives on a Theory in Progress*, edited by J. Mezirow, 71–102. San Francisco: Jossey-Bass.

Benson, W. 1993. "Setting and Achieving Objectives for Adult Learning." In *The Christian Educator's Handbook on Adult Education*, edited by K. Gangel and J. Wilhoit, 158–77. Wheaton, IL: Victor.

Bevans, S. 2002. *Models of Contextual Theology*. Maryknoll, NY: Orbis.

Bloom, B., M. Engelhart, E. Furst, W. Hill and D. Krathwohl. 1956. *Taxonomy of Educational Objectives. Handbook I: Cognitive Domain*. London: Longmans.

Bonk, J. 2008. Personal interview with Perry and Karen Shaw, Overseas Ministries Studies Center, New Haven CT, August 2008.

Bosniak, M. 1998. "Relational Teaching for 'Teacher 2000'." *The Education Digest* 63: 8–11.

Bowles, S., and H. Gintis. 1976. *Schooling in Capitalist America: Educational Reform and the Contradictions of Economic Life*. New York: Basic.

Brookfield, S. 1986. *Understanding and Facilitating Adult Learning: A Comprehensive Analysis of Principles and Effective Practices*. Milton Keynes: Open University.

———. 1987. *Developing Critical Thinkers: Challenging Adults to Explore Alternate Ways of Thinking and Acting*. San Francisco: Jossey-Bass.

———. 2004. "Discussion." Chap. 11 in *Adult Learning Methods: A Guide for Effective Instruction*, 3rd ed., edited by M. Galbraith, 209–26. Malabar, FL: Krieger.

———. 2006. *The Skillful Teacher: On Technique, Trust, and Responsiveness in the Classroom*, 2nd ed. San Francisco: Jossey-Bass.

Brophy, J. 1999. *Teaching*. Brussels: International Academy of Education.

Burke, D. 2010. "Time to Leave the Wilderness? The Teaching of Pastoral Theology in South East Asia." In *Tending the Seedbeds: Educational Perspectives on Theological Education in Asia*, edited by A. Harkness, 263–84. Quezon City: Asia Theological Association.

Bushnell, H. (1861) 1979. *Christian Nurture*. Grand Rapids: Baker.

Caine, G., and R. Caine. 1994. *Making Connections: Teaching and the Human Brain*. New York: Addison-Wesley.

Caine, R., and G. Caine. 1990. "Understanding a Brain Based Approach to Learning and Teaching." *Educational Leadership* 48 (2): 66–70.

Cannell, L. 2005. "Opportunities for 21st Century Theological Education." In *Theological Education as Mission*, edited by P. Penner, 153–70. Prague: IBTS.

———. 2006. *Theological Education Matters: Leadership Education for the Church*. Newburgh, IN: EDCOT.

Cano-Garcia F., and E. Hughes. 2000. "Learning and Thinking Styles: An Analysis of Their Interrelationship and Influence on Academic Achievement." *Educational Psychology* 20 (4): 413–27.

Carr, W. 1997. *Handbook of Pastoral Studies: Learning and Practising Christian Ministry*. London: SPCK.

Cervantes, J. 2007. "Student-Teacher Relationship Important Factor in Learning." Learning Power News January/February 2007. Online at http://learningpower.gseis.ucla.edu/aspirations/articles/story3.html. Accessed 29 September 2009.

Chang, T. M., H. F. Crombag, K. D. J. M. van der Drift and J. F. Moonen. 1983. *Distance Learning: On the Design of an Open University.* Boston: Kluwer Nijhoff.

Cherry, K. 2012. "VARK Learning Styles: Visual, Aural, Reading, and Kinesthetic Learning." About.com Guide. Online at http://psychology.about.com/od/educationalpsychology/a/vark-learning-styles.htm. Accessed 27 May 2013.

Costello, C. 2001. "Schooled by the Classroom: The (Re) Production of Social Stratification in Professional School Settings." In *The Hidden Curriculum in Higher Education,* edited by E. Margolis, 43–60. New York: Routledge.

Cotton, K. 2010. "Classroom Questioning." *School Improvement Research Series, Close-Up #5.* Online at http://educationnorthwest.org/webfm_send/569. Accessed 6 November 2010.

Corcoran, H. 2007. "Biblical Narratives and Life Transformation: An Apology for the Narrative Teaching of Bible Stories." *Christian Education Journal* Series 3, 4 (1): 34–48.

Craik, F., and E. Tulving. 1975. "Depth of Processing and Retention of Words." *Journal of Experimental Psychology: General* 104: 268–94.

Cranton, P. 2006. *Understanding and Promoting Transformative Learning: A Guide for Educators of Adults,* 2nd ed. San Francisco: Jossey-Bass.

Cronshaw, D. 2012. "Reenvisioning Theological Education and Missional Spirituality." *Journal of Adult Theological Education* 9 (1): 9–27.

Csikszentmihalyi, M. 1997. *Finding Flow: The Psychology of Engagement with Everyday Life.* New York: HarperCollins.

Cunningham, S. 2005. "Who Gets to Chew the Cracker? Engaging the Student in Learning in Higher Education." *Christian Education Journal,* Series 3, 2 (2): 302–18.

Dale, E. 1946. *Audio-Visual Methods in Teaching.* New York: Dryden.

Damasio, A. 2005. *Descartes' Error: Emotion, Reason, and the Human Brain.* New York: Penguin.

Dearborn, T. 1995. "Preparing New Leaders for the Church of the Future: Transforming Theological Education Through Multi-Institutional Partnerships." *Transformation,* 12 (4): 7–12.

Deci, E., R. Koestner and R. Ryan. 2001. "Extrinsic Rewards and Intrinsic Motivation in Education: Reconsidered Once Again." *Review of Educational Research* 71 (1): 1–27.

De Gruchy, S. 2010. "Theological Education and Missional Practice: A Vital Dialogue." In *Handbook of Theological Education: Theological Perspectives – Regional Surveys – Ecumenical Trends,* edited by D. Werner, D. Esterline, N. King and J. Raja, 42–50. Eugene, OR: Wipf and Stock.

Dennis, I. 2007. "Halo Effects in Grading Student Projects." *Journal of Applied Psychology* 92 (4): 1169–76.

Dewey, J. 1938. *Experience and Education.* New York: Macmillan.

Dobrow, S., W. Smith and M. Posner. 2011. "Managing the Grading Paradox: Leveraging the Power of Choice in the Classroom." *Academy of Management Learning & Education* 10 (2): 261–76.

Drane, D. 2008. *After Macdonaldization: Mission, Ministry, and Christian Discipleship in an Age of Uncertainty.* Grand Rapids, MI: Baker.

Durkheim, E. (1922) 1956. *Education and Sociology.* Glencoe, IL: Free Press.

———. (1925) 1961. *Moral Education.* New York: Free Press.

Edwards, D. 1988. "Designing Biblical Instruction." In *The Christian Educator's Handbook on Teaching*, edited by K. Gangel and H. Hendricks, 45–60. Wheaton, IL: Victor.

Eisner, E. W. 1994. *The Educational Imagination: On Design and Evaluation of School Programs*, 3rd ed. New York: Macmillan.

Éla, J-M. 1988. *My Faith as an African*. Maryknoll, NY: Orbis.

Elmer, D. 1993. "Inductive Teaching: Strategy for the Adult Educator." In *The Christian Educator's Handbook on Adult Education*, edited by K. Gangel and J. Wilhoit, 135–47. Wheaton, IL: Victor.

ENQA. 2009. *Standards and Guidelines for Quality Assurance in the European Higher Education Area*, 3rd ed. Helsinki: European Association for Quality Assurance in Higher Education.

Escobar, S. 2004. "What Is the Ministry?" The Lexington Seminar. Online at http://www.lexingtonseminar.org/stuff/contentmgr/files/97a7fb6dc4048b98b5a4634b94c8d193/doc/escobar_ministry.pdf. Accessed 13 August 2012.

Esterline, D., D. Werner, T. Johnson and T. Crossing. 2013. "Global Survey on Theological Education 2011–2013: A Summary of Main Findings." Prepared for the WCC 10th Assembly, Busan, 30 October–8 November 2013. Online at http://www.globethics.net/web/gtl/research/global-survey. Accessed 7 October 2013.

Etherington, M. 2011. "The Pygmalion Principle: The Practicum Expectations and Experiences of Mature Aged Student Teachers." *Issues in Educational Research* 21 (3): 259–80.

Farley, E. 1983. *Theologia: The Fragmentation and Unity of Theological Education*. Philadelphia: Fortress Press.

———. 1997. "Why Seminaries Don't Change: A Reflection on Faculty Specialization." *The Christian Century*, February 5–12: 133–43.

Farrah, S. 2004. "Lecture." Chap. 12 in *Adult Learning Methods: A Guide for Effective Instruction*, 3rd ed., edited by M. Galbraith, 227–52. Malabar, FL: Krieger.

Felder, R. M., and L. K. Silverman. 1988. "Learning and Teaching Styles in Engineering Education." *Engineering Education* 78 (7): 674–81.

Fernández, E. 2012. "Engaging Contextual Realities in Theological Education: Systems and Strategies." Paper presented at the ICETE International Consultation for Theological Educators. Nairobi, Kenya, 17 October 2012.

Fernando, A. 2002. *Jesus Driven Ministry*. Wheaton, IL: Crossway.

Ferris, R. 2006. "The Transforming Power of a Learning Orientation." Plenary presentation delivered at the Overseas Council Institute for Excellence in Christian Leadership Development, Osijek, Croatia, 3–7 April 2006.

Festinger, L. 1957. *A Theory of Cognitive Dissonance*. Stanford: Stanford University Press.

———. 1964. *When Prophecy Fails: A Social and Psychological Study*. New York: HarperCollins.

Fink, L. 2003. *Creating Significant Learning Experiences: An Integrated Approach to Designing College Courses*. San Francisco: Jossey-Bass.

Fisher, R. 2008. *Teaching Thinking: Philosophical Enquiry in the Classroom*, 3rd ed. London: Continuum.

Fleming, N. 2012. A Guide to Learning Styles. Online at http://www.vark-learn.com/english/index.asp. Accessed 27 May 2013.

Foucault, M. 1977. *Discipline and Punish: The Birth of the Prison*. New York: Vintage.

Fredericks, D. 2010. "Levels of Questions in Bloom's Taxonomy." TeacherVision. Online at http://www.teachervision.fen.com/teaching-methods/new-teacher/48445. html?page=1&detoured=1. Accessed 6 November 2010.

Freire, P. 1970. *Pedagogy of the Oppressed*. Translated by M. Ramos. London: Penguin.

Fried, R. 2005. *The Game of School*. San Francisco: Jossey-Bass.

Furedi, F. 2012. "The Unhappiness Principle." *Times Higher Education Supplement*, 29 November 2012. Online at http://www.timeshighereducation.co.uk/story.asp?sectioncode=26&storyco de=421958&c=2. Accessed 29 November 2012.

Gardner, H. 1983. *Frames of Mind: The Theory of Multiple Intelligences*. New York: Basic Books.

———. 1993. *Multiple Intelligences: The Theory in Practice*. New York: Basic Books.

Gawronski, B., and F. Strack, eds. 2012. *Cognitive Consistency: A Fundamental Principle in Social Cognition*. New York: Guilford.

Gibson, D. 2012. "Being Trinity." Teaching Theology: A Blog for Theological Educators by Graham Cheesman. Online at http://teachingtheology.org/2012/08/01/being-trinity/. Accessed 14 August 2012.

Gillespie, T. 1993. "What Is 'Theological' about Theological Education?" *Princeton Seminary Bulletin* 14 (1): 55–63.

Goffman, E. 1959. *The Presentation of Self in Everyday Life*. New York: Bantam.

Goleman, D. 1995. *Emotional Intelligence: Why It Can Matter More Than IQ*. New York: Bantam.

———. 2006. *Social Intelligence*. New York: Bantam.

Goodman, D. 2011. "Posing Good Questions." Workshop materials presented at the Church Based Training Symposium, held in Vienna-Mödling, 16–19 May 2011.

Gorman, J. 2001. "'There's Got to Be More!': Transformational Learning." *Christian Education Journal* 5NS (1): 23–51.

Guder, D. 2010. "Theological Formation for Missional Faithfulness after Christendom: A Response to Steve de Gruchy." In *Handbook of Theological Education in World Christianity: Theological Perspectives – Regional Surveys – Ecumenical Trends*, edited by D. Werner, D. Esterline, N. Kang and J. Raja, 51–55. Eugene, OR: Wipf and Stock.

Gurian, M., and P. Henley. 2001. *Boys and Girls Learn Differently! A Guide for Teachers and Parents*. San Francisco: Jossey-Bass.

Habermas, R. 1995. "The Developmental Use of Lecturing." In *Nurture That Is Christian: Developmental Perspectives on Christian Education*, edited by J. Wilhoit and J. Dettoni, 215–23. Grand Rapids, MI: Baker.

Haddad, E., and R. Das. 2012. "Assessing Outcomes: Does Seminary Training Make a Difference in the Community?" Unpublished paper, Arab Baptist Theological Seminary.

Hardy, S. 2007. *Excellence in Theological Education: Effective Training for Church Leaders*. Peradeniya: Lanka Bible College and Seminary.

———. 2012. "Discipleship By Community: The Powerful Impact of 'The Invisible Curriculum.'" Presentation given at Seminario Teológico Centroamericano, Guatemala City, Guatemala, January 2012.

Harkness, A. 2010. "De-Schooling the Theological Seminary: An Appropriate Paradigm for Effective Pastoral Formation." In *Tending the Seedbeds: Educational Perspectives on Theological Education in Asia*, edited by A. Harkness, 103–28. Quezon City: Asia Theological Association.

————. 2013. "Seminary to Pew to Home, Workplace and Community – And Back Again: The Role of Theological Education in Asian Church Growth." Unpublished paper.

Harrow, A. 1972. *A Taxonomy of the Psychomotor Domain*. New York: McKay.

Harvie, P. 2004. "Transformative Learning in Undergraduate Education." PhD diss., University of Toronto.

Heaton, R. 2013. Personal correspondence 30 December 2013.

Hewlett, D. 2010. "Theological Education in England Since 1987." In *Handbook of Theological Education in World Christianity: Theological Perspectives – Regional Surveys – Ecumenical Trends*, edited by D. Werner, D. Esterline, N. Kang and J. Raja, 563–68. Eugene, OR: Wipf and Stock.

Hiebert, P. 1994. *Anthropological Reflections on Missiological Issues*. Grand Rapids, MI: Baker.

————. 2008. *Transforming Worldviews: An Anthropological Understanding of How People Change*. Grand Rapids, MI: Baker.

Hill, C. 2013 "The Benefits Of Flipping Your Classroom." Faculty Focus: Higher Ed Teaching Strategies from Magna Publications. 26 August 2013. Online at www.facultyfocus. com/articles/instructional-design/the-benefits-of-flipping-your-classroom/?utm_source=cheetah&utm_medium=email&utm_campaign=2013.08.26. Accessed 27 August 2013.

Hoeckman, R. 1994. "Ecclesiological Fidelity and Ecumenical Theological Education." *Ministerial Formation* 67: 8–14.

Hough, J. 1984. "The Education of Practical Theologians." *Theological Education* 20: 55–84.

———— and B. Wheeler, eds. 1988. *Beyond Clericalism: The Congregation as a Focus for Theological Education*. Cambridge: Scholars Press.

Huemer, M. (n.d.). "Student Evaluations: A Critical Review." Online at http://spot.colorado. edu/~huemer/sef.htm. Accessed 10 January 2010.

Hunter, G. 2004. "Examining the 'Natural Church Development' Project." In *The Pastor's Guide to Growing a Christlike Church*, edited by G. Hunter III, 105–14. Kansas City, MO: Beacon Hill.

Illich, I. 1970. *Deschooling Society*. New York: Harper & Row.

Issler, K., and R. Habermas. 1994. *How We Learn: A Christian Teacher's Guide to Educational Psychology*. Grand Rapids, MI: Baker.

Jackson, P. 1968. *Life in Classrooms*. New York: Holt, Rinehart & Winston.

Jensen, E. 2008. *Super Teaching: Over 1000 Practical Strategies*, 4th ed. Thousand Oaks, CA: Corwin.

Juengst, S. 1998. *Equipping the Saints: Teacher Training in the Church*. Louisville, KY: Westminster John Knox.

Kachka, P. 2012. "Understanding the Flipped Classroom: Part 1." Faculty Focus: Higher Ed Teaching Strategies from Magna Publications. 23 October 2012. Online at www. facultyfocus.com/articles/teaching-with-technology-articles/understanding-the-flipped-classroom-part-1. Accessed 28 October 2012.

Kahneman, D. 2011. *Thinking, Fast and Slow*. New York: Farrar, Straus & Giroux.

Kang, N. 2010. "Envisioning Postcolonial Theological Education: Dilemmas and Possibilities." In *Handbook of Theological Education in World Christianity: Theological Perspectives – Regional*

Surveys – Ecumenical Trends, edited by D. Werner, D. Esterline, N. Kang and J. Raja, 30–41. Eugene, OR: Wipf and Stock.

Kelsey, D. 1993. *Between Athens and Berlin: The Theological Debate*. Grand Rapids, MI: Eerdmans.

Kennedy, D., Á. Hyland and N. Ryan. 2007. *Writing and Using Learning Outcomes: A Practical Guide*. Cork: University College. Available at http://theologicaleducation.net/articles/view. htm?id=39.

Kherfi, S. 2011. "Whose Opinion Is It Anyway? Determinants of Participation in Student Evaluation of Teaching." *Journal of Economic Education*, 42 (1): 19–30.

Kirk, J. A. 2005. "Re-Envisioning the Theological Curriculum As If the *Missio Dei* Mattered." *Common Ground Journal*, 3 (1): 23–40.

Knowles, M., E. Holton and R. Swanson. 2005. *The Adult Learner: The Definitive Classic in Adult Education and Human Resource Development*, 6th ed. Amsterdam: Elsevier.

Kohl, M. 2010. "Curriculum Development: An Overview." Plenary presentation delivered at the Overseas Council Institute for Excellence in Christian Leadership Development, Taipei, Taiwan, 6–9 April 2010.

Kohn, A. 1999. *Punished By Rewards: The Trouble with Gold Stars, Incentive Plans, A's, Praise, and Other Bribes*. Boston: Houghton Mifflin.

Kolb, D. 1983. *Experiential Learning: Experience as the Source of Learning and Development*. Upper Saddle River, NJ: Prentice Hall.

Kramlich, D. 2013. Personal correspondence 1 December 2013.

Krathwohl, D., B. Bloom and B. Masia. 1964. *Taxonomy of Educational Objectives: The Classification of Educational Goals. Handbook II: Affective Domain*. New York: David McKay.

Landy, D., and H. Sigall. 1974. "Task Evaluation as a Function of the Performers' Physical Attractiveness." *Journal of Personality and Social Psychology* 29 (3): 299–304.

Lane, J. (n.d.). "Sample Verbs for Learning Objectives." Schreyer Institute for Teaching Excellence, Penn State University. Online at http://www.schreyerinstitute.psu.edu/pdf/ SampleVerbs_for_LearningObjectives.pdf. Accessed 27 February 2012.

Lausanne Movement. 2011. "The Cape Town Commitment: A Declaration of Belief and a Call to Action." Online at http://www.lausanne.org/en/documents/ctcommitment.html. Accessed 12 August 2013.

Lawson, M. 1988. "Biblical Foundations for a Philosophy of Teaching." In *The Christian Educator's Handbook on Teaching*, edited by K. Gangel and H. Hendricks, 61–73. Grand Rapids, MI: Baker.

LeDoux, J. 2000. "Emotion Circuits in the Brain." *Annual Review of Neuroscience* 23 (1): 155–84.

LeFever, M. 1995. *Learning Styles: Reaching Everyone God Gave You to Teach*. Colorado Springs: Cook.

Leyda, R. 2009. "Models of Ministry Internship for Colleges and Seminaries." *Christian Education Journal* Series 3, 6 (1): 24–37.

Lindeman, E. 1926. *The Meaning of Adult Education*. New York: New Republic.

Loder, J. 1982. *The Transforming Moment: Understanding Convictional Experiences*. San Francisco: Harper & Row.

———. 1998. *The Logic of the Spirit: Human Development in Theological Perspective*. San Francisco: Jossey-Bass.

Madueme, H., and L. Cannell. 2006. "Problem Based Learning and TEDS' MDiv program." Unpublished paper.

———. 2007. "Problem Based Learning and the Master of Divinity Program." *Theological Education* 43 (1): 47–59.

Marsh, H. and L. Roche. 1997. "Making Students' Evaluations of Teaching Effectiveness Effective." *American Psychologist* 52: 1187–97.

Marshall, T. 1991. *Understanding Leadership: Fresh Perspectives on the Essentials of New Testament Leadership*. Tonbridge: Sovereign World.

Martin, D. 2006. "Verbs to Consider When Writing Aims." Unpublished document.

Marzano, R., and J. Kendall, eds. 2006. *The New Taxonomy of Educational Objectives*, 2nd ed. Thousand Oaks, CA: Corwin.

May, S. 2003. "A Look at the Effects of Extrinsic Motivation on the Internalization of Biblical Truth." *Christian Education Journal* 7NS (1): 47–65.

McCarthy, B. 1996. *About Learning*. Barrington, IL: Excel.

McGrath, A. 2002. *The Future of Christianity*. Malden, MA: Blackwell.

McKeachie, W. 1999. *McKeachie's Teaching Tips: Strategies, Research, and Theory for College and University Teachers*, 10th ed. Boston: Houghton Mifflin.

McLaughlin, V. 2003. "Wizard of Odds: Interview with Bishop Vaughn McLaughlin." *Leadership* 24 (2): 24–29.

McNabb, B., and S. Mabry. 1990. *Teaching the Bible Creatively: How to Awaken Your Kids to Scripture*. Grand Rapids, MI: Zondervan.

Merriam, S., R. Caffarella and L. Baumgartner. 2007. *Learning in Adulthood: A Comprehensive Guide*. San Francisco: Jossey–Bass.

Merseth. K. 1991. *A Case for Cases in Teacher Education*. Washington: American Association of Colleges for Teacher Education.

Meyer, J., and M. Shanahan. 2004. "Developing Metalearning Capacity in Students: Actionable Theory and Practical Lessons Learned in First-Year Economics." *Innovations in Education and Teaching International* 41 (4): 443–58.

Meyers, C., and T. Jones. 1993. *Promoting Active Learning: Strategies for the College Classroom*. San Francisco: Jossey-Bass.

Mezirow, J. 1991. *Transformative Dimensions of Adult Learning*. San Francisco: Jossey-Bass.

———. 2000. *Learning As Transformation: Critical Perspectives on a Theory in Progress*. San Francisco: Jossey Bass.

Miller, D. 1987. *Story and Context: An Introduction to Christian Education*. Nashville: Abingdon.

Miller, G. 1956. "The Magical Number Seven, Plus or Minus Two: Some Limits on Our Capacity for Information Processing." *Psychological Review* 63: 81–97.

Moreland, J., and K. Issler. 2006. *The Lost Virtue of Happiness: Discovering the Disciplines of the Good Life*. Colorado Springs: NavPress.

Murdock, T., and A. Miller. 2003. "Teachers As Sources of Middle School Students' Motivational Identity: Variable-Centered and Person-Centered Analytic Approaches." *Elementary School Journal* 103: 383–99.

Murphy, A. 1999. "Enhancing the Motivation for Good Teaching with An Improved System of Evaluation." *Financial Practice and Education* 9: 100–104.

Myers, D. 1978. *The Human Puzzle*. New York: Harper & Row.

Naftulin, D., J. Ware and F. Donnelly. 1973. "The Doctor Fox Lecture: A Paradigm of Educational Seduction." *Journal of Medical Education* 48: 630–35.

Newman, E. 2003. "Hospitality and Christian Higher Education." *Christian Scholar's Review* 33 (1): 75–93.

Nisbett, R. 2003. *The Geography of Thought: How Asians and Westerners Think Differently .… And Why*. New York: Free Press.

———— and I. Choi, K. Peng and A. Norenzayan. 2001. "Culture and Systems of Thought: Holistic Versus Analytic Cognition." *Psychological Review* 108 (2): 291–310.

Novak, J., and B. Gowin. 1984. *Learning How To Learn*. Cambridge: Cambridge University Press.

O'Brien, J., B. Millis and M. Cohen. 2008. *The Course Syllabus: A Learning-Centered Approach*, 2nd ed. San Francisco: Jossey-Bass.

Ott, B. 2011. *Beyond Fragmentation: Integrating Mission and Theological Education: A Critical Assessment of Some Recent Developments in Evangelical Theological Education*. Eugene, OR: Wipf & Stock.

Palmer, P. 1983. *To Know As We Are Known: A Spirituality of Education*. San Francisco: Harper & Row.

————. 1998. *The Courage to Teach: Exploring the Inner Landscape of a Teacher's Life*. San Francisco: Jossey-Bass.

Parks, S. 2000. *Big Questions, Worthy Dreams: Mentoring Young Adults in Their Search for Meaning, Purpose, and Faith*. San Francisco: Jossey Bass.

Penner, P., ed. 2009. *Theological Education as Mission*, 2nd ed. Prague: IBTS.

Philbin, M., E. Meier, S. Huffman and P. Boverie. 1995. "A Survey of Gender and Learning Styles." *Sex Roles* 32 (7–8): 485–94.

Piaget, J. 1970. *Structuralism*. New York: Harper & Row.

————. 1985. *The Equilibration of Cognitive Structures: The Central Problem of Intellectual Development*. Chicago: University of Chicago.

Pianta, R. 1999. *Enhancing Relationships between Children and Teachers*. Washington: American Psychological Association.

Pierson, G. 1983. *A Yale Book of Numbers*. New Haven: Yale Office of Institutional Research.

Pilli, T. 2007. "Spiritual Development and Mentoring." *The Theological Educator* 2 (1): 3.

Polanyi, M. 1958. *Personal Knowledge: Towards a Post-Critical Philosophy*. Chicago: University of Chicago Press.

————. 1966. *The Tacit Dimension*. Garden City, NY: Doubleday.

Priest, R. 2000. "Christian Theology, Sin, and Anthropology." In *Anthropology and Theology: God, Icons, and God-Talk*, edited by W. Adams and F. Salomone, 59–75. Lanham, MD: University Press of America.

Rhem, J. 1995. "Deep/Surface Approaches to Learning: An Introduction." *The National Teaching and Learning Forum* 5 (1): 1–2.

Rice, L. 1988. "Student Evaluation of Teaching: Problems and Prospects." *Teaching Philosophy* 11: 329–44.

Richards, L. 1970. *Creative Bible Teaching*. Chicago: Moody.

————. 1975. *A Theology of Christian Education*. Grand Rapids, MI: Zondervan.

———— and G. Bredfeldt. 1998. Creative Bible Teaching, rev. ed. Chicago: Moody.

Riebe-Estrella, G. 2009. "Engaging Borders: Lifting Up Difference and Unmasking Division." *Theological Education* 45 (1): 19–26.

Rodgers, C., and M. Raider-Roth. 2006. "Presence in Teaching." *Teachers and Teaching: Theory and Practice* 12 (3): 265–87.

Rogers, A. 2004. "Looking Again at Non-Formal and Informal Education: Towards a New Paradigm." The Encyclopaedia of Informal Education. Online at www.infed.org/biblio/non_formal_paradigm.htm. Accessed 18 October 2012.

Rogers, S., and L. Renard. 1999. "Relationship-Driven Teaching." *Educational Leadership* 57 (1): 34–37.

Rosenthal, R., and L. Jacobson. 1992. *Pygmalion in the Classroom*. New York: Irvington.

Salovey, P., and J. D. Mayer. 1990. "Emotional Intelligence." *Imagination, Cognition, and Personality* 9: 185–211.

Sanders, P. 2009. "Evangelical Theological Education in a Globalised World." Presentation delivered at Centre for Theological Education, Belfast, Northern Ireland, 17 November 2009.

Schön, D. 1991. *The Reflective Practitioner: How Professionals Think in Action*. Aldershot: Ashgate.

Schultz, T. and J. Schultz. 1999. *The Dirt On Learning*. Loveland, CO: Group.

Schwartz, S. 1992. "Universals in the Content and Structure of Values: Theoretical Advances and Empirical Tests in 20 Countries." In *Advances in Experimental Social Psychology*, edited by M. Zanna, 1–65. Orlando, FL: Academic Press.

Schwarz, C. 2000. *Natural Church Development: A Guide to Eight Essential Qualities of Healthy Churches*, 4th ed. St Charles: ChurchSmart.

Seymour, S. 1993. *The Predictable Failure of Educational Reform: Can We Change Course Before It's Too Late?* San Francisco: Jossey-Bass.

Shaw, K. 2008. "Affective Barriers and Bridges to the Communication of the Gospel with Special Attention to Religious Affectivity among Arab Beiruti Sunni Muslim Women." DMin diss., Gordon Conwell Theological Seminary.

Shaw, P. 2006a. "Multi-Dimensional Learning in Ministerial Training." *International Congregational Journal* 6 (1): 53–63.

———. 2006b. "Vulnerable Authority: A Theological Approach to Leadership and Teamwork." *Christian Education Journal* Series 3, 3 (1): 119–33.

———. 2010. "'New Treasures with the Old': Addressing Culture and Gender Imperialism in Higher Level Theological Education." In *Tending the Seedbeds: Educational Perspectives on Theological Education in Asia*, edited by A. Harkness, 47–74. Quezon City: Asia Theological Association.

———. 2011. "A Welcome Guest: Ministerial Training as an Act of Hospitality." *Christian Education Journal*, Series 3, 7 (1): 8–26.

———. 2013a. "Integrated Theological Education: A Practical Model." *The Theological Educator* 5 (2). Online at http://thetheologicaleducator.net/2013/01/16/integrated-theological-education-a-practical-model/#more-720. Posted 16 January 2013.

———. 2013b. "Patronage, Exemption, and Institutional Policy." *Evangelical Missions Quarterly* 49 (1): 8–13.

Shulman, Laura. 2006. "Deep Thinking Skills." Online at www.nvcc.edu/home/lshulman/learning/deepthinking.htm. Posted 16 July 2006. Accessed 6 September 2013.

Shulman, Lee. 2002. "Making Differences: A Table of Learning. The Carnegie Foundation for the Advancement of Teaching." Online at www.carnegiefoundation.org/elibrary/making-differences-table-learning. Posted 1 January 2002. Accessed 6 September 2013.

Siew, Y-M. 2006. "Fostering Community and a Culture of Learning in Seminary Classes." *Christian Education Journal* Series 3, 3 (1): 79–91.

Simpson, E. 1972. *The Classification of Educational Objectives in the Psychomotor Domain.* Washington: Gryphon.

Smail, T. 2005. *Like Father, Like Son: The Trinity Imaged in Our Humanity.* Grand Rapids, MI: Eerdmans.

Smith, F. 1986. *Insult To Intelligence: The Bureaucratic Invasion of Our Classroom.* Westminster, MD: Arbor House.

Smith, G. 2004. "Faculties That Listen, Schools That Learn: Assessment in Theological Education." Online at http://www.lexingtonseminar.org/stuff/contentmgr/files/92fa8d21857 4e393eb9a40a65fc4fc7f/doc/smith_assessment.pdf. Accessed 20 April 2012.

Smith, M. 2001. "David A. Kolb on Experiential Learning." *The Encyclopaedia of Informal Education.* Online at http://infed.org/mobi/david-a-kolb-on-experiential-learning. Accessed 27 May 2013.

———. 2011. "Donald Schön: Learning, Reflection and Change." *The Encyclopaedia of Informal Education.* Online at http://www.infed.org/thinkers/et-schon.htm. Accessed 18 October 2012.

———. 2012. "Non-Formal Education." *The Encyclopaedia of Informal Education.* Online at http://www.infed.org/biblio/b-nonfor.htm. Accessed 18 October 2012.

Sousa, D. 2006. *How the Brain Learns,* 3rd ed. Thousand Oaks, CA: Corwin.

Standish, N. 2005. *Becoming a Blessed Church: Forming a Church of Spiritual Purpose, Presence, and Power.* Herndon, VA: Alban Institute.

Stonehouse, C. 1993. "Learning from Gender Differences." In *The Christian Educator's Handbook on Adult Education,* edited by K. Gangel and J. Wilhoit, 104–20. Wheaton, IL: Victor.

Stray, C. 2005. "From Oral to Written Examinations: Cambridge, Oxford and Dublin 1700–1914." *History of Universities* 20 (2): 76–130.

Suskie, L. 2009. *Assessing Student Learning: A Common Sense Guide,* 2nd ed. San Francisco: Jossey-Bass.

Taylor, E. 2000. "Analyzing Research on Transformative Learning Theory." In *Learning As Transformation: Critical Perspectives on a Theory in Progress,* edited by J. Mezirow and Associates, 285–328. San Francisco: Jossey-Bass.

Tennant, M. 1997. *Psychology and Adult Learning,* 2nd ed. London: Routledge.

Teven, J. 2007. "Teacher Caring and Classroom Behaviour: Relationships with Student Affect and Perceptions of Teacher Competence and Trustworthiness." *Communication Quarterly* 55 (4): 433–50.

Thomas à Kempis. 2003. *The Imitation of Christ.* Translated by A. Croft and H. Bolton. Mineola, NY: Dover.

Thompson, M. 1995. *Soul Feast: An Invitation to the Christian Spiritual Life.* Louisville, KY: Westminster John Knox.

Torres, S., and V. Fabella, eds. 1978. *The Emergent Gospel: Theology from the Underside of History.* Maryknoll, NY: Orbis.

Triandis, H. 1989. "The Self and Social Behaviour in Differing Cultural Contexts." *Psychological Review,* 96: 506–20.

Tufts University. (n.d.). "Verb Worksheet for Preparing Learning Objectives: Behavioural Verbs for Writing Objectives in the Cognitive, Affective and Psychomotor Domains." Online at www.tufts.edu/med/docs/about/offices/oce/Verb%20Worksheet%20for%20Preparing%20 Learning%20Objectives.doc. Accessed 27 February 2012.

Tulving. E. 2000. "Concepts of Memory." In *The Oxford Handbook of Memory*, edited by E. Tulving and F. Craik, 33–43. New York: OUP.

Van Engen, C. 2004. "Centrist View: Church Growth Is Based on an Evangelistically Focused and a Missiologically Applied Theology." In *Evaluating the Church Growth Movement: 5 Views*, edited by E. Towns, C. Van Gelder, C. Van Engen, G. Van Rheenen and H. Snyder, 123–47. Grand Rapids, MI: Zondervan.

Vanhoozer, K. 2007. *Everyday Theology: How to Read Cultural Texts and Interpret Trends.* Grand Rapids, MI: Baker Academic.

Vella, J. 2002. *Learning to Listen, Learning to Teach: The Power of Dialogue in Educating Adults.* San Francisco: Jossey-Bass.

———. 2008. *On Teaching and Learning: Putting the Principles and Practices of Dialogue Education into Action.* San Francisco: Jossey-Bass.

VerBerkmoes, J., J. Bonnell, D. Lenear and K. Vanderwest. 2011. *Research Report: Transformation Theological Education 1.0.* Grand Rapids, MI: Grand Rapids Theological Seminary, Cornerstone University.

Vygotsky, L. (1934) 1962. *Thought and Language.* Cambridge, MA: MIT Press.

———. 1978. *Mind in Society: The Development of Higher Psychological Processes.* Cambridge, MA: Harvard University Press.

Ward, T. 2001. "The Teaching-Learning Process." In *Introducing Christian Education: Foundations for the Twenty-First Century*, edited by M. Anthony, 117–24. Grand Rapids, MI: Baker.

Wazir, R. 2013. "The Contribution of Curriculum Integration to Student Progress." MEdAdmin Sociology of Education paper, Haigazian University, Beirut, Lebanon.

Webb, K., and J. Blond. 1995. "Teacher Knowledge: The Relationship between Caring and Knowing." *Teaching and Teacher Education* 11 (6): 611–25.

Weimer, M. 2013a. "Encouraging Student Participation: Why It Pays to Sweat the Small Stuff." Faculty Focus: Higher Ed Teaching Strategies from Magna Publications. 18 September 2103. Online at www.facultyfocus.com/articles/teaching-professor-blog/encouraging-student-participation-why-it-pays-to-sweat-the-small-stuff. Accessed 18 September 2013.

———. 2013b. "Structuring Discussions: Online and Face-To-Face." Faculty Focus: Higher Ed Teaching Strategies from Magna Publications. 25 September 2013. Online at http://www.facultyfocus.com/articles/teaching-professor-blog/structuring-discussions-online-and-face-to-face/. Accessed 25 September 2013.

Wiggins, G. 1998. *Educative Assessment: Designing Assessments to Inform and Improve Student Performance.* San Francisco: Jossey-Bass.

Wilhoit, J. 1991. *Christian Education: The Search For Meaning*, 2nd ed. Grand Rapids, MI: Baker.

Williams, W., and S. Ceci. 1997. "'How'm I doing?' Problems with Student Ratings of Instructors and Courses." *Change: The Magazine of Higher Learning* 29: 12–23.

Williamson, M., and R. Watson. 2006. "Learning Styles Research: Understanding How Teaching Should Be Impacted by the Way Learners Learn; Part II: Understanding How Learners Prefer to Receive Information." *Christian Education Journal,* Series 3, 3 (2): 343–61.

Willingham, D. 2009. *Why Don't Students Like School? A Cognitive Scientist Answers Questions about How the Mind Works and What It Means for Your Classroom.* San Francisco: Jossey-Bass.

Wilson, R. 1998. "New Research Casts Doubt on Value of Student Evaluations of Professors." *Chronicle of Higher Education* January 16: A12.

Wlodkowski, R. 1999. *Enhancing Adult Motivation to Learn: A Comprehensive Guide for Teaching All Adults.* San Francisco: Jossey-Bass.

———— and M. Ginsberg. 1995. *Diversity and Motivation: Culturally Responsive Teaching.* San Francisco: Jossey-Bass.

Woodyard, J. 1994. "A 21st Century Seminary Faculty Model." In *The M. J. Murdock Charitable Trust Review of Graduate Theological Education in the Pacific Northwest.* Vancouver: M. J. Murdock Charitable Trust.

Wright, N. T. 2008. *Surprised By Hope: Rethinking Heaven, the Resurrection, and the Mission of the Church.* New York: HarperCollins.

Ziolkowski, T. 1990. "The Ph.D. Squid." *American Scholar,* 59 (2): 177–95.

Author Index

Subject Index

Langham Literature and its imprints are a ministry of Langham Partnership.

Langham Partnership is a global fellowship working in pursuit of the vision God entrusted to its founder John Stott -

to facilitate the growth of the church in maturity and Christ-likeness through raising the standards of biblical preaching and teaching.

Our vision is to see churches equipped for mission and growing to maturity in Christ through the ministry of pastors and leaders who believe, teach and live by the Word of God.

Our mission is to strengthen the ministry of the Word of God through:
- nurturing national movements for training in biblical preaching
- multiplying the creation and distribution of evangelical literature
- strengthening the theological training of pastors and leaders by qualified evangelical teachers

Our ministry

Langham Preaching partners with national leaders to nurture indigenous biblical preaching movements for pastors and lay preachers all around the world. With the support of a team of trainers from many countries, a multi-level programme of seminars provides practical training, and is followed by a programme for training local facilitators. Local preachers' groups and national and regional networks ensure continuity and ongoing development, seeking to build vigorous movements committed to Bible exposition.

Langham Literature provides majority world pastors, scholars and seminary libraries with evangelical books and electronic resources through grants, discounts and distribution. The programme also fosters the creation of indigenous evangelical books for pastors in many languages, through training workshops for writers and editors, sponsored writing, translation, strengthening local evangelical publishing houses, and investment in major regional literature projects, such as one volume Bible commentaries like *The Africa Bible Commentary*.

Langham Scholars provides financial support for evangelical doctoral students from the majority world so that, when they return home, they may train pastors and other Christian leaders with sound, biblical and theological teaching. This programme equips those who equip others. Langham Scholars also works in partnership with majority world seminaries in strengthening evangelical theological education. A growing number of Langham Scholars study in high quality doctoral programmes in the majority world itself. As well as teaching the next generation of pastors, graduated Langham Scholars exercise significant influence through their writing and leadership.

To learn more about Langham Partnership and the work we do visit **langham.org**

CPSIA information can be obtained
at www.ICGtesting.com
Printed in the USA
LVHW101116240321
682308LV00003B/105

9 781783 689576